18th CENTURY ENGLISH FURNITURE

THE NORMAN ADAMS COLLECTION

Christopher Claxton Stevens
and
Stewart Whittington

Antique Collectors' Club

© 1983
C. Claxton Stevens and S. Whittington
World copyright reserved
ISBN 0 902028 88 X

First edition 1983
Revised edition 1985
Reprinted 1987
Reprinted 1989

British Library CIP Data
Stevens, C. Claxton
    18th century English furniture.
    1. Furniture, English — History
    I. Title   II. Whittington, Stewart
    749.2   NK2529
    ISBN 0-902028-88-X

Published for the Antique Collectors' Club
by the Antique Collectors' Club Ltd.

Frontispiece. A Chippendale period mahogany secretaire cabinet, c.1765. The piece is described on p. 198.

Printed in England by Antique Collectors' Club Ltd., Woodbridge, Suffolk

"It is difficult to ascertain, in many instances, the true value of furniture, by those who are strangers to the business. On this account gentlemen often think themselves imposed upon in the high price they must give for a good article."

Thomas Sheraton, *The Cabinet Dictionary,* 1803, p. 117.

ACKNOWLEDGEMENTS

In the preparation of this book we have drawn extensively on the archives of the firm and renewed acquaintances with and memories of a large number of clients, past and present, to whom we are deeply indebted. In particular we would like to record our thanks to J.A. Floyd, the Chairman of Christie's, for writing the foreword; the Governor and Company of the Bank of England; Christopher Gilbert, Principal Keeper of Temple Newsam House, Leeds; and Mrs. J. Home-Robertson. For the bulk of the photography we are indebted to Raymond Fortt Studios Ltd. who have served us well for some forty years, and for her hours of painstaking typing, we would like to acknowledge our gratitude to Dé Wyld.

FOREWORD

I had the good fortune and pleasure to know Norman Adams for more than 30 years, from my earliest days at Christie's, just after the war, when Norman was already established as a leading dealer in fine English 18th century furniture. Always setting the highest standards himself, he was generous with his knowledge and I shall remember with gratitude the encouragement and advice he gave to a newcomer in the furniture world.

As time passed I came more and more to admire his discriminating taste — quality, clean lines, well figured woods and above all patina. Before any sale of fine English furniture one could say with confidence "Norman Adams will bid for that lot" (and if he did he was seldom outbid!): on other occasions he would buy a table, a chest, a set of chairs or a mirror and only after the sale did one realise that his eagle eye had spotted an unusual feature or some special quality which others had not noticed — the mundane never interested Norman.

All his friends (for his clients invariably became friends) who were regular visitors to Hans Road or to his stand at Grosvenor House will enjoy this splendid book which will stand as a fitting memorial to a truly discriminating dealer and as a tribute to his successors. It is splendid that in a changing world the standards he set are being maintained. I know that Norman would have approved — need one say more?

J.A. Floyd
Chairman Christie's

CONTENTS

COLOUR PLATES

Norman Adams - A History

It is interesting to note how successful businesses move from plateau to plateau, what particular quirks of fate or arbitrary decision or combination of the two cause a business to change direction or seal its fate. With hindsight it is easy to see a number of instances and decisions that have enabled Norman Adams Limited to achieve its present position as one of the leading dealers of fine English furniture. On balance I can now say that our most important decision came in our middle years: the decision not to sell to the trade in the United Kingdom. Norman Adams wished his business to be known not just as a supplier of fine English furniture, but as an unrivalled supplier of a period of unquestioned quality in English furniture — a position where his clients would turn to him alone and know that they were acquiring the very best of that period. How could this happen if the best goods were constantly being creamed off by other dealers? Norman Adams' answer was to build up a business dealing with private collectors. So something over a quarter of a century ago the die was cast and no more dealing was done with the United Kingdom trade. At the time it must have seemed foolhardy. Fifty years earlier Lady Charlotte Schrieber had commented that the name of Chippendale was hardly known, while those of Sheraton, Hepplewhite and Adam, which today are upon everybody's tongue, were then absolutely unknown. The manner in which Norman Adams went about re-establishing their reputations and ensuring a continuing supply of their best quality forms the backbone to our firm's history and gave me the chance to demonstrate in one volume a catalogue of English furniture that I believe today to be unique.

Norman Adams was the elder son of a Bristol schoolmaster and antique dealer. His early upbringing had served to steep him in the mysteries of the antique, living with and handling all the kinds of things in which he would be totally submerged for the rest of his life. In 1923 he set up business in Charles Street, Boston. He was the first antique dealer selling only to the trade. His ploy, entirely unknown at that time, was notably in opposition to the decision I have set down as our lodestone.

He was immediately successful. Dealers and decorators throughout the United States recognised the quality of the goods with which he was able to provide them, but he would not deal with the private collector and turned away both Rockefeller and Henry Ford. He quickly opened another shop in New York, this time as a retail outlet, with equal success, and subsequently in 1928 established an outlet in London, 10 Hans Road, Knightsbridge, where we are to this day. After such early successes in the 1920s, we were confronted with the Wall Street crash, yet still in the late 1930s shipments of furniture were sent every second month to New York and Boston. As we entered the war our interests in America were sold, our London business was closed, 8-10 Hans Road became an air-raid shelter, and we rented a barn in the Cotswolds to house our stock. When the 'all clear' sounded, trading resumed as normal in London. Hidden in our barn in the Cotswolds we found a large collection of gold watches, a hangover from bullion dealing days, accumulated by Norman Adams' father in Bristol, but more important the stock was intact. We were back in business, but the world was a different place. We decided to concentrate on Hans Road, a sense of proportion that I believe saw us well through the following thirty years and has enabled us to build on our reputation, experience and contacts whatever the economic climate. In so doing Norman Adams, I believe, achieved his ambition, to establish a sure outlet for fine English furniture. He died in 1979 a year and a half after his senior director, Brough Barton. For seventeen years they had instilled in me all they knew. They asked me to ensure that as long as stock was available Norman Adams Ltd. would be there to supply it.

With Norman Adams as my mentor, I grew in understanding and appreciation of the beauty of this period of English Furniture and make no apology that my tastes are a reflection of his own. My one wish is to continue the tremendous dealing tradition he began and to encourage others to admire the values of fine English furniture. As a result of his early decisions I am well placed to do this. From that time we always had a selection of furniture of the highest quality for the discerning collector, and a record was kept of every piece that has passed through our hands, including the destination of that piece. This is important since it means that the business has a continuing opportunity of buying back whatever has been sold over the years. In these days of an acute shortage of stock re-acquiring pieces from the past is a most important source. Each of our pieces is special, of good proportion, fine colour and patination, and blessed with a particular charm for which I am constantly on the look out.

In this book, in collaboration with Christopher Claxton Stevens, without whose contribution this book would not have reached publication, we do not seek to be definitive but simply to catalogue the sort of pieces that fall within the Norman Adams tradition. They are objects which make it for me the most desirable of antique fields — they are graceful, charming, functional but not utilitarian, and whilst they may cost a lot of money are never expensive. They are today what Norman Adams set out to deal in — the cream of English furniture.

Stewart Whittington
August 1983

Introduction

There have been few good quality books dealing with eighteenth century English furniture published since the war. This fact is reflected in the number of references made in this volume to comparative pieces illustrated in the earlier pioneer works on the subject. Even the highly important edition of *The Dictionary of English Furniture* produced in 1954 is a work, albeit a much revised one, first printed in 1924-27. A substantial amount of valuable research has been done over the thirty years since that time and indeed since the revised *Shorter Dictionary* appeared in 1964. This book does not set out in any way comprehensively to bring these works up to date but it may be found useful in amplifying certain of their entries.

In any work of this sort, *The Dictionary* not excepted, coverage is sometimes uneven and there may be certain areas which some might consider important that are barely touched upon. For example it may be thought that too little prominence is given to the Palladian taste of the 1730s and 1740s, with its sometimes heavy and rather ponderous designs. Where possible representative pieces have been included to illustrate developments but it must be remembered that they are also representative of a saleable stock, bought according to the individualistic taste which is Norman Adams' legacy to the firm. Sometimes several specimens of the same type are included, for example Carlton House writing tables and tripod tables where the firm has handled a particularly fine and rare selection over the years. Again, in the final section, there are included a number of pieces such as ormolu-mounted vases which may not strictly be termed furniture but which are so closely connected in taste and style as to have a valid place in any collection of the finest eighteenth century English furniture.

In setting about planning the book it was a hard decision how to divide it up most usefully. The result is something of a compromise. Because of specific functional uses it was possible to keep all Dining Room furniture together but several other types of table, chair and cabinet might equally have been used in a variety of rooms so that the arrangement is generally by furniture type and then broadly chronologically within each section. This is intended to facilitate reference, although comparisons of style between pieces of the same period in different sections may not be so easy. Cross reference is made of many of the salient points where possible. To aid the chronology a division into periods is made as follows, with their approximate dates:

William III 1694-1702	Chippendale 1750-1770
Queen Anne 1702-1714	Adam/Hepplewhite 1770-1785
George I 1714-1727	Sheraton 1785-1800
George II 1727-1750	Regency 1800-1830

The use of the names Chippendale, Adam, Hepplewhite and Sheraton to divide up the second half of the eighteenth century is not always a very satisfactory one since certain pieces do not fit easily into such categories. Neither does it mean that a piece so described need have any direct relevance to a design published by any of these men. George Hepplewhite's *Cabinet Maker's and Upholsterer's Guide* is notably retrospective, being published in 1788 two years after his death, while its third edition came out as late as 1794 at which time Thomas Sheraton's first work, *The Cabinet Maker's and Upholsterer's Drawing Book,* was available. No actual furniture made by either man is known. These personalities have been overplayed, sometimes to the detriment of other important craftsmen whose names did not get into print. Nevertheless Norman Adams has traditionally used these terms and they do have a certain advantage in drawing comparisons between the development of style, shape, technique and detail at different periods towards the end of George II's reign and during the long reign of George III.

Except in the few cases where individual items are documented or very closely comparable to documented pieces, it is very difficult to be precise about dating. The dates given are generally the earliest that might reasonably be expected. The quality of a majority of the pieces suggests that they are of London manufacture and therefore generally at the forefront of fashion, although the taste of some of the people who gave commissions did sometimes dictate a more conservative style. Sometimes too it is surprising how long pattern books remained current or were re-issued, well after one might imagine styles to have changed. To give but one example, designs for chinoiserie inspired fret continued to be published as late as 1786 in John Crunden's *Joiner's and Cabinet-Maker's Darling* (which included no fewer than sixty) and even in Hepplewhite's *Guide* of 1788 and 1794.

Clearly many provincially-made pieces, although sometimes of considerable quality, were made ten or twenty years after their London equivalents, while at the other end of the spectrum, as research into bills and other documents continues, surprisingly early dates have been established for features that previously had not been envisaged until later. Such evidence, like the growing attention paid to furniture bearing makers' stamps and labels, is of great interest in this way and can be of considerable use in authentication so long as it is employed dispassionately. However, the primary criterion for assessing the importance of a piece of English furniture must remain the furniture itself and its intrinsic quality. Not that every piece that appears in this book is necessarily of the highest quality, but each merits inclusion if not for this, then for other outstanding features: rarity of form or size, functional ingenuity, elegance of design and proportion or condition with particular emphasis on surface colour and patina.

If it has survived two centuries or more of use, sunlight, dust and damp, no furniture will look the way it did when it was newly made. Something of the brightness that furniture makers sought, particularly towards the end of the eighteenth century, can sometimes be seen on the inside fittings of cabinets that have been exposed to little daylight: the vivid green of stained sycamore known as harewood, the red streaks of tulipwood and many other exotic timbers. There seem to be two schools of thought on the subject: one, as is often done with French furniture, to flatten and clean off the surface of the wood and the mounts in an effort to return them as nearly as possible to their original condition and the other to value the natural uneven surfaces, the fading and mellowing, and the accumulation of dirt and wax forming patina. The former, besides destroying much of the character of the piece, makes its authentication more difficult. This importance of patina is discussed on pp. 18-20 but allied closely to it is the question of how much restoration should be permissible.

Restoration can take three forms: one as a result of natural warping and shrinkage of the wood, lifting veneers and mouldings, another through the wear and tear of daily use and accidents and thirdly through deliberate alteration reflecting changes in fashion and circumstance. The first two of these are inevitable, although the damaging effects of modern forms of heating without ample humidification should not be underestimated. Furniture generally adapts well to changes of environment so long as the change is made very slowly. If such restoration as may be required is not too fundamental and is carried out by a skilful and experienced restorer, it need not affect the desirability or value of the piece too greatly. The same cannot be said of furniture that has been altered in size or adapted to some other use entirely. With the current trend towards smaller homes it is smaller pieces that tend to be much in demand and, being very often rare, they are commonly found in an adapted form. Apart from the dishonesty that can be involved, such alteration frequently ruins proportion and elegance. A sense of proportion is important in assessing furniture and wherever possible in this volume measurements are included, which unless otherwise stated are the maximum dimensions. These may help in comparison which can be difficult between photographs and serve to give an idea of such things as the optimum height of dining chairs, writing tables, etc.

It is not only in modern times that fashionable alterations have ruined furniture. The Victorians had a partiality for refinishing eighteenth century pieces with French polish and carving up and staining black earlier oak. Less seriously, it is quite rare today to find original handles still on a table or piece of cabinet furniture. From the end of the eighteenth century wooden knobs became increasingly popular, growing larger by Victorian times. These were often added where originally there had been none or were substituted for earlier brass handles. In more recent years this trend has been reversed and brass handles returned to fashion. The fact that such a large proportion of the pieces illustrated here do retain their original handles (if they ever had them), and also that many of them remain in outstandingly fine condition, implies that they have not been in constant use and mis-use over the years and that an unusual degree of respect has been shown to them which itself adds to their rarity.

The precise identification of many woods is hard at the best of times and many misguided claims have been made on this complex subject. Where only small amounts of a particular wood have been used, or when the wood has been bleached by the sun, the difficulties are increased. A large number of exotic timbers were imported during the second half of the eighteenth century and used for their unusual colouring and figure mainly in banding and marquetry. Furthermore, because of the large number of different types, it can be difficult to be definitive about the more common woods like mahogany and rosewood. Although descriptions were recorded it has not been possible, particularly in some of the older photographs, to be certain about some of the woods used. It is likewise sometimes difficult to be positive whether brass mounts have been gilded or merely retain their original bright lacquered finish.

This book does not seek to establish any new or definitive rules for the study of furniture. Furniture does not allow that. The only way to assess quality or pick out fakes or altered pieces is by constant close inspection and comparison especially with the best pieces available. Photography may be a poor substitute for the real thing but good photographs with close-ups and a degree of explanation can still be of considerable use, particularly since the vast majority of the pieces included in these pages has never been published before.

Forming a Collection

One of the most rewarding experiences in antique furniture dealing is helping to form a collection. Indeed not only is it rewarding to a dealer, it is also one of his major functions. It is often said that the important aspect in dealing is to find the top quality pieces of good taste with a fine patina and basically they will sell themselves. Whilst this aspect is for the most part true it must be taken a step further by the good dealer in understanding how to place the pieces of furniture in a house, not only to highlight their excellent points but also to bring a room together as a cohesive unit. How many drawing rooms have we all entered which look as if the furniture has just been thrown together without discrimination, taste or thought? We suspect many. Certainly, in our case, a great many. It would be imprudent to suggest to the owners of these drawing rooms that they are a not attractive. But how nice it is when we are asked to help in remedying the all too obvious faults. It is our business to know how rooms should be arranged, we have learned over the years from experience. So we do not find it strange that an antique furniture dealer should not only know about what he sells but also how to arrange what he sells in a room.

The illustrations show a most formidable collection of the finest English eighteenth century furniture displayed in a beautiful late seventeenth century house in the centre of London. The owner of this collection had finely tuned ideas as to how his house should be arranged, thus needing little help from us in that direction. However we took great pride in supplying the vast majority of the pieces (many of which have been discussed in detail in the body of this book) and in so doing have progressed from a dealer/client relationship to a strong bond of friendship.

*A view of the drawing room: *(in bay) an Adam period settee on cabriole legs with original painted decoration, c.1775; (above settee) one of a pair of Adam carved wood and gilt wall lights, c.1780; *(either side of fireplace) a pair of Adam satinwood sidetables with original painted decoration, c.1785; *above which are a superb pair of Chippendale period carved wood and gilt girandoles of tremendous lightness and delicacy, c.1765; (on mantlepiece and on pair satinwood side tables) pairs of Matthew Boulton ormolu and blue-John cassolettes, c.1780; *(over mantlepiece) a Chinese mirror painting of the Ch'ien Lung period depicting Radnor House, Twickenham, c.1780; *a pair of carved Chippendale mahogany stools in contemporary needlework, c.1750; (centre foreground) a Hepplewhite mahogany serpentine Pembroke table, c.1780.*

*A view of the dining room:
a set of 12 Hepplewhite
mahogany shieldback
armchairs, c.1780;
*a Sheraton period 3-pillar
mahogany dining table,
c.1790; *an 18th Century
Waterford glass chandelier,
c.1785; (back wall)
a Hepplewhite mahogany
shaped serpentine serving
table, c.1780; *a
Chippendale carved wood
and gilt oval mirror with
heraldic cresting, c.1760.*

*A view of the library: *(back
wall) a Chippendale mahogany
wing bookcase, the design
illustrated in Chippendale's
Director, c.1755; (far corner,
right) a Chippendale mahogany
carved Gainsborough armchair,
c.1760; (centre background) a
rare Chippendale period drum
library table, c.1765; (right
window) a very rare
Chippendale period mahogany
extending telescope table,
c.1765; *(centre foreground) a
fine Chippendale mahogany
carved tripod table, c.1760; a
pair of Chippendale mahogany
armchairs in the Chinese taste
with fret arms, c.1760.*

** Discussed in detail in body of
book*

17

The Importance of Patina

Running a firm like Norman Adams, which for sixty years has offered top quality pieces to customers in America and Britain, presents the continuing difficulty of finding quality items. Our pieces must be of good proportion, fine colouring but, perhaps more important and at the same time hardest for the inexperienced to understand, with good patina.

Much has been written about the excellence of English antique furniture. Many people, auctioneers in particular, have discussed the fine quality of the articles they handle, often with a minimum of justification. Screeds have been published regarding provenance, maker, design attribution and so on. However, there has been almost no discussion regarding patina. Some clients and collectors understand the part patina plays in the appreciation of eighteenth century furniture and recognise that a piece can stand or fall if it has a good or bad surface, but collectors in general do not.

Due to the scarcity of English furniture possessing patina, there is a great area of ignorance and it is not easy to make comparisons. To take a similar parallel; it is not difficult to buy a bottle of inferior wine and a bottle of first growth claret and compare the two. The first will be lacking in body, acidic, sharp and be completely without character. The second will unfold and flower, and fill the mouth with untold delights. However, they are both perfectly genuine wines and both of the same year. A piece of antique furniture without patina can be compared with the bottle of inferior wine but an equivalent piece with beautiful surface and colour, i.e. possessing patina, can be likened to the first growth claret. The difficulty is putting the two together to demonstrate the difference to the uninitiated.

The word 'patina' is defined in the *Concise Oxford Dictionary* as "incrustation, usually green, on surface of old bronze, esteemed as ornament; gloss produced by age on woodwork". It is the latter part of the definition that is of interest coupled with the information "esteemed as ornament".

Patina is the ageing process which when found on antique furniture distinguishes the poor from the very best. It is that extra ingredient which imparts the finishing touch to a piece of furniture of whatever quality and transforms the surface, giving it lustrous depth. Indeed, a country piece of furniture which possesses a 'fine patina' can often be more highly prized by a discerning collector than a London made piece which has no patina at all.

Patina is formed by a combination of ageing processes caused by rubbing, dusting and waxing coupled with oxidation of the wood and the action of the sun's rays. The action of rubbing and polishing over a period of time produces a fine bronze-like lustre (Colour Plate 1) which increases in depth and mellowness and softens the hard effect of the waxed raw wood. The natural oxidation of the wood causes hardening of the surface which seals in the rubbing and waxing process and at the same time fills in the grain. The addition of sunlight in varying degrees bleaches, fades and changes the colour to the most attractive shades ranging from medium brown through corn colours to golden grey.

Oak, which begins life as dull medium grey, can be transformed to a deep dark brown with rich highlights. The flat yellow colour of raw walnut becomes golden and 'toffee-textured' with wonderful depth (Colour Plate 2). Mahogany loses its uninteresting reddish hue and softens to glorious graduations of nutty brown to golden grey.

Finally, the dirt and dust of years which clings to cavities, corners and sappy areas in the wood plays its part by highlighting the paler mellow surfaces (figure 1). Even the natural grease from finger tips which darkens the areas around handles is an important adjunct of patina.

Patina cannot be reproduced by the makers of fake furniture and its qualities form a significant guarantee against spurious examples. It is formed by a gradual process and takes two hundred and in some cases three hundred years to acquire. Unfortunately many nineteenth century and even present-day restorers have cleaned or stripped off old surfaces and coated the raw wood with French polish, thereby reducing the surface to a flat lifeless and glassy finish much like modern gramophone cabinets and thus completely destroying all character and mellowing that has been acquired.

Colour Plate 1. An Adam serving table, mahogany, c.1780, which possesses the marvellous deep bronze-like lustrous patina which one hopes to find at this period.

Colour Plate 2. A fine George I chest of drawers, walnut, c.1720, demonstrating the wonderful 'toffee-textured' patina that these early pieces sometimes possess. (See also p. 364.)

When judging a piece of furniture various considerations should be taken into account. These should include: balanced proportions combining charm and beauty of line; good quality; the use of first class materials; fine craftsmanship by a cabinet maker aware of the inherent properties of the timber he was using; and, above all, fine colour and patina. Without the latter the piece is lifeless and worth little.

One must remember that in every period and field good and bad objects were made. Just because a piece dates from the eighteenth century does not mean it is attractive or well made. Many people, including unfortunately some dealers, see little difference between a poorly made chest of drawers which has been re-finished and a dilapidated example with original surface. The mere fact that both are eighteenth century is sufficient in their eye. It is the discerning eye that discards the mediocre and selects that which attracts and has merit no matter what its age. However, having progressed that far, the piece that has merit must also possess patina.

Figure 1. An early Sheraton pier table showing in the frieze the ingrained dirt and wax of two centuries which is such an important ingredient of patina.

Figure 2. The beautifully figured and patinated top of the early Sheraton pier table (above), c.1785. It needs an expert to remove skilfully the more obvious marks without disturbing the patina.

Figure 3. A Chippendale period mahogany serpentine commode, c.1760, of fine patina. As shown on p. 372, the doors enclose a series of drawers which are blood red in colour, whereas the exterior, which has been exposed to the air and sunlight, has mellowed to a rich nutty brown.

Figure 4. A Hepplewhite period secretaire bookcase, of fine small size, c.1780, which is beautifully mellowed and patinated both outside and inside the interior of the secretaire drawer.

SEAT FURNITURE

Dr. Samuel Johnson's chair   Circa 1710

Height of back 55ins. (139.7cm) Width of seat 26ins. (66cm) Depth of seat 22ins. (55.8cm)

There are few pieces of English furniture that can be directly associated with such a well-known character as Dr. Johnson (1709-1784). This elm box chair, while not perhaps a piece of great artistic beauty, has just such historic importance. It contains, inside the seat, a contemporary hand-written note to the effect that the chair was the lexicographer's property and was removed from his house near Fleet Street. It was later discovered, with several other Johnsonian relics, in an old house in East Grinstead.

The chair itself is in remarkably untouched state and shows the solidity of the English oak furniture tradition, combined with the comfort of the original braided velvet upholstery in seventeenth century taste and the shaped arms and arm supports of the Queen Anne period.

A William and Mary period walnut stool   Circa 1690

Height 16ins. (40.6cm) Depth 15¼ins. (38.7cm) Width 20½ins. (52cm)

This stool, with its fine original patina, displays the moulded serpentine cross-stretchers with centre finial that were so popular at this period. The bell-shaped turning of the feet is unusual, but stools of a similar type with the inverted baluster legs were made for Hampton Court Palace. This stool has been recovered with early tapestry and fringe.

Compare Rogers, fig. 78, Edwards, vol. III, p. 173, fig. 28. An identical stool is illus. in Symonds, 1921, fig. 26.

A finely carved William III period walnut armchair Circa 1695

Height of back 54ins. (137.2cm) Height of seat 18ins. (45.7cm)
Depth of seat 19ins. (48.2cm) Width of seat 23ins. (58.4cm)

It is very unusual to find a chair of this type in such original condition and with such a rich golden brown patina. Its proportions, and in particular the arms, are very much of the Charles II period, but the serpentine cross-stretchers, the turning of the legs and the design of the back all show influences that came into England with William III in the last decade of the seventeenth century. The use of the scrollwork and foliage in the back is reminiscent of designs by Daniel Marot (1662-1752), an émigré Frenchman who came to England from Holland between 1694 and 1698. His engravings had a substantial influence on contemporary furniture design and it is possible that he made drawings for other immigrant French furniture makers such as Jean Pelletier who worked at several great English houses.

The chair may be compared with one illus. in Edwards, vol. I, p. 248, fig. 68, and an armchair from the collection of Brig. W. Clark, in Rogers, fig. 63. In both of these the backs are carved as three separate splats.

A rare Queen Anne period gilded gesso settee Circa 1705

This settee, which was displayed by the firm at the Grosvenor House Antiques Fair in 1951, is one of the most unusual items of gesso furniture recorded. The use of gilding on carved gesso, or composition of parchment size and whiting, which originated in Italy in the Middle Ages, became fashionable in England at the end of the seventeenth century with the entry of numerous craftsmen from France. The frequent use of foliated strapwork in the carved decoration recalls designs by Bérain and Marot, although the design of this settee, with its waisted back and seat set in matching narrow moulded frames, is very English in conception. The presence of show-wood, as opposed to stuffed over, arms is an early example of their reintroduction after they had gone out of fashion on settees following Charles II's reign.

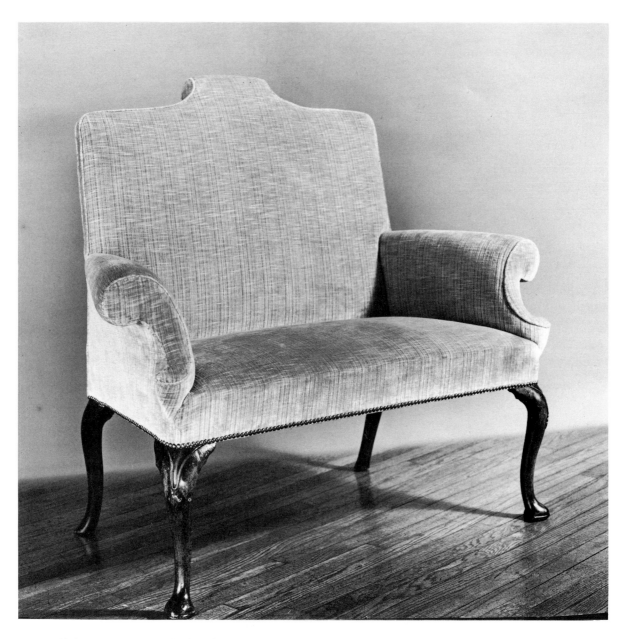

A small Queen Anne period walnut settee   Circa 1705

Max. height 42ins. (106.7cm) Max. width 44ins. (111.8cm) Depth 19ins. (48.2cm)

The small size and the long graceful cabriole legs with no stretchers at front or back, are rare features. The back still retains the height typical of the turn of the seventeenth/eighteenth centuries, and the bold outward curve of the arms, cut away at the front, is echoed in the scroll cresting of the back. The finely patinated legs, with their restrained carving of a lappet and a single husk (or catkin of *garrya eliptica*), stand on club feet still shaped as hooves, formalised from those found on the earliest cabriole legs. The lack of stretchers, so often seen with cabriole legs at this period, gives the piece uncluttered lines and is a further indication of its quality.

Colour Plate 3. A George I period walnut settee, c.1725. The piece is described on p. 37.

An early George I period walnut armchair   Circa 1715

Height of back 35½ins. (90.2cm)
Height of seat 18ins. (45.7cm)
Depth of seat 18½ins. (47cm)
Width of seat 24ins. (61cm)

Set on graceful cabriole legs and pad feet — at the back as well as the front so that it looks well from all angles — the simplicity of this solid walnut chair belies many subtle points of quality. All four legs are edged at the knees with attractive C-scrolls, while the slightly serpentine shape of the top relieves the otherwise square back which is matched by the front seat rail. The well-shaped arms, formed in the scrolled-over or shepherd's crook manner which was fashionable particularly in the second decade of the eighteenth century, are finished off with moulding where they meet the seat rails.

An early George I period walnut wing armchair   Circa 1715

Such was the prevailing Dutch influence at the end of the seventeenth century, that wing armchairs, like other chairs of the period, tended to be tall and thin proportionally and not conducive to comfort. By the second decade of the eighteenth century, however, the proportions had changed and the example illustrated is a particularly well balanced one, on four cabriole legs and with a seat wide and deep enough to be as comfortable as it looks. The front legs, neatly moulded along the edges of the ears and carved with a scallop shell and single husk, end in ball-and-eagle's claw feet which were becoming fashionable at the time. These are perfect specimens of this motif with the balls spherical, not flattened, and grasped securely between four talons.

Colour Plate 4. A Chippendale period mahogany side chair, c.1755. The piece is described on p. 44.

A George I period walnut stool   Circa 1725

Height 17ins. (43.2cm) Depth 18¾ins. (47.5cm) Width 24ins. (61cm)

The good, clean lines of this piece serve to emphasise the colour and deep patination of the timber. The more naturalistic acanthus leaf carving on the knees, that also embraces the ears or corner brackets, is a development from the previous examples although the husk is still present. The use of the loop with its little incisions in the carving is unusual, as is the chamfering of the legs which gives the pad feet an almost webbed appearance. Such features demonstrate the individuality of the carver who shaped the legs and in turn give the piece an individual charm.

A stool of similar form with veneered rather than solid seat rails is illus. in Gilbert, Furniture at Temple Newsam *etc., fig. 373.*

A George I period walnut corner or writing chair

Height of back 32¾ ins. (83.2cm) Height of seat 18¾ ins. (47.6cm)
Max. depth 24ins. (66cm) Width across arms 28¼ ins. (71.7cm)

The scallop shell and husk motifs coupled with C-scrolls at the edges are again used to great effect on the front of the four elegant cabriole legs of this chair. The shell overlaps the serpentine seat rail and so visually links the curves of the two elements.

The chair is made of solid walnut to which time and use have given a mellow colour. It is strongly constructed with three turned columns, yet has several refined touches, such as the paper scrolls at the sides and serpentine mouldings at the bases of the solid splats, which are themselves thinly cut and subtly shaped laterally.

Corner chairs were an English fashion that developed during the first half of the eighteenth century, probably from the Dutch East Indian Burgomaster chairs. Their original purpose, although probably as gentlemen's writing chairs, has never been clearly established and all too often their unusual form makes them appear ungainly. The present example is a notable exception.

The corner chair may be compared with a suite of settee and side chairs of very similar feeling from the Master's House, Peterhouse, Cambridge, illus. in Cescinsky, 1937, p. 169.

A George I period Irish solid walnut armchair

This chair, in untouched condition, has built up a deep dark patina and a natural polish characteristic of the hard, dense and heavy timber of which it is made. In spite of its robustness, however, there is a great deal of movement and interest in the three dimensional shaping of the concave back, which is emphasised by the free flowing movement of the leaf decoration. The arms, like the back, have restrained touches of carving, the wooden saddle seat is scooped out to the human form for comfort, and the four well-balanced cabriole legs are carved at the front. On the knees the rather amusing, flat-carved lions' heads with wrinkled noses are typically Irish in feeling and the quality of the piece as a whole amply illustrates the high standard of which the best Irish craftsmen were capable.

The treatment of the legs of a single chair illus. in Edwards, vol. I, p. 264, fig. 121, has much in common.

36

A pair of George I period walnut single chairs

Circa 1720

Height of back 39ins. (99cm) Height of seat 17ins. (43.2cm)
Depth of seat 17¼ins. (43.8cm) Width of seat 20½ins. (52cm)

These chairs, with their fine colour, illustrate well some of the best ways in which the Continental, particularly Dutch, influences of the late seventeenth century were developed into a very English style of chair. The waisted shaping of the backs, echoed in the vase-shaped splats, is still much the same as on some of the late seventeenth century Marot-influenced chairs, but now with much more of a sculptural, three-dimensional shaping to fit the human form in greater comfort, sweeping down gracefully into the back legs. The veneered seat rails are cut away at the bottom so that they do not appear too heavy, a feature which makes for a smooth transition to the finely shaped cabriole legs with their full acanthus leaf carving, including the ears, and ball-and-claw feet.

A comparison may be drawn with the form of the back and treatment of the legs of a settee illus. in Cescinsky, 1937, p. 178, from which the superior shaping of the current examples is evident.

A George I period walnut settee

Circa 1725

Height of back 39ins. (99cm) Height of seat 18¼ins. (46.4cm)
Depth of seat 21ins. (53.4cm) Max. width 60½ins. (153.8cm)

This settee, also illustrated in Colour Plate 3, p.29, shows well a fine rich patina. It stands on six cabriole legs, the front three again with well-developed carving which incorporates the rather earlier shell motif, and ball-and-claw feet. The open arms are finely shaped and terminate in eagles' heads, a decorative device introduced from France about 1720, while the proportions of the back are lower and squarer than on settees made earlier in the century.

The cushions are made from fragments of seventeenth century Brussels tapestry.

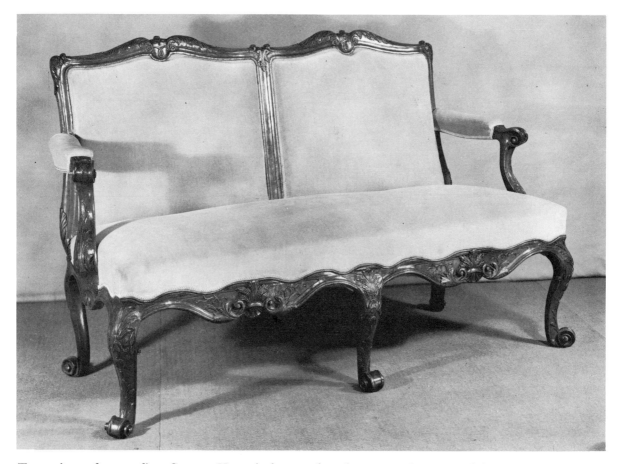

Two pieces from a fine George II period carved mahogany suite comprising two settees and five armchairs   Circa 1750

Settee: Height of back 37½ins. (95.3cm) Height of seat 17ins. (43.2cm)
Depth of seat 26ins. (66cm) Width 60ins. (152.4cm)
Chair: Height of back 37ins. (94cm) Height of seat 17½ins. (44.5cm)
Depth of seat 19ins. (48.3cm) Width 24ins. (61cm)

Two of the signs of particular quality in a piece of upholstered seat furniture are a shaped or carved show-wood seat rail and a similar framing to the back. This suite incorporates both of these, with good serpentine shaping (that on the sides happily accommodating the arm supports) and fine acanthus carving. Each piece stands with solid dignity on cabriole legs, in the carving of which are still discernible the shells, husks and C-scrolls noted on much earlier chairs. The upturned scrolls of the feet, however, which continue the outline curve of the legs so smoothly and are balanced to some extent by the scrolled ends to the arms, are a new device introduced from France about the middle of the century, as part of the rococo vocabulary.

There are several examples of chairs of similar feeling such as a pair in the Untermyer Collection, illus. in Hackenbroch, pl. 74, and a group which is so similar to the present suite as probably to be from the same workshop, including a set of four armchairs formerly in the Leidesdorf Collection which have hairy paw feet, and a single chair given to the Victoria and Albert Museum (W. 42-1947) by Mr. F.D. Lycett-Green and illus. in V. and A., English Chairs, pl. 66, which has straight-topped aprons to the seat rails. It is also instructive to compare the similar handling, yet with the introduction of neo-classical decoration, of the giltwood suite designed for Sir Lawrence Dundas by Robert Adam in 1764, illus. in Macquoid, vol. III, figs. 196-8.

Provenance: Swaines Hill Manor, Hampshire.
The late Marjorie Wiggin Prescott, Belle Haven, Greenwich, Connecticut, U.S.A.

A Chippendale period carved mahogany Gainsborough chair   Circa 1755

Height of back 39½ins. (100.4cm) Height of seat 18ins. (45.8cm) Width of seat 26ins. (66cm)

In some ways this armchair has much in common with the previous example. The overall shape, particularly the carving of the legs, is very similar. Yet the whole feeling here is less monumental and a little more gracious, and the carving is particularly fine and crisp. The sweep of the back legs balances the rake of the back and all four legs are carved in a similar fashion, the shells or plumes on the front knees hipped slightly into the seat; the arm supports are tenoned into the seat rails from above, which leaves the front and side show-wood seat rails free for some lively and inventive acanthus scrollwork and plumage, which is matched in the treatment of the arm supports.

Carving of this sort on such friezes that are set at a slight diagonal angle is often associated with Irish manufacture.

Colour Plate 5. A pair of Chippendale period mahogany Gainsborough chairs, c.1760.
They are described on p. 45.

A fine Chippendale period mahogany Gainsborough chair

Circa 1755

Height of back 39ins. (99cm) Depth of seat 23ins. (58.4cm) Width of seat 28ins. (71cm)

Here all four legs are both carved and cabriole, matching at the front and back so that, free-standing in the middle of a room, the chair would look balanced and attractive from all angles. An unusual feature is the finely serpentine-moulded show-wood seat rails with three-dimensional shaping that sweeps into the curve of the legs. The arms also are carved and shaped in every plane and the top of the stuffed back serpentine shaped so that there is barely a straight line in the whole piece. The feet on this chair illustrate another type of foot popular at the period, the knurl foot, which scrolls under and inside rather than outside as in the French scroll, thereby giving another rounded surface for inventive carving. The detail also shows the way in which castors could be concealed in hollows under the feet. The term 'Gainsborough' to describe such a comfortably-proportioned upholstered armchair of this period with its typical arm pads and concave arm supports, is, in fact, a modern one. Contemporary records use the term 'French' chair.

Examples of a not dissimilar type but with show-wood frames to the backs as well as the seats may be found in Chippendale, 1762, pl. XX. Chippendale advises the covers to be 'nailed with brass nails'. There is a pair of the same period with shaped seat rails at Temple Newsam House illus. in Gilbert, no. 77.

Provenance: The Arthur Leidesdorf Collection.

A pair of Chippendale period mahogany side chairs   Circa 1760

Height of back 37¾ ins. (95.8cm) Depth of seat 16¾ ins. (42.5cm) Width 23¼ ins. (59cm)

A comparison with the last illustration will show at once the change, around the middle of the eighteenth century, to a greater elegance and feeling of lightness in keeping with the qualities of mahogany. The cabriole legs on this pair of chairs have quite similar constituent parts to previous examples, the scrolled front feet, the acanthus above them and the carving on the knee which, instead of the residual shell, now takes the form of cabochons, convex ovals derived from jewellery, set amongst C-scrolls. Yet there is a new slenderness and elegance both in the front legs and the balanced curve of the back ones. The rectangular backs too curve gently backwards to give comfort and visual satisfaction.

The same lightness, including the use of the cabochon motifs and scroll feet, is evident in some of the designs in Chippendale, 1762, especially pl. XI, and Ince and Mayhew.

Ex collection Lord Keith, The Wicken, Castleacre, Norfolk.

A rare Chippendale period mahogany side chair   Circa 1755

Height of back 41¾ ins. (106cm) Height of seat 18½ ins. (47cm) Depth of seat 22ins. (55.8cm)

This superbly patinated chair (see also Colour Plate 4, p. 32) has carving on the knees of a very similar type to the last. The knurl feet, too, are carved with cabochons and acanthus. Other signs of quality in this piece are the hipped corners which run the legs into the seat rails, the serpentine front rail and the subtle use of gadrooning along the bottom edges. However, the particular rarity of the piece is the fact that it still possesses its original tapestry covering, possibly made at the Fulham manufactory. This depicts birds in landscapes and is framed around the edges of the back and seat with fruit, flowers and acanthus foliage which bring the carved wood and covering together in a meaningful whole.

The handling of the carving on the legs is similar to that of a settee at Temple Newsam House illus. in Gilbert, no. 328, and there is similar bird and floral tapestry on a chair from the Mulliner Collection, illus. in Brackett, p. 212.

One of a pair of Chippendale period mahogany Gainsborough chairs   Circa 1760

Height of back 38ins. (96.5cm) Height of seat 17ins. (43.2cm)
Depth of seat 23½ins. (59.6cm) Width of seat 26¾ins. (68cm.)

A further example of a finely proportioned chair set on four similar cabriole legs, each carved and hipped with a scrolled-over shell. The flat scrolls and acanthus carving of the arms and supports match closely, the rounded ends corresponding with the tightly scrolled French feet. The carving and edges are emphasised with original gilding, a manner of enrichment used as a contrast to the bronze-like early mahogany in interior decoration and on furniture, particularly of the second quarter of the century. The front seat rails are gently serpentine in shape, echoing the top rails.

See also Colour Plate 5, p. 41.

An unusual chair with wings from Hornby Castle (see provenance below) and clearly by the same maker is illus. in Edwards, vol. I, p. 289, fig. 199.

Provenance: 10th Duke of Leeds, Hornby Castle, Yorks.

A fine pair of Chippendale period mahogany oval stools

Circa 1755

Width 23¾ins. (60.5cm) Depth 18ins. (45.8cm) Height 18½ins. (47cm)

These stools remain in remarkably original condition with no restoration whatsoever. The seat rails, with a quadrant retaining moulding at the top, are veneered with vertical grain on to beech, the carving of the legs not encroaching on these at all. This carving makes excellent use of the broad knees with extremely crisp and deep cutting of the acanthus that embraces them. It is unusual, and a sign of quality, that in almost every case on at least one side the ears are not separate pieces of wood but carved from the same block as the legs, which would have made for a considerable wastage of timber. The long side scrolls of each leg run smoothly into the deeply scrolled toes with further foliage rising from them and oval blocks beneath. It is a further tribute to the comparatively small amount of use that these stools have had that the original petit point needlework covering on one of the drop-in seats still exists, albeit in a fragmentary condition.

See also Colour Plates 6a and 6b, p. 60.

Provenance: The late Major F.H.T. Jervoise, Herriard Park, Basingstoke, Hants.

A fine pair of Chippendale period mahogany stools

Circa 1755

Height 16ins. (40.6cm) Depth 17ins. (43.2cm) Width 22ins. (55.8cm)

All the seat rails of these stools (see also Colour Plate 7, p. 69) are serpentine in shape and at the same time shaped at the bottom, rising at each corner to small scrolled hips. The cabriole legs are both moulded and carved, which emphasises their smooth curves down to small scroll feet raised on pads in the French fashion of which there are several examples in Chippendale's *Director*. The gros and petit point floral needlework is largely contemporary in date but not original to the stools. The presence on each stool of a letter 'F' branded at each end beneath a royal crown makes it possible that these stools were made for Frederick, Prince of Wales, father of George III. If this is the case the fact that he died in 1751 would make them very early and pre-Director examples of this elegant rococo style.

Two pieces from an outstanding Chippendale period mahogany suite comprising a settee and eleven single chairs

Circa 1760

Settee: Height of back 37½ins. (95.5cm) Height of seat 18ins. (45.7cm)
Depth of seat 21¾ins. (55.2cm) Max. length 73ins. (185.5cm)
Chair: Height of back 37½ins. (95.5cm) Height of seat 18ins. (45.7cm)
Max. depth 24ins. (61cm) Max. width 25ins. (63.5cm)

The design of the backs of this suite is based, with minor variations, on a design that uniquely appears twice (plates XIII and XIV) in the 1762 edition of Chippendale's *Director,* and it became probably his most popular chair back. It combines elegant scrolled curves with the cabochon motif at the top, here matched on the knees of the cabriole legs, and a touch of Gothic in the mouchette at the base. The whole is finished off with judicious carving of acanthus twists and rocaille, the fine quality of which is apparent in the details.

The settee is a particularly good example of a triple chair back, each one with its two uprights for extra strength. It is interesting to note that the whole length of the top rail is carved from a single length of wood, a tribute to the carver, and the fact that the finest mahogany available at this time lent itself to such work in a way that walnut never could. The drop-in seats are all covered with the original gros point needlework in flower and foliage designs, that on the settee based on three sections. This is an extremely good condition through having had nineteenth century covers protecting it.

Amongst other chairs based on the same Director *pattern, some examples are illus. in Gilbert,* Chippendale, *vol. II, p. 83, one set being at Nostell Priory; there is a pair at Temple Newsam House (no. 74 in Gilbert), all the foregoing having straight legs; an armchair at the Victoria and Albert Museum (W.46 — 1925) illus. in Edwards, vol. I, p. 278, fig. 164; and a single chair illus. in Macquoid, vol. 3, fig. 183, both of these having cabriole legs, but of a slightly earlier type than the present suite.*

Provenance: Assheton Craven-Smith-Milne, Esq., Hockerton Manor, Southall, Nottinghamshire.
Sotheby's, 10th March, 1933, Lot 178.
Sir Robert Wilmot Bt., Pitcairlie, Newburgh, Fife.

A Chippendale period walnut armchair   Circa 1755

Height of back 39ins. (99cm) Height of seat 17¾ins. (45cm)
Depth of seat 19ins. (48.2cm) Width of seat 24ins. (61cm)

This chair, apart from its fine quality of craftsmanship and carving, presents an interesting mixture of elements. In the first place it is made of walnut and its cut-away seat rail and the shaping of its cabriole legs and ball-and-claw feet are not dissimilar to the pair of chairs of circa 1720 illustrated on p. 36. Yet the carving has a rococo naturalism very different from the earlier formal motifs. Likewise the back is very much lighter in feeling, the moulded uprights tapering out to meet the curvaceous top rail and the splat opened out with piercing and carving. Touches such as the gadrooning on the shoe at the base of the splat, the acanthus scrolls on the tops of the arms and the subtle running up of the carving from the knee on to the seat rail give added quality to the piece.

The elements in the splat are very much of the Chippendale *Director* period although hardly a trace of the traditional ball-and-claw foot will be found in that work.

An armchair with square legs, the back of which is clearly copied from the same source including the drapery-like carving along the top rail, is illus. in Cescinsky, 1937, p. 287.

50

A Chippendale period mahogany single chair from a set of four   Circa 1760

Height of back 38½ ins. (98.8cm) Height of seat 16¾ ins. (42.5cm)
Depth of seat 18¼ ins. (46.4cm) Width of seat 21 ins. (53.4cm)

Although not perhaps based directly on any published design, the carving of the splat on this chair is of quite exceptional quality. The outline of the traditional vase shape is still discernible and it is filled with fine Gothic ornament and delicate acanthus scrolls on a complex interlace framework which gives structural strength. The classical and the Gothic blend together in a way that the finest eighteenth century designers managed so successfully. In order not to detract from this *tour de force,* the rest of the chair relies on clean cut grandeur: the serpentine-fronted seat rail of finely figured solid timber, the well-moulded front legs chamfered on the inside edges, and the uprights, shaped at the back to avoid heaviness, with a touch of foliage to link them to the top rail. This piece also illustrates the new fashion of the square leg, probably used at first mainly on chairs in the so-called Gothic and Chinese styles, and the return of the stretcher to chairs of quality after about half a century. It is interesting to note that the flat facing of the uprights might point to North Country manufacture.

An arm and one of six single chairs from a set of Chippendale period mahogany dining chairs

Circa 1760

Armchair: Height of back 36½ ins. (92.8cm) Height of seat 18¼ ins. (46.3cm)
Depth of seat 18¼ ins. (46.3cm) Width of seat 23½ ins. (59.6cm)
Single: Depth of seat 17¼ ins. (43.8cm) Width of seat 23ins. (58.4cm)

This is a well-proportioned set with serpentine front seat rails and moulded uprights, front legs and arm supports. The splat is based on a design published in the 1762 edition of the *Director*. Its

elements include a mixture of formalised scrolls and lambrequins which might have been found on bed hangings sixty years earlier, a touch of acanthus foliage on the top rail, and interlace that is probably more Chinese in inspiration than Gothic. The flat surface of this interlace is bevelled at each cusp in the same way as is clear on the Chippendale plate.

Pl. IX of Chippendale, 1762, shows the design on which the splat is based. Two chairs in similar taste with foliage clasps at the ends of the top rails, the property of the Worshipful Company of Drapers, are illus. in. Brackett, p. 210.

A Chippendale period
mahogany armchair   Circa 1760

Height of back 38ins. (96.5cm) Height of seat 18ins.
(45.7cm) Max. width 27ins. (68.5cm)

Another chair with a pierced splat well carved with
interlace and touches of foliage in a basic *Director*
manner. Here the top rail curves downwards at the
ends into the moulded uprights — a last reminder of
the earlier typical arched back — and the moulding is
carried on with a slight twist in the curved arm
supports. The generously proportioned seat is
supported on square legs with moulding on the outside
edges and joined by rather attractive and unusual
rhomboid stretchers.

Chairs based on the same design are illus. in Edwards, vol. I,
fig. 194, and Coleridge, fig. 170.

An unusual Chippendale period mahogany corner or writing chair
Circa 1760

Height of back 32ins. (81.2cm)
Height of seat 17¾ins. (45cm)
Max. depth of seat 25¼ins. (64.8cm)
Width across arms 28¼ins. (71.8cm)

Typical of a number of chairs at this eclectic period, the design above the seat rail is in the classical/Gothic idiom, while below, between the fluted square legs, the blind fretwork is Chinese. The composition of the splats and uprights is hardly in Chippendale *Director* style (indeed probably none of the best London makers were producing corner chairs by this period), yet the small-scale carving is exquisite and even amusing. The uprights, rounded at the back and flat at the front are based on fluted and stop-fluted columns, the tops of the side ones kinked outwards. The capitals take the form of quite elaborate drapery lambrequins. The splats also, beneath the tendril-like foliage and ogee interlace, are based on three columns with entablatures sprouting leaves, the outer columns kinked and the centre ones perched precariously on acanthus leaves.

A Chippendale period mahogany stool   Circa 1765

Height at centre 18½ ins. (47cm) Max. height 19¾ ins. (50.2cm)
Depth 15¾ ins. (40cm) Width 23¼ ins. (59cm)

This stool combines a satisfying curvilinear design with refinement of detail. The scrolled ends of the wooden seat, dipping in the centre like an unrolled parchment scroll, are echoed in the tight upward-scrolled feet. The legs are moulded at the sides and joined by turned stretchers, while the arched stretchers, which support an early use of the circular patera motif, are cusped: the merest hint of Gothic in what is otherwise a classically inspired piece.

This is a particularly fine example of a type of which there are many known, particularly at Oxford University, in Brasenose College Library, the Divinity School at the Bodleian Library, the Old Radcliffe Observatory and twenty-six in Christ Church Upper Library. These latter are the most interesting, in that probably twenty-four of them were supplied by Thomas Chippendale in July 1764 at a cost of £1 10s. 6d. each, see Gilbert, Chippendale *pp. 164-5. It is uncertain whether the design for these stools was Chippendale's own or whether he improved on an already existing local type. Another example is illus. in Jourdain and Rose, fig. 29. Ince and Mayhew also have quite a closely related design on pl. XXXIV.*

   The same outline shape may be found in a set of painted rococo hall stools at Petworth House, Sussex, which may be a little earlier in date, and some stools formerly at Coleshill House, Berkshire, illus. in Edwards, vol. III, p. 182, fig. 57.

A Chippendale period mahogany 'Cockpen' armchair from a set of seven   Circa 1760

Height of back 37ins. (94cm) Height of seat 18ins. (45.7cm)
Depth of seat 21ins. (53.3cm) Width of seat 24ins. (61cm)

Much the majority of furniture produced in the 'Chinese' taste of the mid-eighteenth century was made in a severely anglicised style with little relevance, except in elements of the decoration, to Chinese originals. This chair, in spite of being made of mahogany instead of bamboo as Sir William Chambers would have advocated, is closer to the true Oriental simplicity than most. The square back is filled with lattice-work, or 'Chinese railing' as it was called at the time, all of round section in imitation of bamboo, the four main struts subtly curved. This curve is echoed in the lower back rail, the dipped seat, the arms, which are the most traditionally English part of the piece, and the outward sweep of the legs which is most unusual at this period. The simple moulding at the front of the legs emphasises this sweep.

The term 'Cockpen' derives from the presence of similar chairs in the private pew of the Laird of Cockpen in the church at the village of that name near Dalhousie Castle, Dalkeith. The type would appear to originate from a designer working in the Edinburgh area. Another, identical, is illus. in Edwards, vol. I, p. 285, fig. 188, from Lennoxlove, East Lothian.

Provenance: The late Sir Charles Lockhart Ross, Balnagown Castle.

An arm and a single chair from a set of Chippendale period mahogany dining chairs Circa 1770

Besides the fine quality of their craftsmanship, these chairs are interesting examples of the transition between the Chippendale and Adam styles. The square moulded legs joined by stretchers, the serpentine front seat rails and the moulded arms are all very similar to those on the set illustrated on p. 53, but the backs exhibit several new tendencies. The top rails have high-arched centres and curve smoothly with continuous moulding into the uprights, while the splats, although still slightly Gothic-inspired, have a symmetrical roundness that is moving towards the lyre shapes of the 1770s. The carving includes acanthus curls and husks, but also palm fronds and honeysuckle (anthemion), motifs not to be found in the *Director* or its contemporary pattern books. Even the husks are joined by tendrils. These are the first signs of the new neo-classical style that was steadily to change the design and decoration of all fashionable furniture. The single chair has its original double French nailed leather seat.

There is a chair of similar shape but slightly more developed in the splat and arms at the Victoria and Albert Museum (503-1907), illus. in V. and A., English Chairs, *pl. 85.*

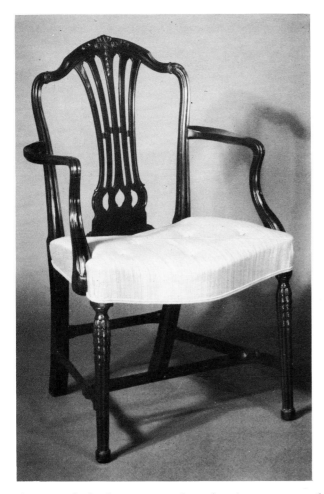

An armchair from a set of twelve (two arm and ten single) Hepplewhite period mahogany dining chairs
Circa 1775

Armchair: Height of back 38¼ins. (97.2cm) Height of seat 18ins. (45.8cm)
Depth of seat 19ins. (48.2cm) Width of seat 23¼ins. (59cm)
Single: Height of back 38¼ins. (97.2cm) Height of seat 18ins. (45.8cm)
Depth of seat 18ins. (45.8cm) Width of seat 22½ins. (57cm)

See Colour Plate 8, p. 69, which also shows a single chair. The upper halves of these chairs conform to a fairly common overall pattern of the period. The moulded shape of the backs and arms is much like that of the previous armchair, and the crisply carved anthemia, rosettes and husks are classical motifs annexed to splats which, in spite of their simple vertical ribs, still have Gothic details like the trefoil head to each slit and the mouchettes at the bases. Indeed the piercing of the splats in this way is a direct development of some of the early pierced splats, sometimes with similar cusps at the tops, of the 1730s and 40s.

Below the dipped seats the features become much more unusual. The uncommon rhomboid stretchers are identical in construction to those on the chair on p. 54, while the attractive front legs would appear to be without parallel. They are circular and tapered with a reel turning at the top and husk chains hanging over reeding below. In some ways they anticipate the turned legs with stiff leaf or 'tassel' tops of the end of the century, but at the same time the way that the reeded legs meet the circular plinth feet is perhaps reminiscent of hexafoil section Gothic columns.

Comparisons of the backs of these chairs may be made with that on a chair in the Victoria and Albert Museum illus. in Tomlin, no. Q/4; and a pair in Cescinsky, 1937, p. 335.

Colour Plates 6a and 6b. A pair of Chippendale period mahogany oval stools, c.1755, and detail. The stools are described on p. 46.

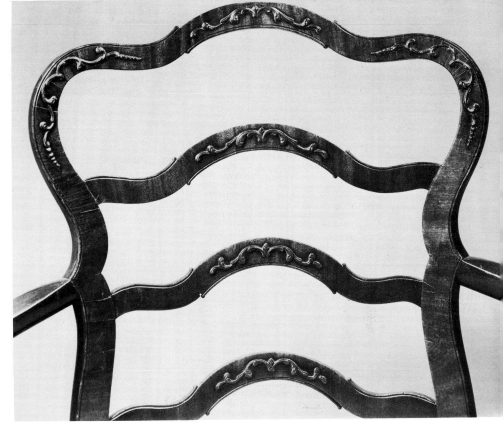

An unusual Chippendale period mahogany ladderback armchair   Circa 1770

Height of back 36ins. (91.5cm) Height of arms 26¼ins. (66.6cm)
Depth of seat 19¼ins. (48.8cm) Width of seat 23½ins. (59.7cm)

Another fashion in the third quarter of the century was the adaptation of the country ladderback chair to the quality manufacture, although there are no designs shown in contemporary pattern books. This example has the unusual feature of cross-grain mahogany veneer on the whole of the front surface of the back and the fine carved trailing foliage applied to it. The 'curvaceousness' of the piece is also noteworthy. The back has a lateral curve as well as a complex outline shape with an arched top rail similar to the two preceding examples, the rungs conforming. The arms, curving to follow the seat rail, have moulded supports with an eccentric twist. The front seat rail itself is serpentine and shaped at the bottom to flow into the carved and moulded cabriole legs and scroll feet with their French lightness. In short, the chair is a fine example of movement.

A fine mahogany window stool, possibly by Thomas Chippendale   Circa 1775

Max. height 26ins. (66cm) Height of seat 16ins. (40.6cm)
Max. depth 20ins. (50.8cm) Max. width 57ins. (144.8cm)

Window stools, or window sofas as they were often called in the eighteenth century, were designed to fit into the space in front of a window without obstructing the view. This one is particularly elegantly designed and well executed in the finest of timber. The scrolled ends balance very well the sweep of the French cabriole legs while the deep concave mouldings curve smoothly up from the toes into the frieze, widening in the centre to take a crisply carved acanthus spray. The seat rails themselves are sightly serpentine in outline and the corners have small scrolled hips and husk pendants.

The stool retains its original webbing and gilt nails but the silk damask covering has been replaced.

Also worth noting is a sketch by John Linnell at the Victoria and Albert Museum, illus. in Hayward and Kirkham, fig. 59, of a chair in very much the same taste inscribed 'six of these Lassells' which may well refer to the Lascelles of Harewood House.

Provenance: The Earl of Harewood, Harewood House, Yorkshire, whence it was removed along with a pair of long stools *en suite.* Thomas Chippendale's commission to furnish Harewood House was the most valuable of his career and ran from 1767 to 1778, in which time he provided a large amount of seat furniture of a variety of types. However, because of the brevity of most descriptions and the loss of some accounts, positive identification is in this case impossible.

A fine Hepplewhite period mahogany armchair

Height of back 37ins. (94cm) Height of seat 17½ins. (44.5cm) Width of seat 23½ins. (59.7)

With a chair like this English furniture gets nearer contemporary French work than at any previous period. Only the choice of wood, some minor points of construction, quality of carving and a generally different air of refinement serve to differentiate the two origins. The front legs and shaped serpentine seat rail are quite close in treatment to the previous window stool, hipped at the corners, here with foliage on the feet and a classical urn in the centre of the frieze. The arm supports twist outwards and are moulded in the same way as the outside edge and front surface of the back frame. This is an irregular, cartouche shape, broadening from bottom to top with a cresting carved with an urn and husks to match the seat rail, a conceit reminiscent of walnut and beechwood chairs made a century earlier. The arms and tops of the legs are also linked in with husk carving.

Variations on this type of chair, although not appearing in pattern books, were common at this period and made by Cobb and other fashionable makers, following the practice in Paris of rococo-style chairs being placed in strictly neo-classical interiors.

A reasonably close comparison with this chair may be made with a Linnell drawing in the Victoria and Albert Museum illus. in Hayward and Kirkham, fig. 60.

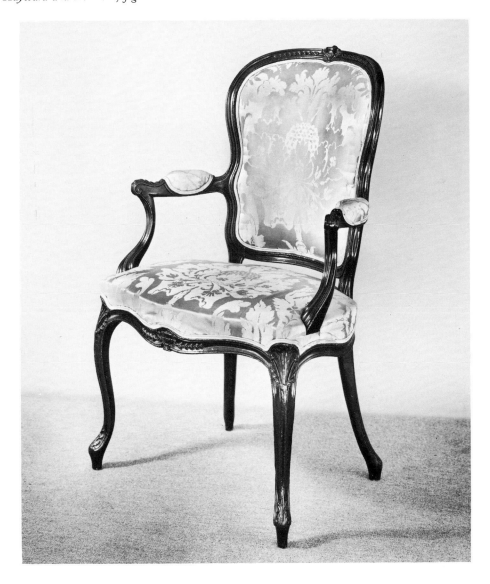

A pair of Hepplewhite period mahogany armchairs

Circa 1775

Height of back 35½ ins. (90.2cm) Height of seat 16½ ins. (42cm)
Depth of seat 21ins. (53.4cm) Width of seat 24ins. (61cm)

In their design, these examples have much in common with the chair on p. 63, including the tendril-like curls at the ends of the arms and similarly moulded serpentine seat rails and legs which end in the scrolled 'French' feet that Hepplewhite in his *Cabinet-Maker and Upholsterer's Guide* calls a 'desirable terminal'. The backs are a little lower in proportion but the front legs, comfortably balanced with the splay of the back ones, have the same length and elegance which is a point of differentiation from the French tendency towards dumpiness. Other signs of quality are the show-wood seat rails and the framing of the backs. Here the latter have the unusual feature of carved husk trails all round the top edges, with rose heads in the centre.

A Hepplewhite period settee with original off-white and green painted decoration   Circa 1775

Max. height of back 37ins. (94cm) Height of seat (with cushions) 21½ins. (54.5cm)
Max. depth of seat 26ins. (66cm) Max. width 73ins. (185.4cm)

The outline of this settee, with its serpentine top rail and unusually high padded ends that run to the front edge, is very much of the Chippendale period or even earlier. By 1775 the usual fashion was for arms to sweep downward. The moulded French cabriole legs, four each at front and back, are noteworthy for their long elegance which is accentuated by the use of (original) brass cup castors. The stiff-leaf carving, diminishing as it climbs the curved show-wood front edges, and at the tops of the legs and in the centre of the frieze, is well executed and emphasised by the painting. The idea of decorating furniture in this way, which tends to lighten its appearance, is another French influence and a practical application of the idea of complete interior design that Robert Adam advanced so successfully.

Chippendale, 1762, pl. XXIX, contains a design for a settee of the same sort of shape in a rather more florid rococo style.

A rare Hepplewhite period cream painted and gilt armchair from a set of four   Circa 1780

Height of back 37½ ins. (95.2cm) Height of seat 17ins. (43.2cm)
Depth of seat 19ins. (48.2cm) Width of seat 23ins. (58.4cm)

A chair giving an impression of being completely neo-classical — in French terms Louis XVI rather than XV — though the design is a distinctive and inventive English one. The oval back is reeded and ribbon-tied in the manner of the Roman fasces, with a finely carved bow as a cresting. An inner oval frame is inset with a copper panel, painted with a spray of summer flowers on a yellow ground, which is joined to the outer frame by six paterae and foliage. The painting is of excellent quality with a different design on each chair.

The slender arms continue the moulding into acanthus scrolled ends with the patera motif picked up at the centres of the scrolls. The fluted baluster arm supports rising from the side rails, which the front legs match though in an inverted position, are uncommon so early. They seem to look forward more to the double-curved arms and turned supports, normally running vertically into the front legs, that are associated with later, Sheraton period, furniture.

Another chair in this set is illus. in Musgrave, fig. 72. A suite of painted and gilded seat furniture in the Lady Lever Art Gallery, Port Sunlight, shows affinities, the armchairs and ends of the settee having oval backs moulded with ribbon tied 'fasces' reeding and vase-shaped splats painted with classical scenes and similar flower sprays to the current example. An armchair is illus. in Edwards, vol. I, plate XVI.

The painting on the central oval is probably by the same hand as the decoration on a pair of cabinets, one illus. in Jourdain and Rose, pl. 12-13. The fluted baluster arm supports are to be found on a set of very different giltwood chairs made in 1769 by Ince and Mayhew for Croome Court, illus. in Musgrave, fig. 63.

Provenance: Lord Roundway, from the Cabinet Room, Roundway House, Wiltshire.
The late Marjorie Wiggin Prescott, Belle Haven, Greenwich, Connecticut, U.S.A.

A Hepplewhite period mahogany stuff-back armchair   Circa 1780

Height of back 37ins. (94cm) Depth of seat 20ins. (50.8cm) Width of seat 24½ins. (62.2cm)

A chair of very elegant proportions that closely follows the best of the Adam tradition. The oval back is comfortably shaped in all three dimensions, its concave moulded show-wood frame carved with fluting which is picked up on a slightly larger scale in the finely shaped serpentine seat rails. These latter have the little half round at the bottom of each flute that is found on seventeenth century oak furniture. The arms are deeply moulded and run into the supports, which in turn curl inwards to meet the seat rail at the front corners and then run down into fluted, inverted baluster legs. An unusual feature is the use of demi-paterae as cappings to the legs, carved on the rounded front corners.

A similar giltwood chair formerly at Langley Park, Norfolk, is illus. in Edwards, vol. I, fig. 207, the only notable differences being in the detailing of the front and back legs.

Colour Plate 7. A pair of Chippendale period mahogany stools, c.1755. The stools are described on p. 46.

Colour Plate 8. An arm and a single chair from a set of twelve Hepplewhite period mahogany dining chairs, c.1775. They are described on p. 59.

A Hepplewhite period mahogany settee   Circa 1780

Height of back 32ins. (81.2cm) Height of seat 16¾ins. (42.5cm)
Depth of seat 23ins. (58.4cm) Width 47ins. (119.4cm)

This settee has much in common with the previous piece and illustrates the typical flowing shape of the backs of settees of this period, ending in moulded inswept arm supports. The fluted, slightly serpentine front seat rail again meets the corners with curved paterae, this time in rectangular frames, and the side rails, similarly fluted, curve round the back in a similar fashion to those on the chair. The fluted tapered legs are headed with twist-fluted decoration and end in fluted feet: both unusual touches.

An open-armed settee illus. in Cescinsky, 1911, vol. III, fig. 246, has a fluted seat rail and tapered fluted legs headed by similar curved paterae cappings.

A pair of Hepplewhite period mahogany stuff-back armchairs   Circa 1780

Height of back 37ins. (94cm)
Height of seat 17ins. (43.2cm)
Depth of seat 22ins. (55.8cm)
Width of seat 24½ins. (62.2cm)

In his *Cabinet Maker and Upholsterer's Guide*, George Hepplewhite wrote: "Chairs in general are made of mahogany, with the bars and frame sunk in a hollow, or rising in a round projection with a band or list in the inner and outer edges." The use of such a hollow concave moulding with defined edges to it is well illustrated in the backs of these chairs. The top part of the moulding is further carved with husk trails rising to a deeply carved oval patera set so it projects on either side of the moulding and marks the apex of the chair. The moulded arms in this case curve down to join the side rails, and below the serpentine front seat rail the legs are square and tapered with fluting. The back legs conform in shape and are set at a splay well judged to balance the chairs in profile.

Colour Plate 9.

A superb Hepplewhite period mahogany armchair   Circa 1780

Height of back 36½ ins. (92.8cm) Height of seat 18ins. (45.7cm)
Depth of seat 18¼ ins. (46.4cm) Width of seat 25¾ ins. (65.4cm)

This exquisite example of English design and carving skill remains virtually in undamaged and untouched condition. With its well-balanced and elegant shape and the refined carving of bay leaves and honeysuckle (anthemion) in the oval, each tendril cut from a solid piece of mahogany, it stands as an important example of its period. The use of the feather-like palm frond carving on the arms, picked up at the top of each leg, is unusual.

An identical chair is illus. in Cescinsky, 1924, vol. II, p. 249, along with a settee of four chair backs. The author says about the chair (p. 253): "It is doubtful if any Chippendale chair, even of the most ornate ribbon-back pattern, was nearly as expensive to make as the one here."

Other chairs of a similar type with the same anthemion motif, but painted, are illus. in Macquoid, vol. 4, fig. 102, and at Houghton Hall, Norfolk and Ham House, Richmond. Another on the trade card of Vickers and Rutledge of Conduit St. c.1775-80 is illus. in Heal, p. 182, and in the Gillow archive there is a design for a chair of the type dated March 1785.

Provenance: Lady Alfred Paget, daughter-in-law of the Marquess of Anglesey.

A Hepplewhite period mahogany oval back armchair

Circa 1785

Height of back 36ins. (91.5cm) Depth of seat 18ins. (45.8cm) Width of seat 21½ ins. (54.5cm)

Within the moulded oval back the crisply carved pierced splat is close to a design found in Hepplewhite's *Cabinet Maker and Upholsterer's Guide*. Some of the detailing here is unusual, however, in the use of single roses and the acanthus foliage at the top which looks back many years. Down the centre, between the intertwined strips and lotus motif (a touch of Egyptian influence), runs a strip of bead ornament picked out again on the edging of the large pierced semi-patera at the base. The back and arm supports are moulded and the classic square tapered legs with spade feet are decorated with fluting with a moulding in each flute (stop fluting) at the top.

Similar single chairs with stop-fluted legs but with shield backs and inlaid paterae are illus. in Edwards, vol. I, p. 296, fig. 224 and V. and A., English Chairs, pl. 103. The splat appears in a shield-back version in Hepplewhite, 1794, pl. 4.

A pair of Hepplewhite period mahogany single chairs
Circa 1785

Height of back 34ins. (86.4cm) Height of seat 17½ins. (44.5cm)
Depth of seat 18ins. (45.7cm) Width of seat 20ins. (50.8cm)

The fashion that Robert Adam seems to have begun for oval backs was adapted in all sorts of ways, here as a pierced circle with the decorations taking the form of a wheel. The rim is cross-grain veneered, rather than moulded as was the ladderback chair (p. 61), and inside, radiating from a central circular patera, are eight spokes carved as pointed palm leaves which are joined to the rim with large husks. Between these, and as if they were hanging from staples set into the rim, are linked husk swags. The web-like impression that they give is to be found on other pierced oval back chairs of this date.

Exactly the same treatment of a circular back, including the scrolled and moulded supports as here, is to be found on an armchair formerly in the possession of Sir Sydney Greville, illus. in Edwards, vol. I, p. 300, fig. 237. Although not carved by the same hand, there would appear to be a direct influence between these chairs. Another set of six of similar type were included in the CINOA International Art Treasures Exhibition at the Victoria and Albert Museum, 1962 (no. 87). Hepplewhite, 1788, pl. 6, gives a design for a pierced oval back with decoration radiating from a central patera, but by the 1794 edition, this had been dropped in favour of a more modish square backed design.

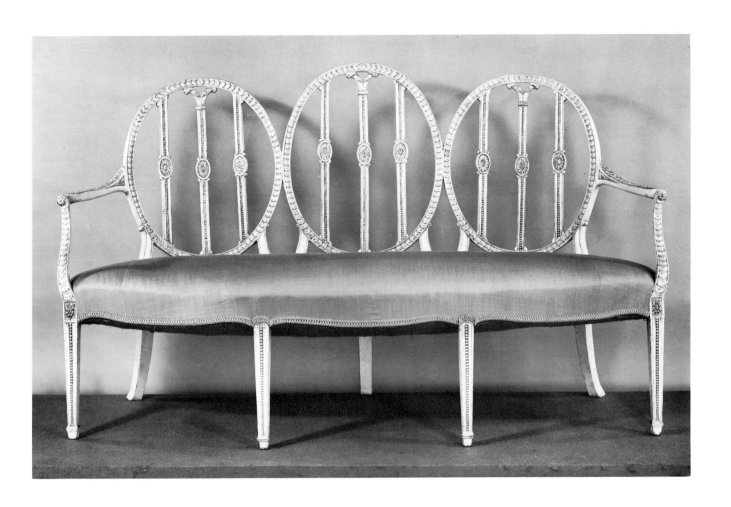

A rare Hepplewhite period white painted and gilded triple chair-back settee   Circa 1780

Here the pierced oval back appears in another form, all three ovals being joined for strength where they touch in lieu of a top rail, the centre one standing slightly higher than the others to good effect. Each contains three vertical splats with oval-framed paterae in the centre and forked acanthus curls at the top of the middle splat. The ovals are carved with an ornament of overlapping discs, a form of guilloche, which continues along the arms and down the arm supports. In contrast the splats and moulded square tapered legs have a channelled bead decoration.

A triple oval chair-back settee with the guilloche ornament and similar rectangular-framed paterae cappings to the outer legs but with pierced splats, is illus. in Edwards, vol. III, p. 99, fig. 68. Vol. I, p. 299, fig. 233 of the same work depicts an armchair of similar handling with the bead ornament on the oval and arm supports and the centre splat with two paterae, while closer still is another armchair, illus. in Cescinsky, 1931, pl. 256. All these are made of mahogany.

A Hepplewhite period mahogany shield-back chair from a set of ten   Circa 1780

Height of back 37½ ins. (95.2cm) Height of seat 18ins. (45.7cm) Width of seat 21ins. (53.3cm)

Besides the oval, the most popular shape for chair backs at this period was the shield. This chair represents one of the seemingly endless variations on the shield back, the slight outward turn and scrolls at the end of the top rail being unusual. The back consists of three splats, the middle one with a central patera reminiscent of the oval chair-back settee (p. 75). Round the patera and diminishing above and below it, is an example of true classical guilloche carving: two bands intertwined into a plait, with a strange use of husks, almost like a bunch of tulips, at the top. The side splats are subtly shaped and carved with lotus and diminishing beads. Added refinement is shown in the little curls carved at the ends. Most of the surface of the back has channelled mouldings, while the front legs are square, tapered and wave-moulded, supporting a dipped seat and joined by stretchers.

An identical chair, except for an inlaid central patera, is illus. in Cescinsky, 1937, p. 344, and another with a serpentine seat rail and no stretchers in Macquoid, vol. 3, fig. 172.

**An arm and a single chair from a set of eight (two arm, six single)
Hepplewhite period mahogany shield-back dining chairs**   Circa 1780

Armchair: Height of back 37ins. (94cm) Depth of seat 18ins. (45.7cm) Width of seat 22ins. (55.8cm)
Single: Height of back 36½ins. (92.7cm) Depth of seat 17ins. (43.2cm) Width of seat 21ins. (53.4cm)

In this case all the members have fairly uniform convex channelled mouldings while the arms run into the side rails in the earlier fashion rather than to the front corners. The pierced single splats follow in the same tradition as those on the set of twelve chairs (p. 59), even to the vestigial trefoil heads to the piercings. The ribs themselves have concave mouldings, as do the scrolls that enclose ribs in a grid form in the lower half. The crestings have carved ribbon-tied wheat ear sprays, a motif that was becoming popular at the time. Another innovation is the inlaid boxwood paterae in the centre of the splats, a hint of fashion for marquetry cabinet furniture at this date.

It is interesting that of two very similar chairs to this set, illus. in Cescinsky, 1937, p. 341, one has an inlaid patera and one a carved one, as if the pattern was offered to clients with this choice. The same situation may be noted in the comparisons made to the chair in Colour Plate 11, p. 80.

A fine pair of Hepplewhite period mahogany heart-back armchairs   Circa 1780

Height of back 37¾ins. (96cm) Height of seat 18ins. (46cm)
Depth of seat 20ins. (53.4cm) Max. width 23¾ins. (61cm)

The patina on these chairs combined with the quality of their shaping and carving makes them exceptional. The heart shape, which is made up of three interlaced loops rising from a semi-patera, has flat channelled mouldings. The slender festoons of drapery that cross the heart are realistically carved, as if they are a single length of material threaded through the loops at the top and tied under the arms. In the centre are three ribbon-tied ostrich feathers, the badge of the Prince of Wales' party, inclining forwards, again with great realism. These backs are well raised from the seats and the arms, moulded and with the most graceful shaping to join the side rails, are set high. These factors and the moulded square tapered legs without stretchers, combine to make chairs of superb proportions and with a notable air of lightness. Each chair is stamped inside the back seat rail with the maker's initials 'R.E'.

This particular pattern of chair back may have been associated with Gillows. An armchair and a side chair are included in their records for 1788 and in their Cost Book for 1797 is a drawing and specifications for a mahogany armchair, illus. in Cescinsky, 1911, vol. III, fig. 383. The cost of this is given as £1 15s. 6¼d. An identical example to the present chairs is shown as fig. 168 in Macquoid, vol. 4, and there is a similar one with arms joining the front corners in the Victoria and Albert Museum, illus. in Tomlin, no. P/5.

A fine pair of Hepplewhite period giltwood shield-back armchairs   Circa 1785

Height of back 37ins. (94cm) Height of seat 17ins. (43cm)
Depth of seat 19ins. (48.3cm) Width of seat 22ins. (56cm)

The concave shape and rounded bottoms of these backs (Colour Plate 10) make for a smoothly flowing line which is accentuated by the reeded frames and picked up again in the serpentine-fronted seat rails. The shields are elegantly raised well above the seats on moulded supports, while the arms have particularly graceful outward double curves ending in dainty scrolls before flowing, moulded, downwards and forwards to meet, with more scrolls, the front legs which are continued above the seat rails. The legs are square tapered and fluted, capped with crisp paterae and end in shaped feet.

A similar overall shape is illus. on a painted chair in Cescinsky, 1911, vol. III, fig. 221, which has feet, arm supports and the joins of the arms to the back carved with lotus in just the same way.

Two fine Hepplewhite period mahogany shield-back armchairs from a set of four   Circa 1780

Height of back 37¼ins. (94.6cm) Height of seat 17½ins. (44.5cm)
Depth of seat 19ins. (48.2cm) Width of seat 24¾ins. (62.8cm)

This type of piercing for the shield back, with five reeded slender ribs curving and swelling to follow the outline shape, was one of the more popular designs chosen by Hepplewhite. These examples (Colour Plate 11) are particularly fine ones for their shaping and the restrained but exquisite carving. The backs have a deep lateral curve, the ribs rising from large semi-paterae to meet the top rails with single husks and rippled bean pods. The front surface of the shield, its supports that run down into the back legs, and the arms and arm supports all have flat channelled mouldings; the fronts legs are similarly treated but have waves in the channels.

The arm supports meet the seat rails at the front corners, as on the previous chairs, with lotus petal carving and paterae but without the upward extension of the leg, which makes a smoother flow. Again the arms meet the supports in two different planes, marked here with neat rosette paterae; perhaps visually a more satisfying method of construction than the single rather lame curve that was sometimes used. These chairs also exhibit such refinements as little scrolls where the back supports meet the shields and touches of foliage where the arms meet the backs and on the top rails.

The piercing appears in pl. 9, and a four chair-back settee in pl. 26, of Hepplewhite, 1794. Amongst other specimens with the same form of back are fig. 218 on p. 294 of Edwards, vol. I, and a very similar chair with a little less decoration and shaping on p. 343 of Cescinsky, 1937.

A fine Hepplewhite period mahogany heart-back armchair from a set of six   Circa 1785

The heart shape with its pointed bottom is here particularly solidly cut and deeply shaped laterally; this meant carving from an unusually thick length of timber for the top section which is all of a piece and so expensive to produce.

The design of the back with its inner shield and crisply carved wheat ears, rosettes, lotus and rising plume-like decoration is an unusual collection. The arms are moulded and run without a stop into their supports, down to upward extensions of the front legs. The scrolls, inverted lotus and patera cappings to the legs are similar to the pair of gilded chairs (p. 80). The moulded seat rails and square tapered legs here support caned seats which became popular towards the end of the century, mainly on lightweight painted and 'japanned' chairs. For such chairs Hepplewhite recommends 'cushions of linen or leather'.

Of the show-wood seat rail of a not dissimilar chair, an entry in one of the Gillow Cost Books notes ''Mahog. Seat Rails — Hollow in Length and Crooked side Rails wch. makes a good deal of waste...''.

Provenance: These chairs were made for Ickwell Bury, Bedfordshire, the home of the Harvey family.

One of a rare set of twelve Sheraton period mahogany armchairs   Circa 1790

Height of back 34ins. (86.4cm) Height of seat 18ins. (45.7cm)
Width of seat 21ins. (53.4cm) Depth of seat 18½ins. (47cm)

As an example of the taste for lightweight square-backed chairs, this has all the typical emphasis on vertical and horizontal lines. For such chairs Sheraton recommends the use of Spanish or Cuban mahogany of a clear, straight grain "which will rub bright, and keep cleaner than any Honduras wood", but the latter is permissible where lightness is desired. One of the more popular designs for backs was a filling of this lattice work, here moulded with reeding set below a rectangular plaque, and supported in the lower half on matching vertical ribs. The arms are of the new high-set type abutting the side rails with rounded blocks and the tapering reeded legs are matched by the back uprights, here formed as columns with lotus-type capitals, and the arm supports. Reeding, which was to become gradually thicker and heavier through the Regency period, was at this time often used, as here, with considerable refinement to emphasise the straight lines of the furniture. Unlike many chairs of this period, this has subtle bowed shaping in the seat rails.

A lattice-back chair with similarities in its surround, although not made until c.1809 is illus. in Edwards, vol. I, p. 307, fig. 264, and an earlier painted one on p. 304, fig. 245. The same form of lattice is shown in Cescinsky, 1937, p. 392.

Provenance: Letton Court, Herefordshire.

**An arm and a single chair from a fine set of eight (two arm, six single)
Sheraton period dining chairs** Circa 1790

Single: Height of back 34ins. (86.4cm) Height of seat 17¼ins. (43.8cm) Width of seat 20ins. (50.8cm)

When Hepplewhite's *Guide* was published in 1788 it was generally reflecting styles that had been current for some years. Indeed Thomas Sheraton in comparing *The Cabinet-Makers' London Book of Prices* by Thomas Shearer et al., published in the same year, wrote that it contained furniture designs "more fashionable and useful" than those of Hepplewhite. However, particularly by the revised 1794 edition, the *Guide* did contain a number of forward-looking chair designs in a lighter vein and with rectilinear rather than oval or shield-shaped backs, a form more normally associated with Sheraton.

This set of chairs is a particularly well-executed example with square backs. A motif noted before, the Prince of Wales' feathers, are in evidence, set against and rising from panels of finely figured mahogany veneer emphasised with boxwood stringing between very slender fluted columns. The arms are, as in the last case, of a new type of which the 1794 *Guide* states: "the arms...though much higher than usual, have been executed with good effect for his Royal Highness the Prince of Wales". They sweep forwards and join fluted baluster supports carved with stiff leaves which abut on the side rails.

The tapered octagonal front legs, again edged with stringing, are unusual and echo, inverted, the back uprights beneath the arms.

The set of chairs is based on a design in pl. 1 of Hepplewhite, 1794. Among many similar chairs after the same design, an identical single chair is illus. in Edwards, vol. I, p. 301, fig. 244 and others are at Temple Newsam House (Gilbert no. 89) and in V. and A., English Chairs, no. 105.

An arm and a single chair from a set of eight (two arm, six single) Sheraton period mahogany dining chairs

Circa 1795

Armchair: Height of back 32¾ ins. (83.2cm) Height of seat 18½ ins. (47cm)
Depth of seat 16¾ ins. (42.5cm) Width of seat 22ins. (56cm)
Single: Depth of seat 16½ ins. (42cm) Width of seat 19½ ins. (49.5cm)

Towards the end of the eighteenth century there was a new interest in archaeological classicism, in other words not merely classical motifs used in decoration, but actually copying the shapes of classical furniture so far as they were known. Two of the first popular indications of this, seen in this example, was a backward scrolling of the uprights and the deepening of the top rail into a panel. These chairs also have a lateral curve and reeded decoration to the backs and arms. The front legs are slenderly turned and tapered and inverted for the arm supports.

The crossed arrows and lozenge motif of the back splats, possibly introduced from France by Henry Holland, is found on pl. 38 of Sheraton, 1791-4.

An arm and a single chair from a set of eight (two arm, six single) Sheraton period mahogany dining chairs
Circa 1795

Height of back 33½ins. (85cm) Height of seat 18ins. (45.7cm)
Depth of seat 18ins. (45.7cm) Width of seat 20ins. (50.8cm)

As with the previous set of chairs, the dimensions show, with the exception of the seat height, the generally smaller size of this period compared with earlier ones. In spite of their similar overall shape, these display some unusual features. The top rails, again set between reeded uprights, have two oval piercings flanking a rectangular panel inlaid with satinwood. Curving downwards from this is a splat pierced with fine lattice work which meets the bottom rail in another, smaller, satinwood panel.

The arms curve downwards in an uncommon fashion, starting outside the top scrolls and continuing down to turned supports that are upward extensions of the front legs which meet the seat rails with rounded rectangular panels. There are slender reeded mouldings along the bottom edges of the seat rails.

The pierced oval and lattice pattern has the same inspiration as a painted chair illus. in V. and A., English Chairs, *no. 108.*

An arm and a single chair from a set of eight (two arm, six single) Sheraton period mahogany dining chairs   Circa 1795

Arm: Height of back 32½ ins. (82.5cm) Depth of seat 16¾ ins. (42.5cm) Width of seat 21¼ ins. (54cm)
Single: Depth of seat 16ins. (40.7cm) Width of seat 20½ ins. (52cm)

In many ways these chairs are of a similar form to those on p. 86 with reeded back and arms and matching turned and tapered arm supports and front legs. The scroll of the back is rather more pronounced, flowing smoothly into the arms, the uprights joined with a new development, a symmetrically turned rail, here with a curved reeded section in the centre. Below, the two cross bars and finely pierced centre section carved with flower heads, are slightly bowed laterally, although the top bar, set further back, is straight. Except for the case of ladderback chairs, this emphasis on the horizontal is not found previously in the eighteenth century.

A Sheraton period mahogany armchair Circa 1795

Height of back 33ins. (83.8cm) Height of seat with cushion 18½ins. (47cm)
Depth of seat 18ins. (45.7cm) Width of seat 21½ins. (54.6cm)

The interestingly contrived shaping of this chair makes it an unusual and attractive design for its date. Having a rounded seat, the uprights, which curve away elegantly into the back legs, are set diagonally so that the inside faces frame the scrolled and reeded back, while the other forward faces, picking out the sides of the scrolls with acanthus curls, flow majestically inwards into the double curved and reeded arms. The uprights are joined by emphatically curved crossbars and a turned top rail with a satinwood panel in the centre, in this instance also curved. The baluster arm supports meet the side rails of the caned seat in octagonal blocks, while the slender turned and reeded front legs are capped with unusually shaped paterae. The front seat rail is slightly bowed.

A pair of early Regency period painted armchairs   Circa 1800

Height of back 33ins. (83.8cm) Height of seat 17½ins. (44.5cm) Width of seat 22ins. (55.8cm)

Here again the emphasis is very much on curves, these chairs being typical of the finest turn of the century taste for caned and decorated furniture without the later Regency heaviness. The scrolls of the backs are echoed in the in-swept sabre front legs, another inspiration from the Greek klismos chair, while the arms, curving down as on p. 87 from extensions to the sides of the top scrolls, sweep over the curvaceous arm supports to form a shape like a question mark. The top rails are oval plaques painted with matching classical scenes *en grisaille,* above lattice panels framed with more scrolls. The whole of the chair frames are painted black and their shaping liberally emphasised with gilded lines including fluting shapes on the legs.

A very similar form of back and arms is illus. in Jourdain, 1948, fig. 31.

Two from a set of four Regency period mahogany hall seats

Height of back 33ins. (83.8cm) Height of seat 17ins. (43cm)
Depth of seat 19½ins. (49.5cm) Max. width 33½ins. (85cm)

These ample-sized armchairs with panelled seats and backs conform to the extensive eighteenth century tradition of wooden-seated hall furniture painted with family crests, but are unusual in the use that they make of the new classical forms. The sabre shaping of the front and back legs, which run in a single curve into the scrolled arm supports, picked out with ebonised flutes and roundels, is an attractive feature, while the arms are symmetrically turned as one might expect on the top rails of chairs. The shaped crestings to the backs are carved with honeysuckle, acanthus and flower heads, with two smaller paterae set at the ends of the top rails in the manner of Greek acroteria. Below these are bands of guilloche carving and the crests of the Bowes-Daly family set in ovals hung with carved drapery swags.

A very similar seat made for the family of the Earl of Belmore of Enniskillen, Co. Fermanagh, is illus. in Jourdain and Rose, pl. 17. The Irish connection would seem to be compounded by the existence of another, uncrested, example in an American private collection which bears the trade label of 'P.J. Walsh & Sons, 19 & 20 Bachelors Walk, Dublin'. The scrolled crestings are very similar to one on a settee illus. in Hope, pl. XVIII, no. 5.

A Regency period satinwood couch   Circa 1810

Height of end 31½ins. (80cm) Height of seat 16ins. (40.7cm)
Depth 24ins. (61cm) Max. length 58ins. (147.5cm)

Here is the classic form of Regency couch that was introduced from France and, in an age of
elegance, became very popular for reclining. Its origins go back to the seventeenth century caned
day bed, but the new inspiration was again very much in line with the Grecian revival which
dictated the shape and the inlaid ebony stringing and palmette motifs. The fact that, unlike most
chairs, the normal view of the piece is from the side, meant prominence could be given to the
scrolled end which sweeps into the seat rail and, at the back on a higher level, into a wooden-framed
upholstered arm rest. The short legs are curved outwards in the sabre fashion, joining the seat rails
with gilt-metal patera plaques which are echoed at the tip of the end scroll.

A couch of similar shape is illus. in Jourdain, 1948, fig. 75.

WRITING FURNITURE

A William III period walnut escritoire   Circa 1700

The practice of making, often portable, wooden cabinets with inner compartments and hinged flaps that let down as writing surfaces goes back in Italy and France to the sixteenth century. However, it was probably not until after the Restoration that they were widely manufactured in this country. Sometimes, as in this example, they were set on a chest of drawers base, this one having only three tiers of drawers instead of the usual four in order to get the right writing height for the flap. This piece has a good original surface and well-chosen figured veneers set on the drawer fronts and the centre panel of the fall in mirror fashion — in other words, adjoining slices from the same piece of timber in each case.

Again, as one might expect in a fine example, each drawer is edged with feather banding, as are the edges of the strips of walnut crossbanding on the fall. Between the drawers, the convex cross-grain mouldings on the carcase are typical of the period, as is the broad pulvinated or cushion frieze which conceals a drawer at the top. The sides are veneered in straight-grain walnut which was rather less expensive and used for parts that were not readily seen. The bun feet are original and again typical of the late seventeenth century, unlike so many cases where they were later removed in favour of more fashionable bracket feet. The brass handles are replacements but are of early eighteenth century date, while the keyhole escutcheons are of the late eighteenth century and are surrounded by the clear marks of the original ornate ones, like that on the fall.

An escritoire with similar features but bracket feet is illus. in Cescinsky, 1911, vol. I, fig. 153.

A William III period walnut bureau

A kneehole recess was introduced with practical considerations in mind on the Continent about the middle of the seventeenth century but is not found in England until later. The weight of the falls of large escritoires, such as the preceding example, made them rather unwieldy and the use of the kneehole made narrower flaps a more comfortable proposition. As became the usual practice the top of the recess has an arched apron while at the back is a cupboard door opening towards the right. This is crossbanded, and has feather banding in common with the drawers and fall as in the previous plate. The slightly darker areas, where less sunlight has reached over the years, emphasise the finely faded veneers of the rest of the piece.

The steeply sloping flap derives from those on portable writing boxes that had been made of oak throughout the previous century. On these the lids had opened with the hinges at the top; here it pivots on brass elbow hinges at its base and rests, as a writing surface, on sliding bearers or lopers. Inside are two staggered tiers of drawers and pigeon holes. Characteristic of this early stage of development are the oversailing sides of the top section, although it is not detachable as it would have been previously, the frieze below it being left blank at the front but with a sliding panel inside the top section to give access to the well.

The feet are of the original onion-shaped type, although replaced. The keyhole escutcheons, with their typical punched decoration of the period, and the small brass knobs are also replacements, the outline of earlier handles, themselves probably not original, being visible.

A marquetry bureau of the same type, with drawers in the kneehole recess, is illus. in Edwards, vol. I, p. 128, fig. 10.

A fine Queen Anne period walnut bureau of rare small size

Circa 1710

Width 30¼ ins. (77cm)
Depth 19ins. (48.3cm)
Height 39ins. (99cm)

The colour photograph (see Colour Plate 12, p. 100) brings out the exceptional faded colour and untouched patina of this piece, which is in remarkable condition having its original brass handles and escutcheons with punched decoration and, in this case, bracket feet which are not replacements. The graduated two short and two long drawers again have a feathered border and the fall crossbanding as well as feathering, but both show a new development in the moulded walnut lip that projects over the carcase surround which itself has no mouldings but crossbanded veneer.

The top section is now made as one with the drawers and no longer even appears to be separate, the whole of the sides being veneered in straight-grained walnut, but the blank frieze with a well behind it is still retained at the front. Inside the fall the central door and drawer fronts continue the feather edging but, as was usual, not the projecting mouldings. The waved edging of the partitions is a pleasing feature.

A fine George I period walnut kneehole desk

Circa 1720

Width 30¼ ins. (76.8cm)
Depth 19ins. (48.2cm)
Height 31¼ ins. (79.4cm)

Another type of writing desk popular at the time had a pull-out secretaire drawer whose front, hinged at the bottom, unlatched and made a horizontal writing surface without the need for lopers. This also meant a larger flat surface on top both for practical and decorative use. Within its moulded edge it is quarter-veneered with finely figured walnut of excellent colour set in mirror fashion, crossbanded and inlaid with feather banding. The drawer fronts are similarly finished off and neatly edged with a half-round cockbead, a practice that was just coming in at this time and was to remain popular through most of the century. Above the deep kneehole recess the shaped apron pulls out as a further drawer. The pedestals stand on original bracket feet, two at the front of each, an arrangement which looks more stable than having only outside ones; the brackets being fashioned so as to form a pleasing ogee shape between them.

The brass handles and escutcheons on the drawers are again typical of the period but not original to this piece.

Provenance: The late Marjorie Wiggin Prescott, Belle Haven, Greenwich, Connecticut, U.S.A.

A rare George I period walnut kneehole desk   Circa 1720

Width 37 ½ ins. (95.2cm) Depth 21 ½ ins. (54.5cm)
Height 35 ½ ins. (90.1cm) Writing height 27 ¼ ins. (69.2cm)

This type of fixed secretaire, where the top is hinged about the middle and folds back on itself while the front falls forward as in the previous example, is much more unusual. Cescinsky wrote of it: ''It is of much too rare a form to take a defined place in the chronological arrangement of English furniture, although in that of Holland this secretaire form is better known''. The outside of the top is crossbanded with rosewood which is also rare at this date.

Within the secretaire is an attractive arrangement of pigeon holes and drawers which, like the central door flanked with columns, are veneered in figured walnut and inlaid with holly and ebonised stringing. The outer drawers project forwards and have concave fronts, the right hand one being fitted with ink and sanding bottles. One particularly interesting feature is a rectangular slot in the horizontal surface in front of the central door. This corresponds with a slightly chamfered section of the upper edge of the opened lid, and is for a reading slope or mirror now replaced, which rises through the slot in channels and lays backwards.

As in the previous illustration, the six drawers below have cockbeaded edges, although the kneehole door has an overlapping convex moulding. The desk stands on double bracket feet. The engraved brass handles are original.

Other examples of this type of opening are illus. Symonds, 1923, pl. XXXVI; Macquoid, vol. 2, fig. 126; Rogers, pl. 88.

A rare small George I walnut bureau   Circa 1720

Width 24½ ins. (62.2cm) Depth 18½ ins. (47cm)
Height 40½ ins. (102.8cm) Writing height 31½ ins. (80cm)

This is a piece of unusual but very pleasing form which displays some interesting features. In some ways it looks backwards, being constructed in three sections: a separate bureau top with a single drawer beneath the fall, set within a large convex moulding on three long drawers which in turn fit within a similar moulding on to a low stand raised on four finely shaped cabriole legs with prominent ears and flattened pad feet. The veneered aprons of the stand are cut away as was noted in the pair of chairs of similar date (p. 36), with a little shaping to mark the centre at the front. The fall and each drawer are also veneered with beautifully figured walnut and crossbanded with a prominent band of chequered stringing between. The drawers are cockbeaded. The sides have their panels of straight grained walnut outlined with simpler stringing and are also crossbanded.

Inside the fall, the central door is mirrored with a shaped panel of chequerboard parquetry inlaid in the horizontal surface which is reflected in it. This is a simple expression of the fascination, originating on the Continent in the seventeenth century, that there seems to have been with reflecting images, patterns and perspectives, sometimes in cabinets on a very elaborate scale.

An early George II period red walnut kneehole desk   Circa 1730

Width 35½ ins. (90.2cm)
Depth 22ins. (55.8cm)
Height 29½ ins. (75cm)

Although a piece of simple, well-balanced form, the quality of workmanship and its fine original condition and rich colour make it an excellent example of that unpretentious beauty which is so English. The desk is made of the darker and denser straight-grained walnut sometimes known as Black Virginian that was being imported from the eastern colonies of North America at this period. It was used more than European walnut in the solid, although here it is veneered throughout on oak, a superior feature at a time when cheaper pine was used for most carcase furniture. This must help account for the fact that the piece has no trace of cracks or warping due to movement of the timber. The carcase surrounding the drawer fronts is crossbanded.

All the handles and escutcheons are original with the exception of the right handle of the top drawer.

Colour Plate 12. A Queen Anne period walnut bureau of rare small size, c.1710. The piece is described on p. 96.

A George II period red walnut bureau   Circa 1745

Width 36¼ ins. (92cm) Depth 20ins. (50.8cm)
Height 40ins. (101.6cm) Writing height 31¼ ins. (79.4cm)

The colour and origin of the timber used here is similar to that of the previous desk, although the sides, top, fall and drawer fronts are in this case solid walnut, the drawers and fall with figured veneer added on the outside. The piece is particularly shallow in its proportions. Inside the fall is an unusual arrangement of pigeon holes and drawers with complex and attractive serpentine shaping in the lowest tier. The four long drawers below are graduated.

The bureau rests on four curvaceous ogee bracket feet which, like the serpentine shaping just mentioned, show how even such a solid English piece of furniture displays the influence of the rococo style. The brass escutcheons, which are original, and the handles, which although not original must be very close to what they looked like, also display more adventurous shaping than those on the previous piece.

A Chippendale period mahogany kneehole desk, probably Irish   Circa 1750

Width 48ins. (122cm) Depth 26ins. (66cm)

Early mahogany which came from the West Indies and the use of which gradually increased from about 1730, was dark and straight-grained and sometimes hard to distinguish from Virginian walnut, but in the same way it lent itself to such sturdy, masculine pieces as this. It is of considerable size for a kneehole desk standing squarely on its double bracket feet. The moulding round the top is repeated beneath the top drawers, as might be found on a pedestal desk, although here this top section is not separately constructed. Around the drawers there is crossbanded veneer and in the kneehole two drawers. However, the feature that immediately takes the eye is the extraordinary and amusing frieze drawer above these, carved in a spirited fashion with sinuous foliage scrolls and a central hirsute face in which the keyhole is the mouth. This conception would seem to point to an Irish origin for the desk.

The brass handles are cast in a robust rococo manner while the carrying handles on the sides are of a rather earlier type with pierced, shaped backplates.

A fine and rare small Chippendale period sabicu bureau　　　　　　Circa 1760

Width 24ins. (61cm)

Apart from the rarity of its small proportions and being set on four beautifully shaped ogee bracket feet which protrude to give it a good feeling of stability, this bureau is in immaculate condition and of excellent quality. It is veneered on the front as well as the sides in the most judicious selection of finely figured sabicu of deep golden colour. This is a West Indian wood, heavier and slower growing than mahogany, that was imported and used very sparingly for furniture about the middle of the eighteenth century. Usually it is found in a darker, chestnut brown colour so that this variety, which looks almost like crinkled satin in parts, is rarer still.

The fall and each graduated drawer are finished with stringing of a complex small-scale pattern. The piece retains all its finely cast fire-gilt handles and the original escutcheons except that on the bottom drawer. Two original silver-coloured polished steel keys, although not shown, are also extant. The handles display a new fashion, with small round plates behind the pommels instead of the cartouche-shaped backplates that had been usual under the first two Georges. The escutcheons are also of a new, neater form.

A rare small Chippendale period mahogany bureau   Circa 1760

Width 24ins. (61cm) Depth 16¼ins. (41.5cm)
Height 37¼ins. (95cm) Writing height 29ins. (74cm)

Although of similar proportions, this bureau does not have the same excellence of quality in its construction; indeed the drawer linings are of pine. The drawers are deeper and there is one less than on the previous example. The maker has not attempted ogee feet but tall shaped brackets instead to give sufficient writing height. Yet with the glowing colour and flame figure of the front veneers it is an outstanding example of the importance of patina in making a comparatively simple piece a desirable rarity. The bureau also has an interesting set of original handles, finely chiselled and decorated with beads and pierced circles of leaves.

A Chippendale period mahogany kneehole desk Circa 1765

Width 48ins. (122cm) Depth 21ins. (53.3cm) Height 36ins. (91.4cm)

This desk, of slightly later date than the previous one, shows the use of finely figured Cuban mahogany that was beginning to be imported for use as veneer. It is interesting to notice that on most of the drawers the veneers would seem to have been cut from the same piece of wood and in some cases have been set upside down. The shallowness is an appealing feature and with one drawer fewer either side than that on p. 102 and a panelled door in the recess, the general appearance is less cluttered and better balanced.

This balance is helped by the very fine and neat set of original handles; they are beautifully cast and fire-gilded, the circular plates finished with rope-like guilloche edging that is hinted at again in the keyhole escutcheons and the grips with restrained foliage decoration and tiny flower heads, while the channelled surfaces are chased with minute punch marks. The majority of fine handles seem at this period to have been made in Birmingham and the types continued to be stock-in-trade for a long period.

Handle designs of c.1790-1810, by which time the normal practice was to stamp out the backplates from sheet brass, illus. in Edwards, vol. I, p. 304, fig. 25, show not dissimilar types still current then.

A Chippendale period mahogany centre pedestal desk   Circa 1760

The development of this type of double-sided desk, usually constructed so that the top section of three drawers each side is separate from the two pedestals, goes back to the seventeenth century with an example at Magdalene College, Cambridge, but it was not until the third and fourth decades of the eighteenth century that they gained popularity. Usually they seem to have been made for libraries. Indeed Chippendale's *Director,* which includes designs for eleven in the 3rd edition calls them 'Library Tables', as does Hepplewhite's *Guide.*

This is a good, large example in fine condition with nine drawers each side and rounded outer corners thinly fluted on the pedestals with a panel of Chinese inspired blind fretwork above. Like all except two of the *Director* plates, the pedestals stand on plain plinth bases which give, both visually and practically, greater solidity and strength. Beneath them, as often, are concealed castors. An unusual and practical feature of this desk is the presence of pull-out slides under the top edge to give extra working space. The leather on the top is replaced but the simple swan-neck handles are original.

Pl. LXXIX, Chippendale, 1762, shows a comparable desk of rectangular form with a band of chinoiserie fretwork beneath the top drawers.

A fine Chippendale period mahogany centre pedestal desk Circa 1760

Width 58½ins. (148.6cm) Depth 37ins. (94cm) Height 29¾ins. (75.5cm)

A less massive piece than the preceding one, here the whole is constructed in one which allows the chamfered corners to be decorated with finely carved chinoiserie blind fretwork all the way up. These panels curve forwards at either end to join the attractively protruding rounded shape of the plinth and the top. The top is lined with old leather and, unusual at this period, crossbanded with rosewood, while each side has nine similar oak-lined drawers with satin-like mahogany veneer set round a large recess.

The set of cast and gilded brass handles, with their pierced intertwined scroll plates, the escutcheons and the carrying handles are all original and of very good quality.

Pl. LXXXI, Chippendale, 1762, has ornate handles and protruding rounded corners in this Gothic inspired manner.

A fine mahogany kneehole desk supplied by Thomas Chippendale in 1774

Width 40½ ins. (102.8cm) Depth 22¾ ins. (57.7cm) Height 31¾ ins. (80.6cm)

This desk of superbly figured mahogany and excellent proportions has the hallmarks of Chippendale's quality. The long fitted top drawer retains its baize-lined writing slide, while all the buckle-shaped drop handles, except one, are original. The restrained decoration is limited to a finely carved narrow band of guilloche below the upper drawer and the large key motif on the bracket feet. Both of these are distinctive of Chippendale's workshop; the key based on the ancient Greek labyrinth pattern and a favourite device on furniture of the Kentian period.

The key motif appears in similar fashion as decoration on the feet of a French style commode in Chippendale, 1762, pl. LXVIII. The kneehole desk itself corresponds, with modifications, to a 'Buroe Dressing Table', pl. XLI of the 1754 ed. It is interesting to note that there was this dual purpose of use and indeed the present piece is recorded as being in use in 1828 in a bedroom as a dressing table.

Provenance: Ninian Home, Esq., Paxton House, Berwickshire. Paxton was built to designs by Robert Adam between 1760-70, and on his return to Scotland from the governorship of Granada in the West Indies, Ninian Home commissioned Chippendale and Haig to provide furniture, the accounts for which, between March and July 1774, survive. This desk is invoiced as: "A neat mahogany Buroe Table with Divisions in the upper drawer and a Slider coverd with Green Cloath. . .£6. 12''. Another version of the same piece without the decoration and fine veneers was made for Paxton presumably by Chippendale illus. in Gilbert, *Chippendale,* pl. 417.

Ninian Home : Esq[r]

To Chippendale Haig & C[o]

		£	s	d

1774

March

11. To repairing a mahogany Tambour much broke, and mahogany 2 Brass Sorcurs Nutt &c — " 8 —

May 5. 13 pieces of fine Blue Stripe and Spring paper and 1 piece of Border fine Blue Bedchamber — 11 .. 11 —

16 pieces plain green Stripe paper & Bedding — 5 .. 2 —

Parchment for Size a large matt & packing — " 11 6

6. To a mahogany writing Table with 2 Flaps the middle part overd with Cloath and made to rise & Drawers for paper, Pens Ink, Sand &c on Casters — 3 .. 8 —

A mahogany Night Table & Stool with Slidings, desks and a Stone pan — 2 .. 12 6

To a mahogany Night Table with Sliding Door — 1 .. 3 —

2 large Mahogany fly Tables — 1 .. 2 —

A neat mahogany Bureau Table with Divisions in the upper Drawer & a Slider coverd with green Cloath — 6 .. 12 —

A new Bell and Spring — " 2 6

8 Brass Cranks, 2 Check Springs wire and Staples — " 7 —

A Bell, Tassell & Line — " 1 6

A very large Oval Glass in a Carved & gilt Frame with Ornaments — 16 .. 16 —

Carried Forward — £ 261 .. 19 . 1

A fine and rare Chippendale period mahogany rent table   Circa 1760

Diameter of top 42ins. (106.7cm) Height 31½ ins. (80cm)

An early and exceptional example of a type of table with a revolving circular (sometimes polygonal) top, each frieze drawer lettered alphabetically as a filing system, generally for documents relating to the various properties on an estate. Here the twelve oak-lined drawers, wedge-shaped to fit segmentally, retain their original gilt-brass swan-neck handles, fitting neatly round the inlaid ivory letters.

In the centre of the leather-lined top is a hinged flap which gives access to a money well for the collection of rents from tenants. This is opened by a lock in the attractively engraved central brass plate, the escutcheon to which is opened by a secret spring-loaded catch.

The square base of the table has reeded canted corners and four large square panels of beautifully figured veneer in moulded surrounds. One of the panels opens as a door to give access to a cupboard. The table stands on four bracket feet of finely moulded ogee profile.

A rent table with a secret locking mechanism and in very similar taste is illus. in Cescinsky, 1937, p. 357.

A Chippendale period mahogany drum table Circa 1770

Another circular table — this time with eight wedge-shaped drawers — similarly veneered and inlaid alphabetically within the grips of the brass handles. Whether this type, without the central money well, was made for the same purpose as rent tables or for filing of some other type is uncertain. The edges above and below the drawers are crossbanded rather than moulded which is a slightly later feature, but the finely proportioned solid mahogany tripod base, with its baluster stem and high-arched legs ending in slightly pointed toes, shows this to be an early example of its type. Drum tables seem to have been introduced about the middle of the century and were made for libraries. The Gillow Cost Books call them 'round mahogany library tables'. Almost always the top was lined with leather as a writing surface and invariably it revolves on the pillar for ease of access to the drawers.

A Hepplewhite period mahogany octagonal drum table   Circa 1775

Width of top 49¾ins. (126.4cm) Height 29½ins. (75cm)

The mix of octagonal top and square plinth base is unusual. Alternate drawers, set in a wide central strip of crossbanding, have been made narrower, as a means of dealing with the problem of fitting drawers all round into the awkwardly shaped central area. By this means, all eight drawers fit together, each with normal rectangular shaped linings. The handles though not original, are a cast set of the period. The base, with one side opening as a door to the interior, is of solid timber rather than veneered, and impressively panelled with different levels of moulding.

A fine and rare Chippendale period mahogany oval centre kneehole desk   Circa 1770

Width 73ins. (185.4cm) Depth 49ins. (124.5cm) Height 30ins. (76.2cm)

The faded figured veneers of this piece are quite outstanding, and with every drawer and cupboard door having either a convex or a concave surface an enormous amount of skill was necessary. The fact that the desk remains in such excellent condition is a tribute to the maker.

The plan comprises four deeply curved recesses beneath kneehole arches, each with three shaped, astragal-moulded panels with surrounds of radially laid quartered veneer. The centre panels are dummy doors, as are the drawers in the frieze above. Between the kneeholes are cupboard doors with similarly moulded panels, the drawers above having fine gilt-brass swan-neck handles. Flanking each of these doors are moulded panelled pilasters divided at the bottom of the frieze. The desk stands on a moulded plinth base.

This is possibly the earliest known example of a desk of this type, although there is one of similar form, but made perhaps fifteen years later, at Horse Guards, Whitehall, used by the first Duke of Wellington. Pl. 30, Sheraton, Drawing Book, gives comparable designs for a "library table" with rising book rests fitted to the end drawers, saying that "this piece is intended for a gentleman to write on, or to stand or sit to read at" and that the pattern had already been executed for the Duke of York, "excepting the desk-drawers".

Provenance: Lady Anne Tree, Mereworth Castle, Kent.
Now the property of the Bank of England.

A Chippendale period mahogany centre writing table   Circa 1765

Width 60ins. (152.4cm) Depth 35¾ins. (90.8cm) Height 30¾ins. (78cm)

The writing table is another useful piece of furniture made mainly for libraries, less massive than a pedestal desk but extremely functional. It is the English version of the French *bureau plat*. As is usual with such tables, the rectangular top, in a crossbanded surround, is leathered for writing on, while the rows of three drawers either side are set high enough to allow a person to sit and write in comfort. A continuous moulding all round the piece divides the top from the four straight square legs which are finished with simple recessed panels, concave at the bottom, above block feet. The mahogany is a good faded colour and the majority of the swan-neck handles original.

An early Hepplewhite period mahogany tambour writing table   Circa 1775

This is an early example of an elegant form of writing table that was to become popular during the 1780s, the table also illustrates early use of the square tapered leg that lends itself so well to such a piece, having more elegance than the straight legs on the previous piece. This development lent itself also to the use of brass socket castors instead of the plate type that screwed into the bottom of the foot. The veneer is well figured and a good colour and there are several features that indicate quality. Inside the semi-cylindrical top, made of narrow strips of mahogany taped together to slide flexibly within channels at either end, is an arrangement of drawers and pigeon holes with two candle slides above. The centre leathered panel of the writing surface rises on an adjustable support to form a reading slope while at each end are pull-out slides, an uncommon feature in such pieces. Below the bold central moulding every edge is finished off with a fine scribed line which emphasises the little cusped brackets at the tops of the legs.

Hepplewhite, 1788, pl. 67, gives a design for a two drawer tambour writing table with a reading slope but with a squared instead of rounded back section, while Thomas Shearer, 1788, published another, similar, in pl. 13, fig. 2. Another writing desk in this same plate has pull-out slides at the ends. There are fine, later, examples of the type at Temple Newsam House, Gilbert no. 430, and Syon House, Middlesex, illus. in Edwards, vol. III, p. 258, fig. 42.

A Hepplewhite period mahogany centre writing table Circa 1780

Width 46ins. (116.8cm) Depth 29¼ins. (74.2cm) Height 30ins. (76.2cm)

Being shallower than the example on p. 114, this has three mahogany-lined drawers in one side and dummy drawer fronts to match on the other. In addition, there is a dummy drawer at either end, a feature which enhances the all-round attractiveness of the table when standing in the middle of a room. The handles, with an unusual style harking back to the much simpler form of ring handle sometimes found on Queen Anne period furniture, are all original except two. The carved oval paterae at the corners form the cappings to square, slightly tapered legs fluted on all sides and ending in block feet, unusually for writing tables, without castors. The solid handling of of the legs is reminiscent of the pair of stuff-back chairs of the same date shown on p. 71, and gives the piece a dignity appropriate for a library.

Colour Plate 13. An early Sheraton period mahogany bonheur-du-jour, c.1790.
The piece is described on p. 127.

A fine Hepplewhite period mahogany centre writing table   Circa 1780

Width 53¾ ins. (136.5cm) Depth 41¼ ins. (104.8cm) Height 29¼ ins. (75.5cm)

Several features of this table, which remains in superb condition, give it unusual quality. The rectangular top, instead of being leathered, is veneered in beautifully toned mahogany, crossbanded round the edge and in intersecting strips on the surface with tulipwood neatly edged with boxwood. The fronts of the three oak-lined drawers each side, as well as the ends, are similarly decorated. The great care that was taken in matching the veneer within these borders is apparent.

The fine original handles, the oval plates following the shape of the moulded corner motifs, were made so that the grips, which are attractively cast with flowers, are fixed to stand proud of the surface. This idea was more usual on French furniture. The legs are square and tapered and moulded with single large flutes. They end in good examples of spade feet, which were known at the time as 'thermed', and plate castors.

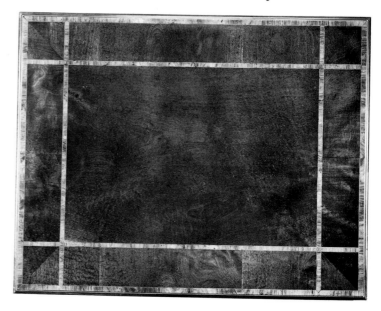

There are identical handles and similar large feet and panelled legs on a sideboard illus. in Macquoid, Vol. 4, fig. 68.

Provenance: General Sir John Moore (1761-1809) who was killed at the Battle of Corunna and is commemorated in Charles Wolfe's poem. There is an inscription in a drawer to him.

Now the property of the Bank of England.

A fine Hepplewhite period mahogany serpentine centre pedestal desk   Circa 1780

Width 57ins. (144.8cm) Depth 33ins. (83.8cm)

To make a serpentine chest or cabinet to stand against a wall is a difficult and time-consuming task, but to attempt a centrally-standing piece like this, serpentine on all four sides, was a real *tour de force* and not likely to be ordered from anyone other than a leading maker. The desk is made in three sections and the drawer fronts had to shaped from mahogany two to three inches thick on an oak carcase. The design is excellent, with canted corners picked out with stringing, one side with nine drawers round the spacious kneehole, graduated down the pedestals, and the other with three matching frieze drawers above two cupboard doors quarter-veneered and with a central oval framed with paler tulipwood crossbanding. The veneers on the drawer fronts and cupboard doors are superbly figured and mirrored with great care either side. The impact of this is heightened by the absence of handles, only the beaded keyhole escutcheons breaking up the surfaces. Both drawers and doors are edged with ebony cockbeads and lined with red cedar.

Chippendale published a design for a serpentine kneehole desk or 'Buroe Dressing Table' as he called it, in pl. LXII of The Director, *1762, and an example based on it is illus. in Symonds, 1921, fig. 95. Another large and fine example of this rare type, at Althorp, Northamptonshire, is illus. in Edwards, vol. III, p. 250, fig. 22. However, a plate of 1788 by Shearer, pl. 2 in the 1793 ed., is closest to the present piece including the use of oval veneers on the doors. It is called a 'serpentine Knee-hole Library Writing-Table' and the considerable costs involved in the making of it are outlined in the text, p. 72. The basic cost without extras adds up to some three times that of the standard rectangular model. Another example with drawers on both sides, and clearly based on the same design, is in the Untermyer Collection, New York, Hackenbroch, fig. 283. The pieces are discussed by John Hayward in* The Connoisseur, *June 1961, pp. 30-3. He computes that the cost of this one to the cabinet maker would have been nearly £12.*

Exhibition: Formerly on loan to Temple Newsam House, Leeds.

A fine Hepplewhite period mahogany centre pedestal desk   Circa 1785

Width 59½ ins. (151cm) Depth 33½ ins. (85cm) Height 30½ ins. (77.5cm)

A common feature on pedestal desks is the arrangement on one side, as shown here, of graduated drawers flanking the kneehole, while the other side has panelled cupboard doors and three drawer fronts above which in this case are false. Like the drawer fronts these panels are veneered in beautifully figured, exactly matching timber. They are enclosed in a rectangular moulding with concave corners and surrounded by a crossbanding of straight-grained mahogany with carved circular paterae set into it. The ends of the desk are treated in the same way, without the crossbanding. Let into the corners are slender fluted and tapered columns, the outer ones with crisply carved acanthus capitals. These are continued downwards to form unusual shaped feet instead of the more normal plinth base. In spite of the difference in types the drawer handles and carrying handles on the ends are all original. The craftsmanship of this piece is of the highest quality.

An unusual Hepplewhite period mahogany library writing desk

Circa 1780

Length 64½ins. (163.8cm) Depth 42ins. (106.7cm) Height 31½ins. (80cm)

A very functional piece for a library and made of finely figured mahogany of good colour, when closed this desk has matching rectangular panels, concave at the corners, on all four sides. The capacious kneehole with its shaped and moulded frieze greatly diminishes the sense of massiveness on the writer's side. Flanking it are doors each enclosing four graduated drawers with unusual posting slots above. The two large doors on the reverse side open to reveal adjustable book shelves, as does one end, the other having dummy doors. The leather and handles are replacements.

Provenance: The Paul Mellon Collection.

A very rare early Hepplewhite period marquetry lady's escritoire   Circa 1775

Width 30ins. (76.2cm) Depth 16¼ins. (41.3cm)
Height 45½ins. (115.5cm) Writing height 28½ins. (72.4cm)

There are many different influences present in this superbly made piece of very fluid design. It would appear to be the product either of John Linnell's firm under strong Swedish influence, or else of Swedish immigrants who had set up their own London workshops. Two young and very skilled cabinet makers, Christopher Fürlohg and his brother-in-law Georg Haupt, left Sweden in 1762 and worked in turn in Amsterdam, Paris and finally London from 1767. Fürlohg stayed here, initially working for Linnell and, from 1772, independently in Tottenham Court Road. He was later to become cabinet maker to the Prince of Wales. Other Swedish craftsmen, including Fürlohg's half-brother Johann Linning, followed so that except in a few cases where pieces are signed, it is impossible to be definitive about authorship.

Nevertheless it seems to have been the Swedes who introduced diaper or trellis pattern parquetry to England from France, and from their homeland and Holland a rich variety of marquetry techniques. The large marquetry medallion depicting classical figures with great delicacy is particularly typical and something that the Swedes made to sell to other cabinet makers in England. Fürlohg is known to have copied paintings by Angelica Kauffman in this way. The medallion is set into a hinged writing slope of a somewhat eccentric outline, more at home in Scandinavia than England, with an ivory balustrade above. The overall marquetry of broad, interwoven bands of satinwood, tulipwood and mahogany has great sophistication. Inside the fall the drawer fronts are of yew wood as is the horizontal surface which surrounds the original leather.

Below are three drawers with a classically draped circular motif in the centre. The base is essentially French; the very elegant cabriole legs are outlined with tulipwood crossbanding and end at the front with scrolled ormolu sabots.

The piece is discussed in Hayward and Kirkham, p. 66 and illus. as fig. 158. The medallion is very similar in feeling to those on a pair of commodes at Osterley Park supplied by Linnell to Robert Child in 1773-74 and illus. in the same volume, figs. 113-6.

A fine and rare early Hepplewhite period mahogany escritoire in French taste   Circa 1775

Width 28 ins. (71cm) Depth 14½ ins. (36.8cm) Height 44½ ins. (113cm)

Like the previous piece, the shaping of this is a real *tour de force,* influenced by the Louis XV style, and yet the construction and uncluttered surfaces bear all the finest hallmarks of English craftsmanship. The curvaceous outline is serpentine in all planes but does not have the bombé exaggeration so typical of German and Scandinavian commodes. It has a gentle elegance, and the purity of line has not been sacrificed to virtuosity of applied decoration. The maker has not even interrupted the visual flow with handles.

The shaped panels are veneered with mahogany which has a deep lustrous patination and an unusual figure that in places is reminiscent of tortoiseshell and is similar in type to that used on the Collector's cabinet shown on p. 201. Each panel of the front is framed with green-stained stringing and straight-grained mahogany, quarter-veneered and laid radially within cockbeading, while the sides have interesting variations of oval shapes. The cabinet doors at the top are dummies and front a deep secretaire drawer which encloses pigeon holes and small drawers lined with mahogany of superb quality and retaining their original handles. Beneath are three drawers, the linings of each specially shaped to fit the carcase outline, and a shaped apron between four tall splay feet which continue the gradual curves to perfection.

A Hepplewhite period mahogany escritoire

Width 30ins. (76.2cm) Depth 16¼ins. (41.2cm)
Height 49ins. (124.5cm) Writing height 27½ins. (69.8cm)

The escritoire form of writing cabinet which was noted at the end of the seventeenth century (as shown on p. 94) is found again occasionally from the Chippendale period onwards. The design of this example is in some ways little changed from the walnut specimen, including the presence of the frieze drawer above the fall, but the type was now more popular in France and it is from there that the influence, as well as the alternative term *secrétaire à abattant,* comes.

The soft, mellow patina of the mahogany veneer of this piece is outstanding. The upper drawer and fall are crossbanded in mahogany with fine chequered stringing attractively shaped at the corners of the fall, while the pair of doors below have moulded panels. The sections are divided with a squared moulding and flanked by slightly projecting stiles crossbanded with kingwood. The whole is supported on panelled square tapered feet. The combination of the unusually shallow proportions and the variation of surface decoration makes this a good example of a type of furniture that can easily appear an uncompromising block of wood.

A Hepplewhite period satinwood escritoire   Circa 1780

Width 35¼ ins. (89.5cm) Depth 16½ ins. (42cm) Height 49ins. (124.5cm)

Another attractive version of the French *secrétaire à abattant,* this is slightly wider than the last example, but still unusually shallow. The pale satinwood panels are crossbanded with tulipwood and inlaid with restrained marquetry consisting of a figure medallion hanging from drapery swags, and on the quarter-veneered doors below, large fan-like paterae, which are matched on the central door inside the fall. Surrounded by crossbanded drawers and pigeon holes, this door discloses further drawers. The large cupboard below contains an adjustable shelf. The legs are tapered and fluted and stand on block feet which are later replacements.

A fine early Sheraton period mahogany bonheur-du-jour   Circa 1790

Width 36½ ins. (92.7cm) Depth 20½ ins. (52cm) Height 41ins. (104cm)

This is another desk of the very highest quality and in original condition throughout. The illustration (also shown in colour on p. 117) shows the heavy, close-grained mahogany of beautiful mellow colour of which it is constructed with contrasting superbly figured wood on the drawer fronts and panels. These are all surrounded with gilt brass astragal mouldings with matching panels which are continued on the back so that the piece can be free-standing. Sheraton says in *The Drawing Book* (1791-4) that where expense is no object, the strength, solidity and effect of brass mouldings on writing desks makes them very desirable.

The superstructure, with its white marble top enclosed in a three-quarter pierced gallery in the French manner, contains six drawers, while below there is a long one, the front of which falls forwards to create a writing surface. There are two deep drawers placed at each end so that the writer is not obstructed when sitting at the table. These drawers are all lined with mahogany and are models of craftsmanship in their construction. The square, slightly tapered legs end in fine large castors.

The achievement of this writing table at least equals that of the very finest contemporary Louis XVI furniture.

There is a similar example in the Collection of the Earl Spencer, Althorp, Northamptonshire.

A fine Hepplewhite period amboyna wood cylinder bureau Circa 1785

Width 33¼ ins. (84.5cm) Depth 18¼ ins. (46.4cm)
Height 42¾ ins. (108.5cm) Writing height 28¾ ins. (73cm)

This is a piece of small size and of excellent proportions and quality of workmanship. The top drawer front is made concave in section to link it to the curve of the cylinder, with above it the original delicate pierced gilt brass gallery. The cylinder itself, a fine expanse of superbly chosen burr veneer which was very difficult to obtain in such a size, opens by pulling forwards the writing slide to reveal a well-fitted interior with four pigeon holes headed with ogee arches. Like the others, the graduated drawers inside are veneered with amboyna and crossbanded with kingwood with a fine line of boxwood stringing between to emphasise the contrast. The sides of the desk, divided by a flat moulding that continues at the level of the writing slide, and the square tapered legs, are similarly treated. The finely cast handles inside the cylinder are original; those outside are later replacements.

Amboyna was one of several woods which became popular for top quality furniture with the late eighteenth and early nineteenth century interest in surface figuring. Imported from the East Indies, it has an extremely attractive figuring of minute curls and knots, resembling yew wood but softer, more uniform and generally of a yellower colour.

A yew wood bureau cabinet, with very similar features but only one drawer beneath the cylinder is illus. in Fastnedge, pl. 74. Compare also the illustration on p.215 of the present work. The design has much in common with pl. 47 of Sheraton's Drawing Book.

129

An early Sheraton period mahogany oval drum table   Circa 1790

Width 60ins. (152.4cm) Depth 48ins. (122cm) Height 30ins. (76.2cm)

Besides its unusual and attractive oval shape, this table has four drawers and four dummy drawers which all retain their original gilded handles of an outline that might be expected on a piece 50 years earlier. However, the uncommon cast detailing, the ends of the crescent shapes being formed as cornucopias, is more in keeping with the period. The base has a very elegant appearance with a plain tapering 'gun barrel' stem, generally a sign of an early date before the heavier Regency turning, and four slender reeded legs with a generous splay ending in square brass caps and castors. The presence of four legs is desirable for extra stability on such a large singly-supported table as this.

A small Sheraton period mahogany drum table   Circa 1790

Diameter 36ins. (91.5cm)

By this period it is usual for edges to have flat crossbandings rather than the earlier solid mouldings and often, as here, to be finished off with boxwood or holly strips. The fine stringing on the three splayed legs carries on this outlining. The drawers however are still cockbeaded. The maker has dealt with the problem of fitting drawers into the circular top in this case by alternating four drawers with four hinged drawer fronts which open as little cupboard doors. The original handles are finely cast with pierced plates and have the unusual and attractive feature of swing grips that stop at an angle to the drawer fronts rather than falling flush (compare with the illustration on p. 118). Again the stem is a pleasing simple slender column or 'gun barrel'.

An early Sheraton period rosewood centre writing table   Circa 1790

Width 48ins. (122cm) Depth 35½ins. (90cm) Height 30¼ins. (77cm)

The original handles here are extremely similar to those on the last piece as is the careful use of boxwood stringing which outlines the edges and frames the drawer-fronts, legs and table ends with a uniform apsidal design. This shows up well against the fine faded veneer of the Brazilian rosewood which was coming into more general use at the end of the century. Wooden mouldings are now completely absent. There are three drawers in either side and the treatment of the friezes at the ends continues the drawer front shapes. The photograph makes clear how the outer edges of the square legs are vertical and the other edges tapered. This gives the necessary optical stability to the table.

A fine early Sheraton period rosewood cylinder bureau   Circa 1790

Width 40ins. (101.6cm) Depth 20ins. (50.8cm) Height 55ins. (139.7cm)

Again this piece shows the use of decorative stringing on the lower drawer front and legs and of squared boxwood-edged crossbandings. It is very much a lady's piece and illustrates the trend towards the end of the eighteenth century of designing such lighter pieces for the drawing room or boudoir rather than the traditional mahogany desk for the library. The soft faded rosewood and bandings of tulipwood and satinwood serve to emphasise this. The piece is enhanced in quality by the fine gilded brasswork of the pierced gallery at the top, the slender corner columns and the oval mouldings round panels of partridge wood on the doors of the superstructure and round the bottom edge.

Inside the cylinder there is a contrast with very pale satinwood veneer on the drawer fronts and a rising reading slope on an adjustable support. All the drawers are lined with red cedar as became usual on the finest cabinet work of this period. The brass lion mask handles are replacements.

In Shearer et al., 1793, pl. 13, there is a cylinder bureau with a superstructure and a reading slope in the pull-out writing slide, called by Shearer "a standing board".

An unusual early Sheraton period mahogany centre writing table   Circa 1790

Width 50ins. (127cm) Depth 26ins. (66cm) Height 29ins. (73.6cm)

Standing on eight slender square tapered legs with boxwood line decoration, the design of this piece was the product of a highly original mind. The rectangular top has a concave centre section each side and a three-quarter pierced brass gallery. It is divided into three leather-lined sections, each crossbanded, the centre of which rises over an interior well. The handles of the two red cedar-lined drawers are original, as are the brass socket castors with typical eighteenth century wide rollers. The legs are capped with carved 'triglyphs', the fluted panels taken from the frieze of the Doric order, inlaid with boxwood. Concave-centre friezes were a refinement often found on furniture associated with Gillow's (compare p. 147).

A rare Sheraton period mahogany architectural writing cabinet   Circa 1790

Width 36½ ins. (92.7cm) Depth 23¼ ins. (59cm)
Height 47ins. (119.4cm) Writing height 30ins. (76.2cm)

Besides the very skilled craftsmanship that went into its making, this piece shows an ingenuity of design which is remarkable. The top portion of the stepped 'roof' lifts up revealing a mirror and a shallow well. This rises above a gallery intricately inlaid with vertical wooden strips in the manner of a balustrade. Below is a central rising tambour enclosing pigeon holes above a drawer concealed as a flight of steps. Flanking this, between inlaid pilasters on plinths, are two horizontal tambours which when open reveal cupboards which in turn slide forward and are hinged to give access to nests of three secret drawers behind when operated by a secret spring underneath. Beneath are further drawers, a chequerboard floor and the three flights of steps each of which slides out as a drawer but only when released by pulling forward the writing slide. There are carved paterae on the divisions matching the frieze of the pilasters above and vertical banding on the edge of the slide. At the sides are further slides. The frieze contains three drawers which are controlled by a lock on the centre one. Finally the substantial weight of the piece is borne on eight quite slender square tapered legs and brass castors.

Clearly the design of this cabinet is strongly influenced by the work of David Roentgen, the leading German cabinet maker who was patronised by Louis XVI and Marie Antoinette, and who produced many ingenious mechanical contrivances often devised by Peter Kintzing. The mahogany secretaires in the form of Greek temples which he provided for Catherine II of Russia after 1783, although more solemnly neo-classical, have similarities in details such as the use of paterae and the stepped tops.

The scale of the piece and use of small patterned marquetry decoration is also reminiscent of a Dutch grande secrétaire illus. in Hinckley, 1960, p. 125.

Provenance: The late Marjorie Wiggin Prescott, Belle Haven, Greenwich, Connecticut, U.S.A.

Colour Plate 14. A Sheraton period mahogany centre writing table, c.1795.
The piece is described on p. 143.

A rare small Sheraton period mahogany Carlton House writing table   Circa 1790

Width 42ins. (106.5cm) Depth 24ins. (61cm)
Height 37½ins. (95.2cm) Writing height 29ins. (73.8cm)

This is a superb example of the use of 'fiddle-back' mahogany, with the figuring that is prized so much for the backs of violins. It is effectively contrasted, especially on the back of the D-shape, with panels of flame-figured mahogany veneer. The stringing is of ebony and boxwood and the drawers are all lined with mahogany and red cedar. The gilt brass moulded edges, pierced gallery and handles are original. Additional writing surface is provided by a slide in the long frieze drawer. There is also the interesting feature sometimes found on these tables of two posting slots in the top surface which have brass covers and give access to the concave-fronted corner cupboards. The legs are turned and tapered and headed with reeding reminiscent of tassels, a popular motif of this time. The form of the superstructure with the stepped tiers at the sides, follow closely that of such tables made by Gillow's.

Cescinsky, 1911, vol. III, pp. 338-40 gives illus. of two from the firm's Cost Books, one titled "Carleton House Table" of 1796 and one with an arched recess in the frieze as made for the Earl of Derby in 1798. An illustration in Edwards, vol. III, p. 257, fig. 41, is also very similar and veneered in fiddleback mahogany.

Provenance: Millards Hill House, Frome, Somerset.

A fine early Sheraton period mahogany Carlton House writing table   Circa 1790

Width 53¾ ins. (136.5cm) Max. depth 30ins. (76.2cm)
Height 42¾ ins. (108.6cm) Writing height 31½ ins. (80cm)

The origin of the term 'Carlton House' has never been pinpointed. It is used to describe this very functional type of writing table with a low superstructure that encloses the sides of the writing area as well as the back. However, from the fact that the term was in use in Gillow's Cost Books as early as 1796, and that a rosewood table of this sort at Buckingham Palace is said to have originated in the Prince Regent's bedroom at his London residence, Carlton House, it would seem reasonable to conclude that one of the first examples might have been made for him. The type was clearly popular for a while, although it is rare to find such a fine selection in original condition as are shown here.

Carlton House tables were designed to be free-standing, so that here the back of the D-shape is beautifully veneered and banded in keeping with the front. The superstructure has a shaped mahogany gallery and is fitted with cupboards and small drawers with two further drawers beneath the concave-topped wings. Once again the use of decorative stringing may be noted. The unusual striped banding, reminiscent of that on the writing cabinet shown on p. 135, runs all round above the frieze and is of purpleheart and boxwood. Purpleheart (or amaranth as it is also known) is used again for the crossbanding and panels on the square tapered legs. The brass handles with their squared form, typical of the end of the eighteenth century, are original, as are the small buckle-shaped ones. The leathered writing surface can be drawn forward and rises on an adjustable support as a book rest.

Shearer et al., 1793, contains a plate (pl. 21) signed Hepplewhite but published in 1792, six years after George Hepplewhite's death, which is similar in form and is called "A Gentleman's Writing Table". It is interesting to note that the specifications (p. 78) for the very basic version of the piece which has just the same dimensions as the current example, priced the cost of making it at £8, much the most expensive item in the whole book, and this only the cost due to the journeyman making it, not the price to be charged to the customer. Sheraton, on pl. 60 in the Appendix to the Drawing Book, *has a smaller version with a platform stretcher which he calls "A Lady's Drawing and Writing Table". This has just the same inlaid panels and crossbanding. Other examples with concave wings and square legs are illus. in Fastnedge, pl. 46; and two early examples in Jourdain and Rose, pl. 97, and Edwards, vol. III, p. 257, fig. 40.*

Provenance: The Hon. Mrs. A.E. Pleydell-Bouverie (the family of the Earls of Radnor).

A Sheraton period mahogany Carlton House writing table   Circa 1790

Width 55½ ins. (141cm) Depth 29½ ins. (75cm)
Height 37½ ins. (95.2cm) Writing height 29½ ins. (75cm)

Again veneered in fiddle-back mahogany, this example has a great deal in common with that on p.137. The overall shape, however, is rectangular with the D-shaped centre well surrounded by drawers in a slightly different arrangement. The gallery and mouldings are of mahogany although once again the original squared handles are retained. On the front ones may be noted the introduction of the distinctive Bramah locks with their circular escutcheons. These were patented in 1784 and came to be used quite regularly by some of the finest makers.

Although a little larger in size, it is interesting to note that the table detailed in the Gillow Cost Book for 1796, which was of "mahogany fine veind ven^r" with "satin and rosewood bands and strings" was costed at £17.8.8d. and estimated to take 351 working hours to make. In Sheraton's description of his "Lady's Drawing and Writing Table", he notes that "the rising desk in the middle" will serve to draw upon; and the small drawers below the coves at each end will be found convenient for colours''. He intended the drawer in the middle of the front for keeping drawings and the top to be lined with green leather or cloth.

A satinwood table of this type but without the upper tier of drawers is illus. in Jourdain, 1948, fig. 128. There is a similar mahogany table in the Red Drawing Room at Uppark, Sussex.

Provenance: The Dukes of Leeds, Hornby Castle, Yorkshire.

A rare small Sheraton period rosewood Carlton House writing table

Circa 1795

Width 41½ins. (105.5cm) Depth 24ins. (61cm)
Height 35ins. (89cm) Writing height 30ins. (76.2cm)

This example is rectangular both outside and inside the superstructure but in spite of its simpler shape, the fine rosewood veneers with bandings of tulipwood edged with boxwood on all four sides are of excellent quality. It has six oak-lined drawers although the brass handles on the frieze drawers are replacements. Once again there is also the rising book rest on an adjustable support, or as Sheraton terms it in the *Drawing Book,* a ''writing flap which rises behind by a horse''. The legs are turned and tapered with an attractive inlay of boxwood lines and dots.

Provenance: Viscount Rothermere, Daylesford, Gloucestershire.

A Sheraton period mahogany writing table

Circa 1790

Width 54½ins. (138cm) Depth 28½ins. (73cm)
Height 46ins. (117cm) Writing height 29½ins. (75cm)

A table with a slightly different kind of superstructure, this is still of a quality comparable to that of the Carlton House tables. Beneath the low pierced brass gallery, four drawers each side flank a centre cupboard which is enclosed by two sliding tambour doors. The lower surface of this cupboard has, most unusually, a slab of mottled yellow and pink marble set into it. Below the writing surface which is crossbanded and mahogany veneered rather than leathered, is a centre drawer with a deep double-fronted drawer either side, set round a kneehole arch and all framed with crossbanding. All the drawers are lined with fine mahogany and display a good set of squared handles and early stamped Bramah locks, bearing their original untouched lacquer. The legs are turned with slender reeding and without capitals.

A Sheraton period mahogany centre writing table

Circa 1795

Length (max.) 75ins. (190.5cm) Depth (max.) 33¾ins. (85.7cm)
Height 30¼ins. (76.8cm) Kneehole height 23¾ins. (61cm)

Shown also as Colour Plate 14, p. 136. It is the rounded projecting corners that give this impressively sized table its special character. It is an idea first used on certain card tables in the early part of the century (see the table illustrated on p. 288). Beneath the convex moulded top edge the corners are faceted and continue down into turned tapered fluted legs with vase-shaped capitals. The writing surface is divided by crossbanding into three leathered sections and below are five drawers each side arranged round a kneehole arch, a similar arrangement to that on the last piece. The handles are later replacements.

HOLWOOD PARK.

A fine early Sheraton period mahogany centre writing table made for William Pitt the Younger   Circa 1790

Width 56ins. (142.2cm) Depth 31¾ins. (80.6cm) Height 29½ins. (75cm)

As one might expect of a piece made for a wealthy politician, this is clearly the work of a top cabinet maker. The finely figured veneers are carefully chosen and crossbanded with tulipwood edged with boxwood. The three drawers at the front are balanced with dummy ones on the reverse side and at the ends. They retain their original squared gilt brass handles with chamfered corners and Bramah locks. At the sides the flanking drawers are deeper than the centre ones and shaped at the inside bottom corners to accommodate a slight kneehole recess very much in the manner of Louis XV *bureaux plats* but extremely rare in English examples. The corners of the table are slightly chamfered above turned and fluted and elegantly tapered legs. The leather on the writing surface is also original.

Provenance: A silver plaque on the table reads: ''Mr. Pitt's writing table, left at Holwood in memory of his ownership of the place, bequeathed by Lord Cranworth to Mr. Alexander and presented by Mrs. Alexander to Lord and Lady Derby 1882''. Pitt purchased the Holwood Estate in Kent in 1785, two years after becoming Prime Minister, and sold it in 1801. The writing table was sold by the Earl of Derby and the executors of the Lady Stanley decd., 1969.

Now the property of the Bank of England.

An early Sheraton period mahogany writing table   Circa 1790

This is another example of the use of rounded corners that project from a rectangular top, this time on a table of smaller proportions. The effect is most attractive. The turned tapered legs are again fluted and this time topped with 'tassels'. The three drawers in the frieze have their original handles of a distinctive patera and drapery swag type that are found at this period, sometimes on furniture associated with the firm of Gillow's. Another interesting feature is the small flush locking drawers of uncertain purpose which have been let into either end. The frieze itself has a pleasing decoration of contrasting mahogany veneer and crossbanding, especially on the rounded corners which are picked out in vertical strips with prominent mouldings above and below.

A Sheraton period mahogany writing table Circa 1795

Width 54ins. (137.2cm) Depth 29ins. (73.7cm) Height 28½ins. (72.4cm)

This piece is very much in the style of the firm of Gillow's which, although based at Lancaster, from the 1770s transported a lot of their furniture down to London for sale. Two quotations about the firm sum up their qualities well. Thomas Pennant in 1776 called them "ingenious cabinet makers...who fabricate most excellent and neat goods at remarkably cheap rates" and a German, Nemmich, called them in 1807 "the first grade salesmen and manufacturers in London. Their work is good and solid, though not of the first class in inventiveness and style." Their emphasis was on function and quality without elaboration, in a price range that more than just the wealthiest classes could afford, and this made them the most successful manufacturers of the period.

The fine timber, the sharply carved reeded and tapered legs headed with recessed rectangular panels, the outlining in cockbeading and the concave centre coupled with the arched kneehole are all typical of the firm. However, it is unusual that the feet of the table were never tapered to take castors.

A writing table of similar form is illus. in Cescinsky, 1911, vol. III, fig. 324.

A Sheraton period mahogany escritoire   Circa 1800

Width 32¼ ins. (82cm) Depth 13¾ ins. (35cm) Height 52½ ins. (133.5cm)

This is an example of unusually shallow proportions and panels of particularly fine flame veneer and demonstrates a lot of French influence (see p. 125). The panels of the fall and cupboard doors are elaborately surrounded with ebony stringing, mahogany crossbanding, boxwood stringing and further mahogany. The drawer between has stringing of brass and handles that are later replacements. The interior of the upper section is fitted with four satinwood-veneered drawers below adjustable shelves and the cupboard below with a shelf. As has been noted on two writing tables, the corners of this piece have rounded projections, here with engaged columns capped with stiff foliage in the Corinthian manner, above gently tapered reeded shafts and nulled 'toupie' feet of the French type.

A Sheraton period mahogany kidney table made by Gillow's   Circa 1795

Width 54ins. (137.2cm) Depth 23½ins. (59.7cm) Height 29ins. (73.7cm)

The kidney shape became quite popular for tables towards the end of the eighteenth century. As Sheraton delicately puts it, the shape is so called "on account of its resemblance to that intestine part of animals". In *The Cabinet Dictionary* of 1803, he says "some are made for writing and reading at, and having a rising desk in the centre, with piers of drawers each end. Others are made for ladies' work tables, with only a shallow drawer under the top."

This example has the general characteristics of a leathered top with a central section that rises on an adjustable support as a reading slope and three mahogany-lined frieze drawers which retain their original oval gilt brass handles. The frieze is veneered so that the grain of the wood runs vertically. The legs are turned and slightly tapered and uncommonly slender. It is no surprise that such a well made, useful and unpretentious piece should be stamped GILLOWS LANCASTER on the top edge of the centre drawer.

A kidney table of similar proportions is illus. in Cescinsky, 1937, p. 368. Designs with pedestals are to be found in Shearer et al., 1793, pl. 22 and in Sheraton, Drawing Book, pl. 58, and with cross-shaped end supports on pl. 45 of the Cabinet Dictionary.

An early Sheraton period satinwood kidney table   Circa 1790

A smaller table than the last and made for a lady's bedroom or boudoir, this has similar tapered legs joined by a shaped galleried platform stretcher as the "Lady's Drawing and Writing Table" on pl. 60 of the Appendix of Sheraton's *Drawing Book*. The top has a matching curved wooden gallery with a centre leathered rising slope while the rest of the surface is veneered in satinwood which lends itself so well to this kind of elegant feminine furniture. The edge and that of the platform below are crossbanded in tulipwood. The frieze has three drawers, the small side ones cunningly concealed among the series of boxwood-edged panels and opened by springs beneath. The boxwood is emphasised with very fine ebonised lines which are also used on the legs to enhance the slender appearance.

An early Sheraton period satinwood cheveret   Circa 1790

Width 15½ ins. (39.4cm) Depth 12¼ ins. (31.2cm) Max. height 43ins. (109.2cm)

The term cheveret or sheveret is found in the Gillow Cost Books in 1790, used to describe this type of small table with a drawer in the frieze and a separate bookstand with carrying handle and fitted with drawers resting on top. This is a fine example made, as they usually were, in satinwood with tulipwood crossbanding round the drawers and the edges of the concave-shaped platform stretcher. The tiny turned ivory knobs and the curved wooden lifting handle are typical, but the square, tapered legs have a most unusual and pleasing outward curve to them which serves to give the piece more stability but which one might expect to see more on a chair of the period.

The word cheveret seems also to have been used for other small tables of similar form like the writing table illus. in Sheraton, Drawing Book, pl. 24 and the ''Lady's Work Table''in pl. 25 of Shearer et al., 1793. An extremely close example to the current one is included in Cescinsky, 1911, vol. III, as fig. 321.

A rare small Sheraton period rosewood drum table   Circa 1790

Diameter 26½ ins. (67cm) Height 26½ ins. (67cm)

In looking at the proportions of this piece, it is interesting to notice that the height and the diameter of the top are the same. The balance, combined with the four slightly moulded splayed legs and long slender 'gun barrel' stem, is perfect. The rosewood is of a sort that has faded evenly to a fine golden colour without losing the distinctive grain, which is especially effective in the contrast between the horizontal grain of the drawer fronts and the crossbanding round them. This is smartly finished off with boxwood edging. The table has two full width drawers and two narrower ones in order to fit the linings into the centre space. The handles are later replacements but the shaped castor caps, finely chiselled with a palm frond motif, are original.

A similar table is illus. in Jourdain, 1948, fig. 115.

Colour Plate 15.

A fine Sheraton period rosewood drum table   Circa 1795

Diameter 47¼ ins. (120cm) Height 27¾ ins. (70.5cm)

This is a table of immense quality that has mellowed, like the last, to a most desirable honey colour. Instead of being leathered, the top is veneered in finely figured rosewood with outer bands of tulipwood laid in the feathered fashion that had been popular early in the eighteenth century, and of calamander. The eight drawer fronts in the frieze are quarter-veneered with tulipwood in a similar way. Round the top edge is an attractive band of ormolu beading while each drawer and the bottom edge are finished with brass cockbeading very carefully fitted with screws. The drawers are rectangular and triangular alternately and have linings of red cedar. The triangular drawers slide on centre runners to prevent side to side movement. They are all fitted with locks stamped patent and with 'G.R.' crowned (for George III).

The simple rosewood 'gun barrel' stem is proportionately slender and rests on four reeded splayed legs ending in large brass castors, the caps again cast with foliage which was not uncommon at this period on the finest pieces.

A Hepplewhite period satinwood bonheur-du-jour

Circa 1785

Width 36ins. (91.5cm) Depth closed 17½ins. (44.5cm)
Depth open 27½ins. (69.8cm) Height 48¼ins. (122.5cm)

The origin of the term 'bonheur-du-jour' to describe a lady's small writing table with a cabinet of shelves or drawers above, is obscure but this very feminine type of furniture was developed in France in the mid-eighteenth century and became popular in England towards the end of the century.

This example is made of particularly well-figured and lustrous golden satinwood and has the unusual feature of a mirrored recess in the centre of the superstructure. This is flanked by quarter-veneered doors with oval panels of mahogany. Above, the original leather book spines in fact form the face of a double tambour which encloses a cupboard; another rarity. Above the oak-lined frieze drawer with its contrasting purpleheart banding and original brass knobs, is a writing flap "hing'd to the front with card-table hinges" as *The Cabinet-Makers' London Book of Prices* describes it. The legs are square and tapered, headed with purpleheart lozenges and ending in spade feet. The brass gallery, two mirror plates and the marble base of the recess are later replacements.

There is a design for this kind of desk called "A Lady's Cabinet", including the cupboards and recess, dated 1792 and signed "Hepplewhite" on pl. 23 of Shearer et al., 1793, and a description of it on p. 85.

A fine Hepplewhite period mahogany bonheur-du-jour Circa 1785

Width 31½ins. (80cm) Depth 21ins. (53.4cm) Height 40¼ins. (102.2cm)

Once again effective use is made of contrasting woods from among the great variety of exotic timbers that were available from traders to the wealthier cabinet makers at this period. The cupboard doors and frieze drawer are quarter veneered in tulipwood in an attractive diamond pattern, reminiscent of the French taste, and banded with mahogany of an unusual mottled figure which is also used on the writing surface and two shaped drawer fronts beneath the central recess. The right hand door encloses four small drawers with red cedar linings and the frieze drawer is fitted with a baize-lined writing slide. The whole piece is finished with finely wrought ormolu mouldings on all four sides so that it can be used freestanding, and a pierced gallery. All the mounts are original except the two ring handles on the frieze drawer. The square tapered legs are of exceptional elegance.

A fine early Sheraton period mahogany bonheur-du-jour   Circa 1790

Width 29¾ ins. (75.6cm) Depth 17½ ins. (45cm)
Height 45ins. (114.3cm) Writing height 31½ ins. (80cm)

Another example of beautiful quality, the main veneer here is honey coloured mahogany with fine fiddle-back figuring. The two cupboard doors, one again enclosing small drawers, are quarter veneered with ovals of flame-figured mahogany in the centre, while all the edges around the doors and two centre drawers are crossbanded with tulipwood, as are the edges of the hinged writing flap and two frieze drawers with their matching panels at the sides. The square tapered legs, headed with contrasting dark panels, end in socket castors and are joined by a shaped galleried platform stretcher.

A table of similar form with a platform stretcher at Stourhead, Wilts. is illus. in Musgrave, pl. 164. This was supplied by Thomas Chippendale the Younger about 1791.

**An early Sheraton period rosewood
bonheur-du-jour** Circa 1790

Width 32½ ins. (82.5cm)
Depth 14¾ ins. (37.5cm)
Height 40¾ ins. (103.5cm)

Although similar in its general shape to the
others, the bowed frieze and exquisitely
restrained marquetry give this its own
character. The form is simple: a recess flanked
by two cupboard doors inlaid with classical
urns and banded with satinwood as a foil to the
darker rosewood colour. These each contain
one drawer. The writing surface is similarly
treated with a fan-like demi-patera and ribbon-
tied husk swags, a motif continued on the frieze
drawer front. This and the sides and top, which
has never been galleried, are also edged with
satinwood banding. The handles are later
replacements.

A Sheraton period mahogany Croft writing-cabinet   Circa 1790

Width 18¾ ins. (47.6cm) Width (with flaps) 36½ ins. (92.7cm)
Depth 18ins. (45.7cm) Height 31ins. (78.8cm)

The Croft was another compact and useful piece of furniture that appeared at the end of the eighteenth century, but being of a more specialist nature than the Davenport (see p. 161), it never gained the same popularity and examples are rare. The design as an early kind of filing cabinet was inspired by the Rev. Sir Herbert Croft Bt. (1757-1816) who in 1792 set about revising Dr. Johnson's Dictionary. He envisaged eight or ten of them for large libraries, each containing up to twelve alphabetically lettered drawers in two tiers behind the panelled protective door. Some unusual double specimens are known but always made in the same form.

The square top of solid wood has D-shaped flaps that rest on pull-out lopers, while the frieze drawer is fitted with a writing slide. In the present case the cupboard below contains six drawers and folio compartments. The whole is made of finely faded mahogany and rests on a plinth base. The brass carrying handles are original although those on the drawer are later replacements.

Edwards, vol. II, p. 155, illus. an example made by the firm of Seddon, who add on the maker's label that they may "at any time be moved up stairs or down, without disturbing any of the papers they contain: they may easily be moved on a porter's head..."

A fine pair of Sheraton period painted cabinets on stands　　　　　　Circa 1795

Width 23ins. (58.4cm)

The very elegant stands to these cabinets with their gilded slender fluted legs joined by stretchers, concave at front and back and joined with a centre ring, are very reminiscent of the work of the French ébéniste, Adam Weisweiler. It is interesting to see how English taste has adapted the design, dispensing with the typical ormolu enrichments, and substituting finely painted scenes of cherubs and musical trophies *en grisaille* on a black background where Weisweiler would have used oriental lacquer and bronze or porcelain plaques.

The cabinets are effectively painted with contrasting marbling outside and topped with three-quarter pierced brass galleries. Inside they are finely fitted with arched pigeonholes and drawers all veneered in satinwood. The friezes of the stands also contain drawers. The conception and quality of craftsmanship of these pieces make them outstanding examples of the period.

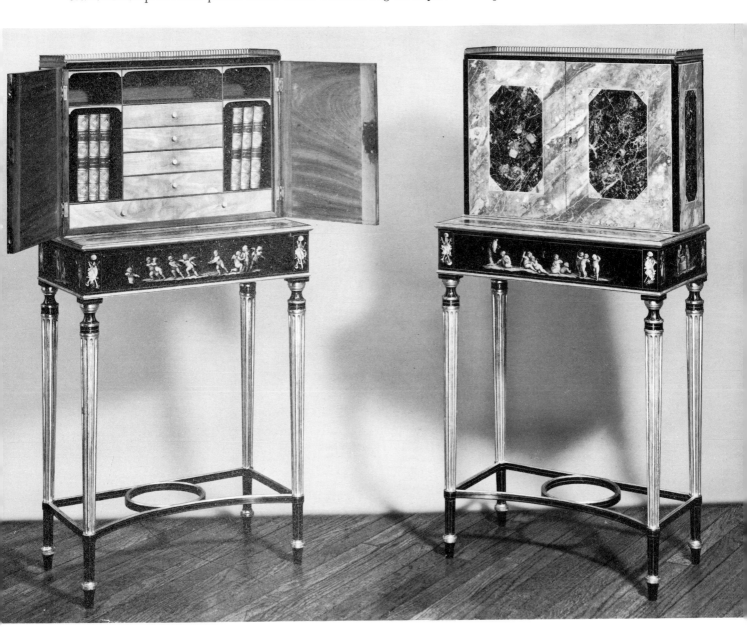

A Sheraton period rosewood centre writing table   Circa 1795

Width 48¾ins. (123.8cm) Depth 32ins. (81.3cm) Height 28½ins. (72.4cm)

The rectangular writing table on twin end supports made its appearance towards the end of the century, often only the absence of end flaps differentiating it from the sofa table (see p. 329). Usually the top was leathered, although here the surface is veneered with faded rosewood and the edge bound with a gilt brass moulding including the rather pleasing re-entrant corners. The frieze contains three red cedar-lined drawers on either side and two matching dummy drawers at each end, all subtly outlined with boxwood stringing. The supports are simple and slender and give the table a lightness and elegance which is increased by the high-set stretcher bar, finished off like the uprights with small scrolled brackets (cf. p. 349).

The re-entrant corners are similar to those on an example illus. in Edwards, vol. III, p. 262, fig. 55.

A Sheraton period mahogany Davenport desk   Circa 1800

Width 14½ins. (36.8cm) Depth 19ins. (48.2cm) Height 33ins. (83.8cm)

The prototype of this compact and functional form of desk seems to have been made by Gillow towards the end of the eighteenth century for a Captain Davenport who afterwards requested several repeat orders of the same model. However early examples of the type, which became so popular during the nineteenth century, are rare and usually of a single square shape like this one. The desk section with its pierced gilt brass gallery, wheeling handle, and leathered writing slope rising to reveal internal drawers, pivots 180° so that it can be used more comfortably with an overhang to accommodate the knees. Below are four drawers with brass knobs and a slide above on one side and matching dummy drawers on the other. The feet are almost bracket feet socketed into large brass castors.

The feet are very similar to those on a Davenport illus. in Edwards, vol. II, p. 202, fig. 1.

A fine early Regency period rosewood centre writing table attributed to John MacLean

Circa 1805

Width 52¾ ins. (134cm) Depth 32¼ ins. (82cm) Height 28½ ins. (71.8cm)

Like the table illustrated on p. 160 the rounded rectangular top is edged with a gilt brass moulding and here leathered with a rising slope on an adjustable support set into the centre. The frieze is faded almost to a honey colour with crossbanding round three mahogany-lined drawers in one side, three dummy drawers in the other and matching panels at the ends, all outlined with fine brass mouldings. Again the end supports are single and slender and here inset with tapered panels of gilded ribbed brass on the splayed legs. Between them is a turned stretcher of beech, painted to simulate the grain of rosewood and used because it was easier to gild on soft wood as has been done on the rings.

Six pieces of furniture are known with the trade label of John MacLean. These and several other associated pieces show a fairly narrow range of types and some very distinctive features such as the kind of rosewood which was originally quite a bit darker in colour, the quality and manner of using the metal mounts and the turning of legs and stretchers. The similarity of this piece to a labelled sofa table would seem to date it to about 1805. The firm advertised themselves as specialising in ''Elegant Parisien Furniture''. Although something of the style and use of mounts certainly has a French Directoire flavour, the interpretation is thoroughly English.

Redburn, p. 31f, gives an account of the firm of John MacLean which is first recorded in 1770 and was bankrupt by about 1815.

A fine early Regency period rosewood drum table attributed to John MacLean   Circa 1805

Diameter 40¼ ins. (102.2cm) Height 28¼ ins. (71.8cm)

The similarity of the gilt brass mounts with the last piece shown is obvious, here reeded along the edges of the drum as well as the inset fluted plaques. Again these are combined with water gilding on the wood of the pillar stem. The red cedar-lined drawers are a mixture of true drawers and hinged doors. They are outlined with boxwood stringing and again surrounded with crossbanding. The three splayed legs are set high with an elegant curve and boxwood decoration between them. It is clear from the photograph that the legs have been shaped from solid rosewood with the greatest possible length of grain for maximum strength.

Redburn illus. an identical table (pl. 42A).

Provenance: The late Mrs. Nesta Sybil Liston, M.B.E., Marlow, Buckinghamshire.

A fine early Regency period mahogany centre writing table　　　　　　　　Circa 1800

Length 72½ins. (184.2cm) Depth 40¼ins. (102.3cm) Height 31ins. (78.8cm)

This imposing table has certain features and excellence of quality reminiscent of Gillow's although, like much of their work after 1790, it is not stamped with their name. The corners have rounded projections to break up the rectangularity of the top which in this case retains its original leather. The frieze is fitted with three drawers on one side and two with a central dummy drawer on the other. The ends have cockbeading to match. Between these are cappings to the legs of sunken rectangular panels similar to those on certain of the Carlton House tables (e.g. p. 137) and at the corners, of inlaid crossbanded fluting like those on the writing table illustrated on p. 146. The

veneers and crossbanding are of a fine mellow colour, as are the eight tapered, turned and reeded legs picked out with ebonised rings. They end in unusual socket castors attractively cast with curling foliage and, like the gilded squared brass handles, original to the piece. The quality of the workmanship is illustrated by the close-up of the centre drawer, the sides and framing of the bottom of the finest mahogany into which are fitted panels to minimise the sagging of so wide an expanse.

　　Provenance: The Hon. Lady Mary Bailey, D.B.E., whose husband Sir Abe Bailey, Bt. (1864-1940) was a well-known South African financier and statesman. A label is fitted to a drawer.

An early Regency period rosewood bonheur-du-jour in the manner of John MacLean Circa 1805

Width 32ins. (81.3cm) Depth 18ins. (45.7cm)
Height 38¼ins. (97.2cm) Writing height 29ins. (73.6cm)

Once again the gilded ribbed motif is to be found on the cappings to the legs while the edges of the frieze, the single drawer and matching side panels and platform stretcher are outlined with gilt brass mouldings. The superstructure, slightly concave at the ends, is topped with a pierced brass gallery matching that of the stretcher and is supported on gilt brass columns with a design of crossed struts between. The legs are turned and tapered and ringed in the manner of bamboo.

Several tables of this type are illus. in Redburn, pls. 38B and 39 being particularly similar.

A fine early Regency period mahogany centre writing table   Circa 1805

Width 50¾ ins. (129cm)
Depth 38¾ ins. (98.5cm)
Height 30¼ ins. (76.8cm)

The mahogany of which this table is made is of a good rich colour with effective crossbanding on the top edge. Its design offers another skilful alternative to the average rectangular writing table and is particularly suited to a centre standing piece. The corners are canted with large crisply carved rectangular paterae capping square tapered sabre legs which are decorated on the outward facing surface with fluting and reeding and pendant husks. Their sides are outlined with ebony stringing. The frieze contains three drawers each side and the ends are similarly finished with thin ebony beading indenting in the centre of each panel, while the bottom edge is marked with an oval beaded moulding. The brass knobs are later replacements.

The quality and style of this table, which has certain affinities with the fine library furniture that was made for various country houses such as Stourhead, provides a possible attribution to Thomas Chippendale the Younger.

A writing table from Heveningham Hall, Suffolk, illus. in Jourdain, 1948, fig. 139, has similar paterae and something of the same feeling.

A fine early Regency period mahogany centre pedestal desk   Circa 1805

Width 59¾ins. (151.8cm) Depth 35½ins. (90.2cm) Height 30ins. (76.2cm)

Besides the wide kneehole, the heaviness here is much diminished by the use of pleated silk behind broad mesh brass grilles in the pedestal doors on both sides. With the growing interest in silks and chintzes towards the end of the eighteenth century this practice became popular in cabinets of all descriptions. The mahogany itself is a mellowed grey-brown colour and is embellished with brass mounts. The three oak-lined drawers on one side are matched with three dummy drawers on the other and panels at the ends, all decorated with brass strips and lotus motifs, which are applied rather than inlaid, as became common in the Regency period. The brass lion mask knobs pick up the impressively large and original lifting handles at the ends. These are enclosed in rectangular brass mouldings with corner roundels, which pick up the form of the cupboard doors. Thus the piece achieves a satisfying feeling of balance.

A Regency period rosewood drum table   Circa 1810

This is a fine display of figured rosewood in a pristine unfaded state. The top is attractively veneered in a complex manner with three crossbandings and four segments of veneer, the grain of each running laterally thus forming a square pattern. The frieze has six small drawers set alternately with blank panels, each outlined with boxwood stringing which is also used to good effect on the tapered concave-sided triangular support which gives the piece enormous character. This rests on carved and gilded lion's paw feet and in turn on a conforming plinth. A table after the same model appears on p. 356.

The components of the distinctive base follow an archaeological type of monopodium table that was made famous by Thomas Hope in his Household Furniture and Interior Decoration, *1807 (pl. XXXIX).*

**A Regency period Irish rosewood centre writing table by
Mack, Williams and Gibton**   Circa 1815

Width 47¾ ins. (121.3cm) Depth 27¾ ins. (70.5cm) Height 29½ ins. (75cm)

The lyre motif was made popular in chair backs by Robert Adam, and by the turn of the century it was being adopted for the supports of sofa and writing tables. Thomas Chippendale Jun. was using the idea for Stourhead, Wiltshire, in 1802.

This table is made of rosewood faded to a soft, grey-brown colour, particularly on the top which is veneered rather than leathered. The two drawers either side are lined with red cedar and, like the matching end panels, the fronts are edged with decorative gilt-brass beading. The lyre supports and splayed legs are crisply moulded, with foliage carving on the knee projections and anthemion mounts. The simple arched stretcher is an unusual feature and gives the piece a sense of movement. The sheet brass knob handles are original. One of the drawers bears a maker's label of Mack, Williams and Gibton of 39 Stafford Street, Dublin, "Upholders to the Rt. Honble and Honble His Majesty's Board of Work".

A table of somewhat similar feeling is illus. in Jourdain and Rose, fig. 109.

A fine Regency period rosewood centre writing table
attributed to Louis le Gaigneur

Circa 1815

Scrolled lyre-shaped end supports are again in evidence on this piece which is an elaborate example of the fashion for brass inlay and mounts made by a cabinet maker of the highest skills. Every available surface has some interesting embellishment including the top which instead of being leathered has a mass of finely engraved brasswork: roundels set in crossbanded surrounds depicting musician figures and scrolling foliage and tendrils with more scrollwork in the spandrels, all surrounded with a *rinceau* border. The roundels are modelled closely on late seventeenth/early eighteenth century French work made popular by André-Charles Boulle, where the brass was generally inlaid with tortoiseshell as opposed to the rosewood used here.

There was a revival of such Boulle work in the Regency period and the Frenchman Louis le Gaigneur, whose 'Buhl Manufactory' at 19 Queen Street, Edgware Road, supplied a library table to Carlton House in 1815, was one of the leaders. The type of cast convex edge moulding is typical of le Gaigneur's work, as are the panels of superbly engraved brass of a more classical nature at the end and on the scrolls of the supports. Even the turned stretcher is picked out with thin brass rings and the end balusters given collars of egg-and-dart. All the ormolu mounts are extremely well cast and finished off which would imply that at a period when mounts could be bought from founders' stock, the more important makers tended to have their own foundries.

A rosewood cabinet at the Victoria and Albert Museum has an identical mask mount in its frieze of Louis XIV style.

170

171

Colour Plate 16. A Queen Anne period burr yew bureau bookcase, c.1710. The piece is described on p. 177.

A Regency period mahogany centre writing table

Circa 1810

Width 60½ ins. (153.6cm) Depth 37½ ins. (95.2cm) Height 30¾ ins. (78cm)

The lion mask and ring motif is here very much in evidence, the handles and corner mounts all being original. The mellow mahogany colour contrasts with the ebony banding round the drawer fronts and end panels. The legs are tapered with an uncommon form of spaced fluting below scrolled foliage capitals and end in lotus carving with plate castors rather than disturbing the lotus motif with brass cups. The Greek key pattern stamped leather on the top is a later replacement.

A similar arrangement of lion mask and ring handles is to be found on a design for a library table from Sheraton's Encyclopaedia, *1805, illus. in Jourdain, 1948, fig. 228.*

A fine Regency period mahogany centre writing table   Circa 1810

Width 72ins. (183cm) Depth 43¼ins. (110cm) Height 30ins. (76.2cm)

The impressive proportions of this table are perfectly balanced and it is a tribute to the craftsmanship that the top shows no signs of sagging. The frieze, with three mahogany-lined drawers either side, is decorated with a large Greek key pattern applied in ebony strips, a motif noted on the Chippendale kneehole desk shown on p. 108 that became very much more popular in the Regency period. At the corners are panels with brass anthemion mounts, while the four octagonal tapered legs, with original octagonal castors to match, are headed with finely carved acanthus scroll capitals of a very similar type to the last example.

BOOKCASES AND CABINETS

A rare William III period walnut bureau bookcase   Circa 1700

Width 36ins. (91.5cm) Depth 21ins. (53.5cm) Height 81ins. (206cm)

The combination of a kneehole base with the early type of separate over-lapping desk section and a cabinet above is uncommon. This example has a particularly attractive faded colour. The structure of the base is similar to that of the piece shown on p. 95, but with a frieze drawer and another above the kneehole recess, which has the unusual feature of double doors. The drawers are feather-banded and the cabinet doors crossbanded, with uniform convex mouldings. The fall has a ledge in the centre of its bottom edge for resting a book, a feature sometimes found on oak writing boxes. Inside are pigeon holes and drawers.

The brass escutcheons are original, although the handles and turned feet are replacements. The cabinet doors may originally have had wooden instead of glazed panels.

A comparison may be made with the form and proportions of a slightly later bureau bookcase illus. in Symonds, 1923, pl. XXIV.

A fine Queen Anne period burr yew bureau bookcase   Circa 1710

Width 39ins. (99cm) Depth 22¾ins. (57.8cm) Height 92½ins. (235cm)

The rich colour (see Colour Plate 16 on p. 172) and original condition of this piece are oustanding. Beneath a broken arched pediment with a walnut cavetto moulding the two mirrored doors bear their original bevelled and shaped plates and enclose adjustable shelves. Beneath are slides for candles to reflect their light in the mirrors. The fall and graduated drawer fronts are crossbanded with golden walnut which makes an interesting constrast with the browny tightly knotted yew wood and on the carcase around the drawers there is a double bead moulding. The fall has a book rest and encloses a well beneath a sliding panel and tiers of drawers and pigeon holes flanking a decoratively inlaid cupboard door between fluted and stop-fluted pilasters. Operated by a spring catch in its top, this whole centre section slides forward to reveal three secret drawers behind and pull-out compartments in the back of the pilasters: a fine example of the intracacies that top quality cabinet makers provided at this period.

The sides of both cabinet and bureau are veneered with burr elm and edged with walnut crossbanding. The bracket feet, also of walnut, are original. The piece retains all its engraved brass handles and escutcheons (except one grip), including the carrying handles on the sides. These display a slightly more elaborate cartouche-shaped outline than was usual ten years earlier. The finial is a later replacement.

A rare Queen Anne period miniature mulberry bureau bookcase   Circa 1710

Width 10ins. (25.5cm) Depth 7¼ins. (18.5cm) Height 23½ins. (59.5cm)

Miniature furniture was made for a variety of purposes: as apprentice pieces to use as portable examples of skills, as samples which could likewise be carried round for submitting designs to potential customers, and for use in shop windows to advertise the wares that were made or were available within. To find pieces surviving from such an early date is most unusual and the fine original condition of this example would suggest that it did not travel very widely. It is an outstanding piece for very often the proportions of apprentice pieces are incorrect. So often features such as locks, crossbanding or the size of burr used are too large. It is a measure of quality that out of context with other items it is not immediately recognisable as a miniature. Except perhaps for the slightly deep fall, everything is immaculately proportioned including the finials, the original bevelled glass mirrored doors with their arched tops, all the mouldings and even two candle slides.

Great care has been taken in selecting veneer, crossbanding it on the front and sides with stringing in between, and fitting the interior with adjustable shelves, pigeon holes and further drawers. The bureau, which as with a full size piece is made separately from the bookcase, is similarly fitted with the horizontal surface inside the fall inlaid with a tiny chequerboard pattern. It stands on four shaped bracket feet. All the brass fittings and locks are original and the whole surface has developed a good patina.

A Queen Anne period walnut secretaire cabinet   Circa 1705

Width 43½ ins. (110.5cm) Depth 20¼ ins. (51.5cm)
Height 84¼ ins. (214cm) Writing height 30¼ ins. (76.8cm)

The ogee-shaped cornice of this cabinet is more unusual than that on the previous piece, emphasised as it is with the complex overhanging mouldings typical of the period and balanced with raised and flat-topped sections at the sides. The space formed between this cornice and the arched doors is filled with a circular mirror, just as the doors have bevelled glass mirror plates. They enclose a variety of graduated drawers veneered in wave-figured walnut, feather-banded and divided with a convex moulding. There are secret drawers behind the narrow centre bottom drawers, reached from behind the square ones either side.

The lower half has a fitted secretaire above three graduated drawers, feather-banded and with double beading on the carcase round them. The front of the piece is veneered in fine burr walnut while the sides, which are not so obviously displayed, as was often the case, are finished in straight-grained walnut. The bracket feet are later replacements, as are the mirrors. The well-engraved brass handles in the cabinet, including the attractive corner ornaments on the door fronts, are original, while those on the lower section are replacements of perhaps c.1730. This was sometimes done in order to make a piece of furniture look more up-to-date, for the same reason that buns were often changed to bracket feet.

The cornice shape is found on an Oriental lacquer bureau bookcase illus. in Symonds, 1923, pl. XXXIX.

A rare George I period walnut standing corner cupboard Circa 1720

Width 30½ ins. (77.5cm) Height 78¾ ins. (200cm)

This is a fine quality piece of small proportions, the angles being canted beneath a well-moulded domed top with a conforming panelled door mirror veneered with twelve sections of burr wood of pleasing mellowed patina and edged with feather banding. Inside, the shaped shelves are crossbanded on the front edges above a most unusual fall-front escritoire enclosing a row of pigeon holes. In the lower section of the piece are five carefully graduated drawers with feather banding and triangular oak linings. These retain their original engraved brass escutcheons and knobs which resemble those illustrated on p. 95. The bracket feet are also original.

A contemporary arched top hanging corner cupboard is illus. in Edwards, vol. II, p. 174, fig. 2.

Exhibition: The C.L. David Collection, Copenhagen.

A George I period walnut bureau cabinet   Circa 1720

Width 38ins. (96.5cm) Depth 22ins. (56cm) Height 88ins. (223.5cm)

In this case the dark timber is probably North American and used in the solid, but with enough figure to give interest to the arched fielded panelled doors. This wood existed side by side with the lighter figured walnut for some time as the latter gradually became scarcer and more expensive, the French supplies having dried up owing to frost damage and export controls.

The shape and mouldings of the broken pediment are similar to those illustrated on p. 177. Inside the cabinet are drawers and pigeon holes with dividers of an attractive wavy outline which are found again inside the bureau. These and the double concave fronts of the drawers and the recess in the central door give a very lively baroque feeling which contrasts with the plain lines of the outside.

Below, the drawers retain their original brass handles and are still edged on the carcase with double beading. The bun feet are replacements but probably copy originals replaced at a time when bracket feet had become the norm.

The piece is comparable with the slightly more developed mahogany one illus. as fig. 44 in Edwards, vol. I, p. 143.

Colour Plate 17a (opposite). The Murray writing cabinet shown open. Colour Plate 17b (above left). The Murray writing cabinet shown closed. Colour Plate 17c (above right). Detail of the Murray writing cabinet.

The Murray writing cabinet — a highly important George II period ormolu-mounted and brass inlaid mahogany writing cabinet from the workshops of John Channon   Circa 1750

Width 44ins. (112cm) Depth 29ins. (73.5cm) Height 96ins. (244cm)

The Murray writing cabinet (Colour Plates 79a, b and c) has been called "perhaps the most spectacular English piece of eighteenth century furniture extant" (J. Hayward) and "a *tour de force* of the English cabinet-maker's craft" (R.W. Symonds). It is a piece of furniture of the grandest conception and proportions, excelling both in the quality of its cabinet work, its mounts and its engraved brass inlay. The front and sides are of full serpentine shaping, technically so difficult to perfect, with corner pilasters. They are veneered with the very finest figured mahogany of a lighter colour than that usually encountered at this date. The pilasters, coved cornice, the shaped panels on the doors, the surrounds of the lower drawers and all the wooden mouldings are crossbanded with a slightly paler wood with a dark grain, probably padouk. The carcase of the lower part is of deal with an oak backboard, while the interior of the doors is veneered on oak. Elsewhere all is mahogany.

The piece is made in four sections including two parts to the entablature. The base, which has proportions reminiscent of a Régence commode, has four drawers lined with mahogany, the upper of which is fitted with pen trays and compartments as a writing drawer and has a sliding board with its original green baize. This drawer slides forwards with the concave-fronted corner trusses as supports in the manner of an architect's table. It runs on brass wheels with great smoothness, as does the whole piece on four heavy brass castors concealed beneath. Above, the two deep doors open easily on pivot hinges at the top and bottom and glide on rollers of similar precision, having stops to prevent them from moving over 90°. The presence of drawers and paper racks within their depth is an idea of extreme rarity. Apart from the veneered fronts of these drawers being slightly shaped, they match exactly the array of drawers, pigeon-holes and racks with adjustable shaped dividers, which are found in the body of the cabinet. All are lined and dovetailed with mahogany of superb quality and thinness. A door in the centre reveals further drawers and a most ingenious system of hidden spring catches and sliding panels gives access to no less than seventeen hidden drawers and compartments. The whole of the contents of the cupboard slide out and it is interesting that the mahogany of which they are made, without employing any veneer, is a very different, darker and more purple variety than that used throughout the rest of the piece. Its grain has a white fleck typical of that of West Indian origin. It would therefore seem possible that this section was made in a different workshop. The ring handles, however, match those of the rest of the cabinet.

The quality of the brass mounts fitted to the cabinet is exceptional even by French standards which at the time were the highest in Europe. The corner pilasters of the upper part have trusses of female heads, perhaps nereids, with scrolls and scallop shells that tie in closely with the consoles below, while the winged satyr heads on the base section are again linked to scallop shells as well as foliage and ribbons. All of these mounts are repeated in half section on the rear pilasters. In the treatment of the feet and the massive handles on the main drawers great rococo exuberance is evident in the intricate and lively scrollwork, while the pediment at the top is surmounted with a very bold asymmetrical design which cuts through the low serpentine plinth from which it rises. Either side of it, and from the bottom of the nereid mounts, trail shellwork clusters very reminiscent of the work of silversmiths such as Nicholas Sprimont. These mounts, without exception, are deeply cast and undercut, finely finished with chasing and fire gilded. There can be little doubt that a French or possibly German master was involved in their making but it cannot be said with any certainty whether they were made in London or commissioned from Paris. In either case the strongly developed rococo style displays the very latest French taste.

Besides the inlay, brass is also employed elsewhere on the piece for mouldings including the cockbeading on the main drawer, for the dentils of the cornice where wooden cores are sheathed with it in a most unusual manner, and for the figures that stand at the front corners of the plinth above. These are of a very different and more classical style than the other mounts and their gilding is not the same colour, which implies a different origin, although the presence of the corner pedestals would seem to signify that statues were intended. It is remarkable that they are cast in solid brass instead of hollow cast, a technique which might denote slightly less sophisticated English manufacture, although their quality is by no means indifferent. It is also interesting that the figures, which represent Bacchus after Jacopo Sansovino and the Medici Venus, are extremely close to, and the same size as, a series of hollow cast bronze statues made by Massimiliano Soldani in Florence at this time, some of which were brought back to England.

The third important element in the piece is the brass inlay of the most intricate and elaborate kind. This takes the form both of fine stringing and engraved motifs. The inlaid lines about $\frac{1}{12}$in. thick are used throughout, outlining each drawer with amazing precision as well as edging every thin partition inside the top section and the writing drawer. The crossbanding on the fronts of the doors is picked out with brass stringing and similar shaped panels are echoed on the sides of the doors as they open, and the central cupboard door inside. The serpentine sides and plinth above the cornice are also decorated in this manner. Human fallibility is illustrated on the right hand door where it is evident that the gouge slipped at one stage and a strip of wood was inserted.

The use of engraved brass is confined to the outside of the piece and mainly to the front where even the brass stringing is engraved with two lines along its length. The main design is a complex arabesque interlace, used at the corners and sides of the doors and repeated on the drawers below. Across the join of the doors two further sections of this arabesque are interwoven, at the top with a bacchic head and winged monsters from which hang a naturalistic vine with grapes, and at the bottom with reclining figures of Mercury and Flora.

The detail of every part of these designs is minutely engraved with consummate skill, perhaps showing the hand of an engraver of silver and gold. It is clear that they were engraved before being set on to the cabinet since a less skilled hand has filled in a very thin band on the edge of the brass strip that was fixed to the left hand door. It is interesting to compare the rather conservative nature of this arabesque design of a type that was popular in France under the influence of Jean Bérain at the end of the seventeenth century, with the mounts which, as has been said, were the very height of fashion. Much of the engraving retains an inlay of red resin or mastic which is an unusual feature and may be parallelled in certain German engraving of the period. Incorporated in the engraving of the vine is a concealed keyhole covered with a flush flap which is released by a spring operated by pressing a certain point in the engraving with a spike. The cabinet retains two such spikes (also used for working the springs on the secret drawers) with its two steel keys, themselves fashioned with the greatest precision and care.

The techniques of metal inlay on furniture had been introduced to England from the Continent by the royal cabinet maker Gerrit Jensen at the end of the seventeenth century. Many different craftsmen, several of whose names are now lost, were probably producing brass inlaid furniture in London at the time that the Murray writing cabinet was made. Most of them seem either to have come from or had links with Germany where the engraving of bone, mother-of-pearl and marquetry as well as brass, was a particularly skilled craft. Amongst these were Frederick Hints of Newport Street, Leicester Fields (see p. 290), Gern of St. Johns Square, Clerkenwell, J. Graveley and the great German cabinet maker Abraham Roentgen who worked in London between 1733 and 1738. The attribution of this piece, and indeed quite a number of others, to one name in particular, John Channon, is based on comparisons of style and detail with a pair of large bookcases engraved with his name and dated 1740, made for Sir William Courtenay at Powderham Castle, Devon. The late John Hayward in his article in the *Victoria and Albert Museum Bulletin* for January 1965 drew convincing links between many of the group including their construction, the use of fine mahogany drawer linings, and the type of brass stringing and inlay employed. He noted others that have concealed keyholes similar to the Murray cabinet.

Apart from a writing cabinet formerly in the Leverhulme Collection discussed by R.W. Symonds in *Country Life*, 7th May, 1948, and 13th January, 1950, which does not have metal mounts but is very clearly by the same hand as this, it is with a small group that share mounts from the same moulds that the closest comparisons can be drawn. These include a mahogany commode at the Fitzwilliam Museum, Cambridge, which is serpentine at the front and has the same nereid angle mounts and handles as the Murray cabinet (illustrated in A. Coleridge, *Chippendale Furniture*, 1968, fig. 63); another commode at Temple Newsam House, Leeds, serpentine at front and sides, with identical mounts to the last (illustrated in C. Gilbert, *Furniture at Temple Newsam etc.*, vol. I, no. 222); a straight-fronted chest of drawers on a low stand with the same handles (illustrated in P. Macquoid, vol. 3, fig. 128); and closest of all, a library desk in the Victoria and Albert Museum (W.4-1956) which was made with minor differences as one of a pair, the other being sold at Sotheby's 12th February, 1965. It is thought that this pair might have been made for the library at Powderham Castle. The Powderham bookcases themselves are made of what is probably rosewood and have no ormolu mounts but rather decoration of carved and gilded wood. However the dolphins carved on the corner plinths are very similar to two ormolu ones at the bottom of the Victoria and Albert Museum desk. The dolphin is found elsewhere as a general decorative motif in the eighteenth century but it also happens to be the family crest of the Dukes of Devon (Courtenay). Another link between the two is the presence of a band of inlaid brass Greek fret across the cornices of the bookcases and outlining the top of the Victoria and Albert desk (but not its pair). The Temple

Newsam commode is also decorated in this fashion, the fret in all three being slightly different.

Besides these details and similarities in the quality of cabinet work, the whole conception of these pieces, and indeed that of the Murray cabinet, shares a strong Germanic influence. The large proportions and particularly the dramatically designed pediment with its deeply gouged embrasures have a marked South German baroque feeling to them. Similarly the Victoria and Albert desk with its exceptionally complex shaping in every plane shows that great German love of technical virtuosity, as does the smothering of the surface with ormolu mounts, mouldings and inlay. It does, however, have no inlay of engraved brass, which the Powderham and Murray pieces do. The Murray cabinet, although again Germanic in feeling and comparable to some of the furniture made for example in Potsdam, makes no sacrifice of proportion and outline to the enjoyment of its exceptional features that have already been discussed.

If the authorship of the Powderham bookcases and Victoria and Albert desk are accepted as one and the same, there can be no doubt between the Victoria and Albert and Murray pieces. The nereid and satyr mounts, the feet and handles on the latter are all on the former. Each drawer is similarly outlined in brass stringing, although the brass mouldings on the Murray cabinet are plain and not cast with decoration as on the other. The mahogany veneer of both pieces is of the same colour and figure and the banding on the top edge of the desk into which the brass key pattern is inlaid is the same padouk. Structurally too, the top drawer of the desk (although not its pair) pulls forward on the corner trusses as supports, and the linings are again comparable. The desk is even raised on similar castors.

Too little is still known about John Channon. With a father and elder brother each named Otho, the family had German connections and comparatively humble origins in Exeter. He seems to have been baptised in 1711, came to London at some time after 1733 and was established on the west side of St. Martin's Lane by 1737, apparently living there until 1783. How such a man could have progressed to being responsible for the making of some of the finest pieces of furniture ever constructed when he was only 30 to 40 years of age and still be almost unknown to us today, must be one of the greatest mysteries in the study of furniture. We have perhaps one measure of his contemporary importance in the payments made to him for apprenticeships. In 1741 when he was described as a joiner he charged £25; in 1752, as a cabinet maker, £15 was asked for, whereas in 1762, the sum was £50. By way of comparison Thomas Chippendale in 1754 is recorded as charging £20. Channon was clearly a man who built up a large and successful workshop. John Hayward, in the *Victoria and Albert Bulletin* article already cited, saw a progression in style and development of the brass-inlaid furniture associated with him which culminates in the ormolu-mounted pieces. He makes the valid point that since Continental influence is still so strong at this stage, further immigrants must have joined the workshop and brought with them the latest styles and techniques. The flow of such craftsmen, particularly from Germany, in and out of this country was probably more widespread than has hitherto been realised. Thornton and Fitz-Gerald in the October 1966 *Victoria and Albert Bulletin* further suggest a working relationship between Roentgen and Channon.

References: R. W. Symonds, 'A George II Writing-Cabinet', Country Life, Jan. 13th, 1950; 'A Magnificent Dressing-Table', Country Life, Feb. 16th, 1956; 'Rediscovering Old Furniture', Country Life, Oct. 18th, 1956; J. Hayward, 'English Brass-inlaid Furniture', V. and A. Bulletin, January 1965; Coleridge, fig. 64; Edwards, vol. I, p. 140 and fig. 45; Edwards, Shorter Dictionary, p. 80, fig. 26.

Provenance: Sir William Keith Murray, 9th Bt. of Ochtertyre, nr. Crieff, Perthshire, the family seat for over 500 years. By family tradition, the cabinet was made for a predecessor, presumably Sir Patrick Murray, 4th Bt. (b.1707, succ.1739), although the present house, on a lower site, only dates from c.1790.

Christie, Manson & Woods, 30th June, 1949, Lot 30.

The late Major Arthur Bull, Brynderwen, Usk, Monmouthshire.

Exhibition: English Taste in the 18th Century — Royal Academy Exhibition, 1955-6, no. 180.

A George II period mahogany wing cabinet Circa 1745

This well-balanced cabinet dates from the Palladian period popularly associated with the name of William Kent when the heavy classical taste in architecture was reflected in interior decoration and furniture, which was generally made of this dark and dense mahogany. In spite of its architectural feeling, topped with a broken triangular pediment and the tops of the wings sweeping upwards in the manner of a Dutch gable, it is quite shallow and, standing on bracket feet instead of the more usual plinth base, appears less heavy than most examples of the period. The centre section is slightly breakfront. The finely carved but restrained decoration on the mouldings is very much in keeping with this and a good selection of the types in use at this time: acanthus and egg-and-dart on the pediment, ribbon and rosette framing the glass panels and bead and reel on the cornice of the wings and on the bottom section. The three panelled cupboards contain shelves. The glazing bars are later replacements.

The original purpose for which this piece was made is uncertain. Symonds, 1921, p. 80, calls such early mahogany china cabinets of great rarity, illustrating an example of similar shape as fig. 66, which type, he goes on, originally invariably had mirrors fitted to the panels in the upper part and were intended not as display cabinets but more as decorative pieces. However Macquoid, vol. 3, fig. 90, illus. a glazed cabinet then at Blenheim Palace which he says was probably made to contain some of the Marlboroughs' fine collection of china. Another with very similar mouldings to the present example is illus. in Edwards, vol. I, p. 84, fig. 15 and a slightly later example, with simple glazing bars in Coleridge, fig. 33.

A Chippendale period mahogany bureau bookcase

Circa 1760

Width 42¼ins. (107.5cm) Depth 20¾ins. (52.5cm) Height 88ins. (223.5cm)

Many cabinets on bureaux were made originally with wooden panelled doors and later glazed so that they might be used for display or books. In the example shown opposite, left, the fielded panels with their matched figuring have been left and the chinoiserie feeling of the bold cusping at the top is carried on in the band of blind fret round the base of the cabinet.

The fall encloses a fitted interior which includes the use of false leathered book spines either side of the central door. These are obligingly dated 1759 and 1760. However the bureau section is particularly noteworthy for the carving of its base. It has rosette and ribbon carved along the bottom edge and convex bracket feet with husks and acanthus, pierced right through the brackets. The swan-neck handles are later replacements.

The piece is based on a 1753 design by Chippendale that appears as pl. CIX in the 1762 edition of the Director. *This has a similar fret band, feet and even the slight projection in the centre of the cornice.*

A fine Chippendale period mahogany collector's cabinet

Circa 1760

Width 43ins. (109.2cm) Depth 19½ins. (49.5cm) Height 68ins. (172.8cm)

This is another piece, shown opposite right, which was never intended as a display cabinet but which shows great excellence of craftsmanship and of timber, with solid mahogany sides and doors, the latter with two pairs of fielded panels veneered with beautifully matched timber and crossbanded. The top section, which is shallower than the base, is still markedly architectural in form, the arched panels with prominent keystones and imposts between tapered pilasters, panelled and carved with suspended foliage and fruit. Above is a deep frieze similarly carved with ribbon-tied swags between two console brackets below a dentil cornice projecting at the ends. The lower cabinet has shaped panels with corner rosettes and rests on bracket feet. This contains grooves for sliding shelves and a deep tray that moves forwards on brass rollers while the upper part is also fitted with sliding shelves and thirty small mahogany drawers. The brass escutcheons are not original.

The piece is illus. in The Connoisseur *Oct. 1960, p. 79, and in Hinckley, 1971, pl. 97. There is a very similar cabinet, clearly from the same workshop, in the Martin Gersh Collection, New York.*

Provenance: Miss Blanche Brooking, great-granddaughter of 1st Earl of Harrowby.
Now on display at Temple Newsam House, Leeds.

A fine Chippendale period mahogany wing bookcase   Circa 1760

Width 97½ ins. (247.5cm) Depth (sides) 18¾ ins. (47.5cm)
Depth (centre) 20¾ ins. (52.8cm) Height 104ins. (264.2cm)

This splendidly proportioned bookcase is constructed of first quality mahogany with well-matched figured veneers in the lower part. There is particular interest in the fact that it is closely based on designs published for Chippendale's *Director* in 1753, the glazed top section on Plate XCI and the bottom on Plate XC. The former, with its broken triangular pediment and centre plinth, the dentil cornice and moulded geometrical glazing bars, differs only in the lack of the diamond decoration at the intersections on the doors. The base with two sections of four graduated oak-lined drawers flanked by cupboard doors with fielded panels that enclose adjustable shelves, has precisely the same form as the Director plate but with the positions of doors and drawers reversed. The mouldings above and below and the plinth base also conform. Even the good set of original chiselled brass handles resemble those in the Chippendale drawing.

A small Chippendale period mahogany cabinet   Circa 1760

Width 31½ ins. (80cm) Depth 18½ ins. (47cm) Height 73ins. (185.5cm)

Although not an important piece in itself, it is very interesting to compare this illustration with the last, since it shows the way that a less significant, probably provincial, but nevertheless skilled, cabinet maker adapted the same Chippendale *Director* plates. The broken pediment with central plinth and dentil cornice are just the same and the thirteen-pane pattern of glazing, although broadened in proportion for the single door, even has the refinement of the concave-sided diamond decoration at the central intersections seen in Plate XCI. The three graduated drawers below retain their original swan-neck handles and oval escutcheons which show a degree of conservatism. Being a less massive piece of furniture, the maker has finished it off with four nicely shaped ogee bracket feet instead of a plinth.

A fine Chippendale period mahogany secretaire bookcase   Circa 1760

Width 39ins. (99cm) Depth of lower part 18ins. (45.5cm)
Depth of upper part 12ins. (30.5cm) Height 89ins. (226.2cm) Writing height 32ins. (81.2cm)

This secretaire bookcase of unusually shallow proportions belongs to the period when mahogany was available of such quality that fretwork pierced as exquisitely as that within the swan-neck pediment could be carved. The scrolls of the pediment itself are also finely carved with acanthus and the under sides with close-set dentils. The pattern of the thin glazing bars is derived from a Chinese fret, a style taken up again on the top edge of the lower section which is carved with gadrooning in the manner of a pagoda roof.

Below this are graduated drawers bearing their original cast handles, the top two fronts of which form a secretaire enclosing pigeon holes and drawers. All the outer drawer fronts are veneered with exactly matching figured wood and crossbanded between them. The feet are of an elegant ogee shape, finishing the piece with a curve balancing the pediment at the top.

The pagoda edge is found on several Chippendale designs in the *Director,* particularly for 'China cases' in flamboyant chinoiserie style that were much copied in the nineteenth century. It is unusual to find an authentic eighteenth century use.

A secretaire cabinet with many similar features to the current example, including this gadrooning, is illus. in Edwards, vol. I, p. 151, fig. 59.

Exhibition: The International Art Treasures Exhibition, Victoria and Albert Museum, 1962, no. 121.

Colour Plate 18. An Adam period mahogany collector's cabinet-on-stand, c.1775. The piece is described on p. 201.

A Chippendale period Chinese lacquer cabinet-on-stand

Circa 1760

As very often happened in the eighteenth century, this cabinet was made in England using black and gold lacquer cut from larger panels, often screens, imported from the Far East. In this case these panels are of very high quality but it is evident that they depict fragments of larger designs. The depictions on the doors, outside and inside, have no sense of continuation from one to the other, although the fronts of the two drawers inside continue through. The smaller scale panels on the pair of doors above these and on the sides are more complete in themselves and may have been cut from lacquer boxes.

The strip of blind fret along the top inside the cabinet matches the pierced wooden gallery above and the diagonal emphasis is again to be seen in the complex patterns of fret on the frieze and square legs of the stand, picked out in gold on a black background. The top edge moulding of the stand is carved with ribbon and rosette, and in the centre of the frieze is the bold mask of a Chinaman wearing a ruff. Often such cabinets have elaborate Oriental lock plates and hinges that tend to disfigure the lacquer panels to which they are fixed, in the same way as the ormolu mounts sometimes do on florid French furniture. In this case the mounts are Western and discreet leaving the lacquer to speak for itself.

Colour Plate 19. One of a pair of Adam period serpentine secretaire bookcases, c.1770. The piece is described on p. 203.

A Chippendale period mahogany bureau bookcase   Circa 1765

As the detail shows, like the piece illustrated on p. 192, this has another splendidly detailed pediment of similar swan-neck form, this time with rose-heads carved at one end of the scrolls and flowers and foliage at the other. Whereas the style of the other tended towards chinoiserie, here the taste is Gothic. The finely pierced and cusped fret is Gothic inspired, the cornice has pointed arched machicolation rising from inverted bell shapes, and the glazing bars of the doors form interlaced Gothic arches. The interior of the bureau is well fitted with contrasting crossbanded edges and the unusual feature of a door at either end. The writing fall is adjustable. The graduated drawers below have contemporary but not original handles and the piece rests on particularly small and light ogee bracket feet.

A very fine Chippendale period mahogany secretaire cabinet   Circa 1765

Width 43½ ins. (110.5cm) Depth 21¼ ins. (54cm) Height 89½ ins. (227cm)

The quality of design, craftsmanship and materials here are exceptional and can be seen in colour in the frontispiece. Often the presence of a secretaire drawer gives a feeling of bottom-heaviness by making a piece high-waisted, but in this case the proportions are very satisfying visually and the splayed bracket feet finish off the base with a fine touch of elegance. A great deal of trouble is also taken to avoid its appearing too box-like, with the slightly recessed centre three drawers below the frieze with its contrasting breakfront centre tablet and triglyph ends. The single cabinet door below the arched dentil cornice, with its central projection resting on a console, is also flanked by recessed stiles. The moulded glazing bars offer yet another variety of the seemingly endless patterns to be found at this time.

The quality of the timber and the restrained carved decoration are evident from the details. The almost satin-like close-grained texture meant a sharpness of edges and carving unsurpassed at any other period. The pineapple and acanthus finials are works of art in themselves and the use of paterae in the corners of the doors and centrally in the frieze give a sense of homogeneity, as do the husks suspended above and in swags on the long drawer below. This centre plaque (shown below) is comparable to that on a medal cabinet supplied by Thomas Chippendale for Nostell Priory in 1767, illustrated in Gilbert, *Thomas Chippendale,* pl. 99. The frieze drawer is fitted with a baize-lined writing slide with shaped divisions beneath while the cupboards contain slots for vertical folio racks. The set of chiselled brass handles is completely original.

Provenance: The late Marjorie Wiggin Prescott, Bell Haven, Greenwich, Connecticut, U.S.A.

A Chippendale period mahogany wing bookcase   Circa 1765

Width 86ins. (218.5cm) Depth (centre) 23ins. (58.5cm)
Depth (sides) 20ins. (50.8cm) Height 90½ins. (230cm) Height of base 36½ins. (92.5cm)

This is another finely proportioned wing bookcase with superb veneers that glow with rich original patina. Like the piece illustrated on p. 190 it has the traditional form of thirteen pane glazed doors but in style it has moved away from the architectural pediment in favour of a moulded cornice carved with an unusual lappet design and narrow fluting. The four doors in the base are each panelled with shaped astragal mouldings and have carved paterae at the corners. The edge above is carved in a similar fashion to the piece on p. 192 but with the more usual English convex gadrooning rather than the Chinese pagoda type. The moulded brass edging to the centre right-hand doors is another touch of quality although the brass escutcheons were added later.

Provenance: Brigadier R.D. Ambrose.

200

A fine Adam period mahogany collector's cabinet-on-stand   Circa 1775

Width 19½ ins. (49.2cm) Depth 14½ ins. (37cm) Height 47¼ ins. (120cm)

This cabinet (also shown as Colour Plate 18, p. 193), meticulously finished in every aspect, was clearly commissioned by someone with a collection of medals or something similar which could have been displayed on the close-set flat mahogany trays that slide out on runners. Below them is a shallow drawer. The outside surfaces of the cabinet and the top of the stand are veneered in richly coloured mahogany with a carefully-chosen and unusual figure that most closely resembles tortoiseshell. The door panels with moulded surrounds and indented corners are crossbanded with contrasting stripy timber. The attractively shaped ogee feet raise the cabinet and give it poise and lightness as an entity in itself. It fits on to four pegs in the top of the stand.

The stand has a frieze of well-drawn marquetry paterae alternating with triglyphs and with outstepped corners capping square tapered fluted legs. The concave square feet are unusual in form. Both top and base are further matched by having every astragal moulding applied with great care in cross-grained kingwood.

One of a fine pair of Adam period serpentine secretaire bookcases   Circa 1770

Width 44ins. (111.8cm) Depth 22½ins. (57.2cm) Height 82½ins. (209.5cm)

Shown opposite far left and also in Colour Plate 19, p. 196. The product of a top quality maker, this bookcase illustrates the return to fashion of marquetry and parquetry for surface decoration and how well it could be adapted to the clean and straightforward lines of English furniture. The lattice pattern, with the four-petal flowerhead in the centre of each division, was known in Europe as a common border on imported Japanese cabinets and boxes, and also on the brocade covers in which the latter came. From the middle of the century Oeben, Carlin, Riesener and other great French ébénistes used versions of it, although it is not often found in England. Here the serpentine sweep of it, right across the lower doors and uninterrupted by fussy ormolu escutcheons and handles, is very effective. Another version is shown on p. 397. Throughout the piece the keyholes are hidden as two petals of the flowerheads.

The lattice is picked out with green-stained lines edged with boxwood on a ground, probably of sycamore. Each panel on the doors, secretaire drawers, sides and horizontal surfaces above the secretaires have re-entrant corners and are edged with a diagonal banding of rosewood. Even the attractively shaped bracket feet are rosewood veneered and carefully finished to match. It is also noticeable how each panel is specially made with the size of the design that best suits its shape and position. Thus the single bands round the glazed cabinet doors are planned to make an agreeable join at the corners. The fronts of the small drawers inside the secretaires continue the motif on a background of harewood (sycamore) that still retains its original green stained colour.

The locks in the lower part were clearly specifically made for the purpose. Those in the doors are slightly curved in shape and fashioned so that the keyholes could be set well away from the edges. In the deep secretaire front there is a double lock which also releases a section of the baized writing surface inside to reveal compartments within. The cabinets above and below contain adjustable shelves. It is interesting that there are no signs of the upper doors ever having received the glazing bars which would normally be expected at this period.

Provenance: Airth Castle, Falkirk, Scotland.

A fine Adam period serpentine secretaire bookcase   Circa 1770

It is at once obvious that this piece (illustrated opposite right and in the detail), which Norman Adams handled nearly thirty years before the ones described above, is from the same workshop and differs only in minor details, the most obvious being the presence of astragal glazing bars. Also on the top section the dentil cornice has a bead inserted between each dentil and only the right hand door has a full-width central stile although the trellis-pattern is shaped to take this into account. The top edge of the base, unlike the brass edging of the other examples, has an ebonised moulding, as does the division beneath the secretaire drawer and the bottom edge. Furthermore the surround of the panels is satinwood instead of rosewood which makes a pleasing contrast with the darker harewood and the bracket feet differ slightly in their decoration. The secretaire interior also varies in its arrangement. In all these ways the comparison between these pieces makes an extremely interesting study in the way that the age of handmade furniture differed from that of mass-production.

A Hepplewhite period mahogany secretaire bookcase

Circa 1780

Width 49¼ ins. (125cm) Depth 24¾ ins. (62.8cm) Height 102¾ ins. (261cm)

This shows the use of superbly figured and matched mahogany within contrasting radiating surrounds on doors with unused round recessed panels. The apron is shaped and runs into splayed feet which broaden a little towards the bottom in a rather novel manner. The secretaire drawer has two shaped rectangular panels in keeping with the cupboard doors and encloses an originally arranged interior with a hint of chinoiserie influence still present in the projecting pagoda-topped centrepiece. In the door of this is inset a mirror in a complex waved surround of boxwood, the idea of which is followed in the sinuous foliage marquetry on the cants either side and in the scroll tops to each pigeon hole. These hark back to the fretwork of the piece illustrated on p. 192. Below these stepped compartments are six drawers veneered with harewood with a matching panel above. Contrasting banding and minute chequered stringing are used throughout.

The cabinet section has moulded glazing bars centring on an oval, below a frieze inlaid with *trompe-l'oeil* fluting and marquetry conch shells and a thin swan-neck pediment inlaid with stars.

A Hepplewhite period mahogany wing bookcase   Circa 1780

Width 84¾ ins. (215cm) Depth of top (side) 9½ ins. (24cm)
Depth of base (side) 11¾ ins. (30cm) Height 91ins. (231cm) Height of base 35¾ ins. (91cm)

Although an impressive piece made with considerable accomplishment, the unusual design and inclusion of several conservative elements would suggest that this was not made by one of the foremost London makers. Indeed the rarest feature, the perpetual calendar in the centre of the swan-neck pediment is signed Bance, Hungerford. This is probably an early example of the work of Matthew Bance, a watchmaker who is recorded at Hungerford, Berkshire, 1793-97. A wheel barometer by him is noted by Nicholas Goodison (*English Barometers,* 1969) as being set into a late eighteenth century bookcase. The cornice has small dentil decoration and stars carved on the scroll ends. The Gothic inspired glazing pattern is unusual, the four doors set between attached columns, fluted above and abruptly changing to reeding towards the bottom, with fine brass Corinthian capitals. There are similar columns in the lower section but with turned wooden capitals and bases. These divide eight drawers, with their original swan-neck handles, and panelled cupboard doors, the mouldings of which are carried on in narrow vertical panels either side of the breakfront centre. The proportions of the bookcase are exceptionally shallow and not as monumental as might be assumed from the photograph.

A Hepplewhite period mahogany cabinet Circa 1780

Width 49ins. (124.5cm) Depth of base 18ins. (45.8cm)
Depth of top 12ins. (30.5cm) Height 91ins. (231cm) Height of base 37ins. (94cm)

The beautifully matched faded figured panelled doors of the bottom section contrast with the most unusual treatment of the upper cabinet. Beneath a dentil and fluted cornice the doors are glazed with original oval mirror plates in the centre. Rather later, Sheraton, in his *Drawing Book* (1791-4), recommends silk curtains behind the glass, fluted and with festooned drapery at the top, and also talks of using a panel of looking-glass in cabinet doors "which has a pretty effect". Many pieces, perhaps including this one, probably started life with these features and were later altered to clear glass for display purposes as fashion changed (see p. 187). It is interesting to record in this connection George Smith's claim in his *Household Furniture* (1808) that "nothing can distress the eye more that the sight of a countless number of volumes occupying one entire space".

The ovals are framed and joined to the stiles and rails with a very original arrangement of acanthus, husks, paterae, tied cable and other classical motifs finely carved in mahogany. The interiors of both top and bottom have adjustable shelves. The bracket feet are small and finish the piece off neatly.

A Hepplewhite period mahogany wing bookcase Circa 1785

This imposing piece is the product of an inventive mind and is made interesting by the variety of its surface treatment and a number of unusual features. Above the dentil cornice is a vestigial swan-neck pediment that by now has practically no architectural pretension. It is similar to a form given in Sheraton's *Drawing Book* (1791-4) pl. 57, no. 1. Of this he writes that it "should have the facia, or ground board, glued up in three thicknesses, having the middle piece with the grain right up and down". This method of construction gave eighteenth century pierced fret its strength so that so much of it has survived.

Below the upper doors are four pull-out slides with reeded front edges, a very practical consideration since the horizontal surface above the lower section is quite shallow. This part contains no less than three separate fitted secretaire drawers above cupboards in the wings and two small ones in the breakfront centre flanking a kneehole recess with tambour doors to a further cupboard. The arch to this is finished with imposts and fluted pilasters on the side surfaces. The use of finely figured mahogany circles and ovals of varying shapes is interesting. These are crossbanded on the secretaire fronts and recessed with a boxwood edging on the cupboards. Each is surrounded by radiating figured veneer (cf. p. 205). The base has five separate shaped aprons set in varying planes and for such a wide piece of furniture rests surprisingly elegantly on thin splayed feet.

The interesting geometric glazing bars of the four doors show an uncommon diversity of pattern, the centre ones being close to a design in Shearer et al., 1793, pl. 15, no. 8, and the sides to pl. 26, no. 4.

A fine Hepplewhite period mahogany secretaire bookcase   Circa 1780

Width 38ins. (96.5cm) Depth 14½ins. (36.8cm) Height 90ins. (228.5cm)

This piece of rare shallowness and superb figuring and crossbanding on the front provides an interesting comparison with some of the slightly earlier specimens. The elegant swan-neck pediment, finished off with scrolls at the centre and ends, contains pierced fretwork of a kind close to that on the piece shown on p. 192. Again the machicolation of the cornice and Gothic glazing bars closely resemble those shown on p. 197. Yet by 1780 more use is being made of stringing and crossbanding and less of mouldings. The glazing bars are flat and treated in just this way and instead of the dentils in the cornice, there is a contrasting strip of pale wood. The surrounds of the cabinet doors have rosewood crossbanding edged with boxwood on both the inside and outside edges, and the secretaire drawer and cupboard doors below are similarly finished. The oval panelled doors with radiating figured surrounds are particularly striking. Even the bracket feet have inlay in keeping with that on the rest of the piece. The handles and beaded brass edging to the doors are original.

A fine Hepplewhite period mahogany wing bookcase   Circa 1785

There is a striking resemblance between the treatment of the lower doors of this piece and those of the last, even down to the beaded brass edging at the centre. The mahogany veneer used, although just as striking, is of a softer texture and colour with more of a flame or satin-like figure. The cupboards are flanked with five drawers either side, beautifully figured and crossbanded and graduated emphatically from very shallow ones at the top which are matched with the long centre one. The absence of a deeper secretaire drawer enhances the proportions of the whole bookcase which are particularly shallow. The handles are a finely cast original set with patera back plates. It is a further mark of quality that even the plinth is crossbanded in keeping.

The glazing pattern of the doors, all crossbanded, shows variety with rectangular panes in the wings and unusual balloon-like shapes in the centre ones above pointed arches similar again to those of the last plate. Again the stiles and rails of each door are banded on each edge. The frieze above is decorated with an undulating boxwood line. By this date it was becoming increasingly usual for cornices to be flat without pediments.

A similar glazing pattern to that of the centre doors is illus. in Shearer et al., 1788, pl. 1.

A rare Hepplewhite period mahogany secretaire bookcase   Circa 1785

Width 33½ ins. (85cm) Depth of base 20¼ ins. (51.5cm)
Depth of top 15ins. (38cm) Height 81½ ins. (103.5cm)

The theme of ovals, also prevalent at this time in chair backs and interior decoration, is once more very apparent in this superbly made piece. The richly figured ovals of the lower cupboard doors and secretaire drawer front are set in quarter-veneered radiating surrounds and further crossbanded on the outer edge with satinwood. The stiles are also panelled with feathered quartered veneer. The original gilt brass rope-twist handles and patera back plates follow the oval shape and match the tiny engraved paterae in the glazing bars above. These too take the form of linked ovals, crossbanded with and in a surround of tulipwood.

Another extremely rare feature is the use of fillets of mirror glass set into the stiles and frieze of the cabinet, although this does not show to its full attractive effect in the illustration. The secretaire drawer contains drawers and pigeon-holes, the lining of the lower of which slides forward to reveal a well with three tiny secret drawers, one in the thickness of the back edge of the writing surface.

These features and the small size and quality of the piece combine to make it an outstanding one of its period. It was discussed in an editorial article in *The Connoisseur*, June 1965.

This form of glazing corresponds with pl. 26 no. 3 of Shearer et al., 1793. The use of pilasters faced with mirror glass is also found on a cabinet at Badminton House, Glos. (Edwards & Jourdain pl. 124.)

Provenance: The late Capt. E.G. Spencer-Churchill M.C., Northwick Park, Blockley, Gloucestershire.

A fine Hepplewhite period mahogany bow-front secretaire bookcase   Circa 1785

Width 45½ ins. (115.5cm) Depth 22½ ins. (57cm) Height 90¼ ins. (229.5cm)

Another secretaire bookcase (shown above and opposite in Colour Plate 20) made with meticulous care and with the unusual feature of being bow-fronted. As in the previous piece and that shown on p. 214, effective contrasting use is made of thin crossbandings, here of sycamore, to outline edges and in this case also for the flat geometric glazing bars of the cabinet, which match a design in pl. 27 of Sheraton's *Drawing Book.* The cornice has similar machicolation to that shown on pp. 197 and 209.

The stiles of the lower part, front and back, are narrow and project slightly. They and the slender square tapered legs are finished with boxwood stringing, which is also used to outline the finely figured panels on the secretaire and cupboard doors. Those of the latter are particularly attractive with their concave sides. Outside these there is long grain veneer bounded by rectangular mouldings with conforming instepped corners and then cross-grain mahogany inside the sycamore borders.

Within the secretaire drawer are pigeon holes and tiers of small drawers veneered in satinwood with alternate grain to give a herringbone effect. The top centre drawer is integral with the arched tops of the compartments below. A very cleverly devised feature is the writing surface that slides forward with fixed drawers either side for ink and writing implements and three dummy drawer-fronts at the back which when fully forward become indetectable from those above.

A small Hepplewhite period mahogany chiffonier
Circa 1785

Width 20ins. (50.8cm)
Depth 14ins. (35.5cm)
Height 51ins. (129.5cm)

The terms chiffonier and chiffonière seem to have been used first in France and then in England to cover a variety of different forms of furniture, but by the end of the eighteenth century they generally meant a cabinet with shelves or cupboards surmounted by open shelves, generally for books. In his *Household Furniture* of 1808 George Smith described them as "chiefly for such books as are in constant use, and not of sufficient consequence for the library".

This is an early example of fine even colour and quality, once again exhibiting the oval motif on the cupboard doors. Here it is inlaid with crossbanded satinwood into the mahogany. The same thin crossbanding of contrasting colour is used round the edges of the doors and the drawer above. The unusual rectangular gilt handles are original. The upper, open, part has three shelves receding with waved ends and an arched top, all the edges being crossbanded. The piece is raised on square tapered legs of similar type to the last illustration, and has original brass castors.

A Hepplewhite period yew wood cylinder bureau cabinet   Circa 1785

Width 36ins. (91.5cm) Depth 18¼ins. (46.2cm)
Height 64¾ins. (164.5cm) Writing height 30½ins. (77.5cm)

Like the bureau shown on p. 128, this piece is very close to the design on pl. 47 of Sheraton's *Drawing Book*. Here the surface is veneered in yew of a superb faded colour making use of both the close-knotted burr with its irregular cracks, and the streakier grain on the drawer fronts. The contrasting paler crossbanding is in tulipwood with boxwood edging at the corners.

Beneath the pierced brass gallery the short proportions of the cabinet are just the same as those of the Sheraton plate, as is the layout inside the cylinder of four pigeon holes, drawers, the rising adjustable reading slope and even the side containers, for ink and pens which move out with the writing slide. The latter are similar to those on p. 213. The piece shown here does not have the kneehole that Sheraton uses, nor the drawer in the concave frieze above the bureau. The outer handles are later replacements. Originally the doors may well have been silk-lined as Sheraton depicts.

Colour Plate 21.

A Hepplewhite period satinwood secretaire cabinet

Width 33½ ins. (85cm) Depth 18¼ ins. (46.4cm)
Height 72½ ins. (184cm) Writing height 29½ ins. (75cm)

This is a piece (shown opposite) unusual both in form and detail and at the same time of considerable quality. The projecting cornice, supported on machicolation, is painted on its upper surface with delicate leaves and the frieze is outlined with tulipwood rectangles while below, the cabinet doors have glazed ovals with silk behind, framed with quarter-veneered satinwood. In the centre of each is a small satinwood oval, quartered to match. Beneath are four small drawers.

The lower section incorporates a secretaire drawer and a most uncommon drop-front cupboard which is quarter-veneered in two sections like the cabinet. Both are crossbanded and have original painted panels in the manner of Cipriani. The sides of both the cabinet and lower half are finished off with shaped panels of dark stringing, the shape of the bottom of which is echoed in the contrasting cappings to the square tapered legs.

A similar form of base is illus. in Edwards, vol.I, p. 156, fig. 76, and Sheraton gives "a New Design of a Lady's Secretary and Cabinet" of 1794 which includes such a door in the Appendix, *pl. 64.*

A fine Hepplewhite period satinwood secretaire bookcase

Width 34½ ins. (87.5cm) Depth of top 12½ ins. (31.8cm)
Depth of base 22ins. (55.8cm) Height 82ins. (208.5cm) Writing height 33ins. (83.8cm)

This cabinet (shown overleaf) is glazed with yet another configuration centred on ovals, this time with moulded astragal bars. Above, the cornice is finished in mahogany with contrasting inlaid paterae, fluting and a lozenge pattern. The serpentine shape of the chest of four drawers beneath the straight fronted top is unusual although noted also on the pieces illustrated on p. 202. Its top edge, like the bottom edge of the cabinet above, is veneered with burr yew. Another assurance that the two belong together is that, like the cabinet doors, the drawers are crossbanded with tulipwood which has faded from its original reddish grain and does not now present such a contrast. Each drawer also has an ebonised cockbead. The top one has a writing slide which encloses an interior fitted with compartments. The fine proportions of the four splayed feet, whose graceful curves into the shaped apron are emphasised with stringing, give a sense of poise and elegance. The gilt brass handles are later replacements.

An exact match to the glazing bars can be seen in Shearer et al., 1793, pl. 15, no. 11.

A Hepplewhite period satinwood secretaire bookcase, c.1785, described on p.217.

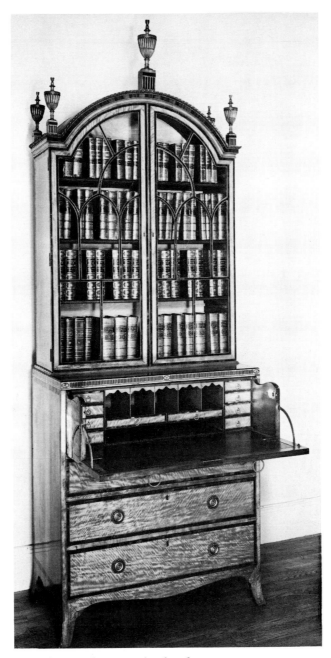

A fine Hepplewhite period satinwood secretaire bookcase Circa 1780

Width 36ins. (91.5cm) Depth of top 12¾ins. (32.5cm)
Depth of base 21ins. (53.5cm) Height 102ins. (259cm) Height of base 42ins. (106.8cm)

The proportions of the arched cornice rising from the horizontal at the sides are similar to those illustrated on p. 177 and it is interesting to compare the difference in treatment over sixty years. Here the idea of an architectural pediment is gone: the tops of the glazed doors conform in shape while the top edge is unusually carved with water-leaf decoration. A set of five finely carved wooden urns set on plinths inlaid with fluting are placed emphatically on top and hark back to the seventeenth century Dutch practice of arranging porcelain vases on the tops of cabinets.

The satinwood in which the piece is veneered is of a particularly mellow colour and contrasts strikingly with the rosewood crossbanding which is used in thin strips round the cabinet doors, on the mixed rounded classical and pointed Gothic patterned glazing bars and round the drawer fronts within the secretaire drawer. The sides of both sections and the five drawer fronts in the lower part, the top two of which form the secretaire, have thicker banding. The top edge of this part is inlaid with tiny paterae and fluting, while the whole is raised elegantly on splayed feet joined by shaped aprons.

A fine small Hepplewhite period satinwood secretaire bookcase

Circa 1785

Width 33½ ins. (86cm) Depth 17¾ ins. (45cm) Height 66½ ins. (169cm)

The simple shape of this piece with its plain rectangular glazing bars belies its very satisfying proportions and great quality of execution. The satinwood used is of a glowing colour and intense figure and is crossbanded with tulipwood on the cabinet doors, secretaire drawer and the cupboard base. This contains three drawers. The frieze above the cabinet is inlaid with fluting which ties in with that on the square tapered feet, and has a painted urn and swags in the centre.

In contrast, for the decoration of the base, the maker has used marquetry in the form of engraved classical deities perched on stiff leaf brackets set in mellowed rosewood ovals, the idea going back to the Swedish immigrants of the 1770s (see p. 122) rather than forward to the painted panels popular in the 1790s. The ovals are superbly framed in quarter-veneered satinwood sunk within an astragal moulding. The secretaire drawer front is divided into two parts with similar mouldings. Each is mounted with a fine rope-twist ring handle framing a circular enamel plaque depicting an urn, slightly differently shaped in each case. The astute attention to detail is continued on the sides, each of which has three panels of rosewood of the same type as that used on the front, framed with satinwood.

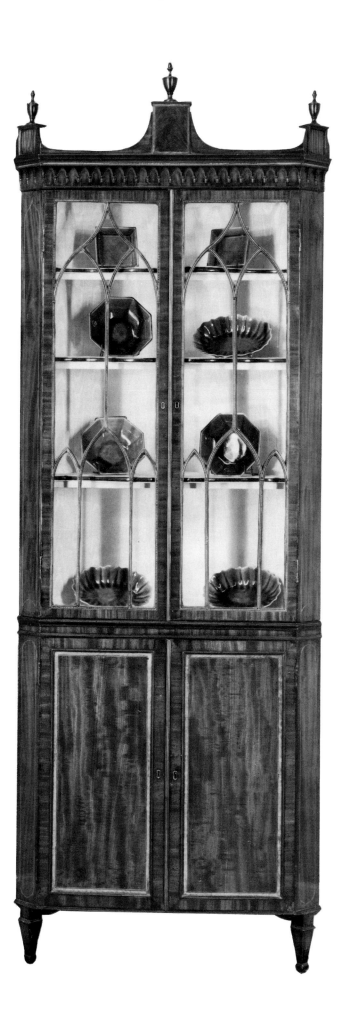

A small early Sheraton period mahogany standing corner cupboard   Circa 1790

Width 32ins. (81.2cm)
Depth of side 21ins. (53.5cm)
Height 93¼ins. (236.8cm)

Perhaps surprisingly in view of their attractiveness, corner cupboards of this quality and with
glazed cabinet tops for display were not
commonly made in the eighteenth century. This
example is low-waisted which gives it a good
balance, and unusually narrow. It retains the
machicolated cornice noted on earlier pieces
which is surmounted by an arrangement of urns
on large plinths of different proportions to those
on p. 219. The narrow doors contain fine Gothic
glazing bars in satinwood. They are framed in
crossbanding of a stripy mahogany and the
chamfered angles are decorated with stringing
with ogee-shaped tops which echo the glazing
bars.

The lower part has two rectangular panels of
long grain mahogany edged with satinwood and
an astragal moulding, and is crossbanded in a
similar fashion to the top. Also like the top the
join of the doors is marked with a brass moulding.
The whole stands on square sharply tapered feet.

*The glazing bars can be compared with Shearer et al.,
1793, pl. 7.*

Provenance: The Arthur Leidesdorf Collection.

A fine Hepplewhite period satinwood wing bookcase   Circa 1780

Width 76ins. (193cm) Depth 13ins. (33cm) Height 103ins. (262cm)

The notably low waist of this piece, besides giving more space for the practical purpose of storing books, decreases the sense of weight and with the very shallow breakfront centre section gives it very satisfying proportions. The upper doors have unusual curved glazing bars which are set most effectively to form a series of regular circles. The meticulously inlaid circular paterae where the circles touch are repeated in the pediment above and on a larger scale in the centres of the doors below. Again above and below the glazed doors are friezes of boxwood-inlaid fluting. All these points are carefully thought out to tie the bookcase together visually. The mouldings are also cogently used to emphasise horizontals while elsewhere all the edges are flat and banded and in the lower section outlined with ebony stringing.

The form of the scrolled pediment is similar to the cresting on the chairs shown on p. 91, but here the details of foliage and scrolls are inlaid and it is surmounted by a squat classical urn. The two central doors in the base enclose adjustable shelves and are flanked with three oak-lined drawers either side, all of similar size and retaining their original chased brass ring handles. The plinth base is veneered in satinwood with vertical grain.

As the sectional reference numbers on the top frieze show, this bookcase was once a centrepiece among several plainer fitted open shelves that stood round the walls of a large library.

Provenance: The Late Capt. E.G. Spencer-Churchill, M.C., Northwick Park, Blockley, Gloucestershire.

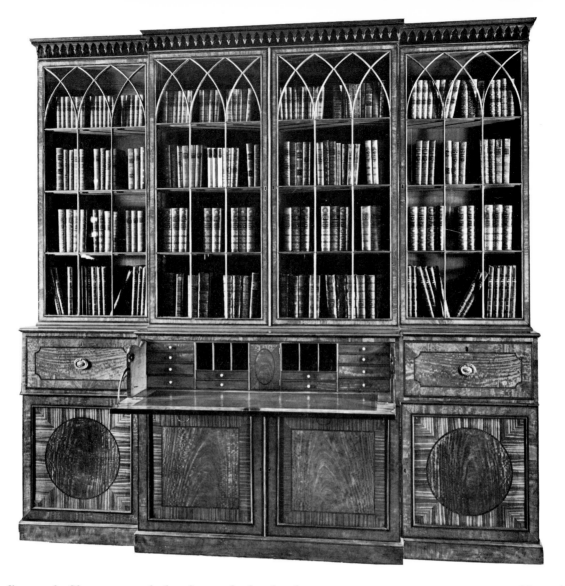

A fine early Sheraton period satinwood wing bookcase　　　　　　　Circa 1785

Width 102½ ins. (260.5cm)　Depth 23¼ ins. (59cm)　Height 100¾ ins. (256cm)

The increasing use of ebony is a pointer towards the taste at the end of the century. The machicolated cornice is made in satinwood to stand out against an ebony veneered frieze while throughout, ebony and boxwood stringing is used plentifully and with great precision for outlining. The satinwood chosen has a markedly rippled figure, very carefully mirrored in opposite panels and with a uniform stripe in the crossbanding and quarter veneering of the lower doors. Here there is still a mixture of inlaid and moulded borders.

One most unusual feature of the piece, which is not immediately obvious in the illustration, is that the thin intersecting Gothic glazing bars are made of gilded brass. The centre join at the top and bottom also has a brass beaded moulding. In *The Cabinet Maker and Upholsterer's Guide,* Hepplewhite says of such ''library cases'' that ''the ornamental sash bars are intended to be of metal, which painted of a light colour, or gilt, will produce a light pleasing effect''. It is perhaps surprising that more examples do not seem to have been made in this way. Above the four panelled doors in the lower section are three drawers, the centre one divided into two panels matching those of the wings and containing a large fitted secretaire interior with graduated drawers. The concave-cornered rectangles on the drawer fronts are continued with three at either end. The handles are of the period but not original and it would appear that, like many other pieces of the period, more than is apparent today, it started life with no handles, the drawers being opened only with keys.

Provenance: The Collection of Sir George Young, Bt.

Colour Plate 22.

An early Sheraton period satinwood breakfront cabinet-on-stand   Circa 1785

The top half of this piece is constructed in three separate sections, the centre of which is given emphasis by being both deeper and raised higher than the wings. It is topped with a depressed segmental pediment, a new shape which architects like Sir John Soane were making popular at this time.

The base is fitted with three mahogany-lined drawers and stands on six slender square tapered legs finished with concave brackets. The decorative stringing of the top is matched in the rectangles with concave corners on the drawer fronts and the legs and ends are outlined in ebony. The handles are later replacements.

A similar segmental pediment is illus. for example in Sheraton, Drawing Book, *pl. 28.*

A Sheraton period mahogany bookcase   Circa 1790

The prevailing style of this finely executed and unusual piece is classical. It is constructed in three
sections of identical size divided by two orders of superbly carved long slender engaged columns,
doubled at the ends. The columns are finely reeded with capitals of the Corinthian order in the top
half of the piece. Those in the bottom half are slightly different. They give an imposing character to
the bookcase without the heaviness that would have been associated with a similar structure in, say,
the 1740s. The horizontal lines are broken up emphatically by the projection of the entablatures and
plinths, the detail showing the complex manner in which they are designed with a plain frieze and an
inlaid dentil cornice. The upper doors have moulded glazing bars of three rounded arches with
capitals, the centre one in each case being larger, while below are three recessed panelled doors,
crossbanded like the top ones.

*A bookcase of very similar form, the columns paired throughout and changing to the Ionic order in the lower tier is
illustrated in Macquoid, Vol. 4, fig. 180.*

A Sheraton period mahogany wing bookcase   Circa 1790

Width 71¾ins. (182.2cm) Depth 16½ins. (42cm) Height 90ins. (228.5cm)

The shallowness of this piece (shown opposite) makes it a rarity as does the very narrow ledge above the bottom section. It is veneered in beautifully figured mahogany, flame-like and mirrored on all four lower cupboard doors and once again stripy in the crossbanding of both parts. The desirability of this latter effect increased towards the end of the century as is seen in the growing use of rosewood and even more emphatically others such as calamander and zebra woods. The importation of paler mahogany with darker contrasting markings shows this same taste.

This bookcase has practically no curved mouldings, all the edges being squared off, another tendency that can be seen in previous illustrations, with the copious use of boxwood for stringing and outlining. This is effectively seen on the recessed shaped rectangular panels of the lower doors. These panels and the pattern of glazing bars are reminiscent of those shown on p. 213, but here the emphasis is much more vertical and heightened by the square tapered legs that are used instead of a plinth base. This tendency is typical of Sheraton's designs.

An example of a similar feeling is illus. in Edwards, vol. I, p. 92, fig. 33.

A Sheraton period mahogany dwarf open bookcase　　　　　Circa 1790

Width 48ins. (122cm) Depth 10½ins. (26.8cm) Height 36ins. (91.5cm)

This is another example of the renewed popularity of the use of columns towards the end of the century. The lobed corner projections have been noted on writing tables (see pp. 143 and 146) and an escritoire (p. 148) the latter having a similar French type of 'toupie' feet. The shape is emphasised here by the moulded brass edging of the top. The engaged columns themselves are reeded with capitals of upright leaves, carefully crinkled, an adaptation that proved more popular for capitals on furniture than directly architectural types. The simple quality of the piece is enhanced by its rare shallowness.

A Sheraton period mahogany chiffonier   Circa 1790

Width 33¼ ins. (84.5cm) Depth 15¼ ins. (38.8cm) Height 44½ ins. (113cm)

Towards the end of the eighteenth century such small bookcases as this became increasingly popular. They usually seem to have been made to fit into recesses or in the spaces between the windows of drawing rooms in contrast to the larger library bookcases. The Gillow Cost Book of 1799 describes the type as a ''moving library''. Most examples are fitted with castors and so were presumably intended to be moved about carrying books from the library for use in other rooms.

The most striking feature of this piece is the finely figured octagonal panels of the doors, recessed within bead mouldings and a radiating veneered surround. Above are three graduated shelves with shaped ends and wooden galleried top. The ends are outlined with ebonised stringing. The bottom edge is emphatically moulded and the feet are turned and tapered.

A small Sheraton period satinwood open bookcase   Circa 1790

Width 22½ ins. (57cm) Depth 13¼ ins. (33.5cm) Height 43ins. (109.2cm)

Besides the brass castors, the mobility of this piece is emphasised by the brass carrying handles. It is a particularly small example and made of mellow satinwood with rich figuring at the sides. The shaping of the ends and gallery is similar to that of the previous piece. Here all the front edges are outlined with ebony stringing. At the bottom is a single drawer bearing its original brass knobs. The feet are again turned and tapered.

A Sheraton period rosewood chiffonier   Circa 1800

Considerable play is made here of the contrast of thin satinwood crossbanding, all edged with very fine ebony lines, and the figured rosewood. Over the years this has faded somewhat but the effect is still striking. The open shelves are graduated as in recent examples with shaping at the sides and with a waved gallery at the top. All the front edges are crossbanded. Below are one long drawer which takes in the centre as well as the two small drawer fronts either side, and three corresponding panels filled with pleated silk, a wide horizontal oval flanked by two narrow lancet shapes. The centre one, surrounded with quarter-veneered rosewood, opens as a door. The divisions are emphasised with diamonds and rectangles and also by the positioning of the six tall turned toupie or peg-shaped feet.

A Sheraton period penwork chiffonier   Circa 1800

Width 36ins. (91.5cm) Depth 17ins. (43.2cm) Height 56½ ins. (143.5cm)

The striking decoration on this chiffonier, known as penwork, was popular in late eighteenth and early nineteenth century England as a development from Oriental lacquer. Although mainly used on boxes and small furniture, for example the tops of tripod tables, it is here employed on a rather larger scale and with great accomplishment. The surface is first japanned black, then the design painted on in white and the details and shading added in black Indian ink with a quill pen which allows for great delicacy. The surface is then varnished.

The panels of birds and flowering plants on the doors have obvious Chinese influence but the overall effect with the borders and small scale flower sprays is also reminiscent of the Anglo-Indian ivory inlaid furniture being produced at this time in Vizagapatan. The wide scallop-edged borders round the doors are finely detailed with a variety of flowers and foliage and continue round the inside edges of the shelves above and the back edges of the sides. All the front edges are picked out with chains of bellflower which very effectively outline the curvaceous nature of the sides and fronts of the four graduated shelves, the gallery at the top and the apron which curves satisfyingly into the thin bracket feet (cf. p. 218).

A Regency period rosewood double-sided bookcase   Circa 1805

Width 30½ins. (77.5cm) Depth 15ins. (38cm) Height 38ins. (96.5cm)

This is a fine example of an unusual type of bookcase, made to stand out from a wall or in the centre of a room and useful as a space-divider. The increasing use of rosewood with brass detailing at this period is illustrated here in a restrained fashion, some of the mouldings being carried out in ebony. The brass gallery is particularly attractively pierced with a heart motif and is lobed at the corners. The engaged corner columns are fluted and the flutes filled with brass reeding which is matched on the front edges of the adjustable shelves. The ends are panelled with strips of brass cast with water leaf and have impressive cast lion mask and ring carrying handles in the centre. The feet are turned with large castors. Again this was probably intended to be wheeled from the library to the drawing room with books for immediate use.

A Regency period rosewood cabinet
Circa 1810

Width 34ins. (86.5cm)
Depth 14½ins. (36.8cm)
Height 70½ins. (179cm)

This is a piece of unusually small proportions with the top shallower than the base. The friezes at top and bottom are crossbanded and there is matching use in both sections of rather fatter reeding than has hitherto been seen, on the horizontal edges and recessed in the pilasters that project just slightly at either side. These have fine brass patera appliqués above and below. The two pairs of doors are glazed with fillets of decorative brass of a type similar to that shown in the last plate. They would probably originally have been panelled with wood or filled with pleated silk (see p. 207). As well as adjustable shelves the upper section has two small drawers. The feet are square and tapered and look back to a type that was current twenty or more years before.

A rare Regency period rosewood revolving bookstand   Circa 1810

Diameter of base 17½ ins. (54.5cm) Height 37½ ins. (95.2cm)

Another form of small bookcase designed to stand away from a wall which came in at this time was the circular bookstand with graduated tiers, each of which revolve independently on a central pillar. Benjamin Crosby took out a patent for this type in 1808 and the mechanism is described in Ackermann's Repository in 1810. In order to fit books into the circular space, there are fixed at regular intervals groups of three false leather book spines with wedge shaped blocks behind them. Some of these spines are original and some replaced.

The edges of each tier are crossbanded with satinwood as is the surface of the base and the piece is well-balanced on four bold cast brass lion's paws.

Other examples of this type are illus. in Jourdain, 1948, p. 140.

**An unusual Regency period
mahogany corner open bookcase** Circa 1805

Depth at side 18ins. (45.8cm)
Height 72½ins. (184.2cm)

Quadrant-shaped and with obvious similarities
in form to the last bookstand, this has seven tiers
carefully graduated in height (in twos except the
bottom one) and each one set back a little
further and shaped at the sides. Once again to
ease the fitting of books, there is at either end of
each shelf a wedge-shaped block fronted with
pairs of half columns shaped with entasis in a
masculine Doric form. These and the three
gilded brass lion's paws which support the piece
emphasise the change of taste from the elegant
and lighter styles of the late eighteenth century
to a feeling of greater solidity and archaeological
correctness of detail.

DINING FURNITURE

A George I period oak dresser   Circa 1720

Width 79ins. (200cm) Depth 20ins. (51cm) Height 33ins. (84cm)

During the early eighteenth century the oak dresser or sideboard which, a century earlier had been present in every major household in its various forms, was generally beginning to give way to the large, marble-topped side table in fashionable dining rooms, and styles gradually became debased. Occasionally a finely proportioned and shallow example such as this is, however, found. Its rarity is much enhanced by its original condition and the rich glowing patina that it retains, the surface varying from golden to almost a smoky black in places. The drawer fronts and moulded top are crossbanded with walnut which adds even more to the variation. The drawers have a lip moulding round them which is copied in panels at either end. They also bear their original handles and escutcheons. Below them and at the ends the aprons are pierced and shaped in a fanciful manner which, with suitable restraint, adds interest to the rectangular lines above. Likewise the three cabriole legs are particularly gracefully shaped, edged at the knees with C-scrolls and ending in pad feet. In common with most pieces of this kind, the back legs are left as square posts.

Although at this period the superstructure of shelves more commonly associated with dressers was making an appearance, many that exist today were only added in the nineteenth century. Certainly its shallowness indicates that this example never had such an addition.

A dresser illus. in Edwards, vol. II, p. 224, fig. 12, has similar shaping in the apron, legs and brasswork.

A large George II period walnut drop-leaf dining table Circa 1735

Width 68½ ins. (174cm) Depth 65¼ ins. (165.8cm.) Height 28¼ ins. (71.8cm)

After the Restoration the innovations in building design that came from the Continent included the construction of separate smaller dining rooms instead of traditional large halls. Dining tables then generally became smaller, a number of small ones often being used in the same room instead of one large. The oval gateleg table continued in popularity into the eighteenth century and gradually developed into this rather more refined type, operating on the same principle of a leg, or occasionally two, at either side swinging out to support a raised flap. Sometimes the legs were cabriole in shape or, as here, turned and slightly tapered ending in pad feet.

This example is particularly unusual for its size, being almost circular with a top of solid figured walnut ovolo-moulded at the edge and joined, as one would expect at this period, with moulded rule joints which conceal the hinges beneath. The expanse of timber is extremely heavy and illustrates the size of some of the trees that were being felled at this time in North America from where it probably would have come. The top also allows a good depth of overhang all round for practical purposes of comfortable seating.

A George II period oak dresser   Circa 1750

Width 80¼ins. (203cm) Depth 18ins. (46cm) Height 33ins. (84cm)

Another particularly shallow example, this is made of oak that has mellowed to a golden brown colour which contrasts with the darker mahogany crossbanding on the drawer fronts. While having turned baluster front supports in the traditional fashion that goes back to the seventeenth century, there are several unusual features which show contemporary influences and give it a special character. The five drawers are cockbeaded and retain their original escutcheons and swan-neck handles. The lower ones are subtly deeper in size. They are arranged round an arched recess which has no function in the way that it would have in a kneehole desk but rather looks forward to the sideboards of the last twenty years of the century.

A bold complex moulding which runs all round the visible sides of the piece frames the arch with a square head, the slight architectural flavour continuing in the diminutive keystone in the centre. The spandrels are most attractively pierced. The front outside corners of the dresser are also neatly finished with short fluted quarter columns, while the ends are given some interest with a shaped apron below, the shaping also appearing in brackets at the tops of the slender supports at the front. The whole stands on a plain plinth or pot board raised on simple shaped bracket feet.

A George II period mahogany dresser   Circa 1750

Width 73½ ins. (186.5cm) Depth 19½ ins. (49.5cm) Height 36½ ins. (92.5cm)

This is an interesting example of a type of furniture that was by now mainly confined to oak pieces made in the country, being made with greater refinement and in the fashionable wood. Its sophistication is apparent if the treatment of the centre section with its fluted pilasters on high plinths and finely moulded arch with imposts and prominent keystone is compared with that of the previous example. The architectural centre is balanced at the front corners with fluted quarter columns very similar to those on the last piece, above rusticated quoins. Either side are three oak-lined graduated drawers. Their brass handles and escutcheons, although of the period, are later replacements as is one hinge of the finely figured central door. The piece rests on ogee bracket feet which again bear comparison to the last illustration.

A fine Chippendale period mahogany dumb waiter

The dumb waiter seems to have been an English invention: a refreshing change when so much of our furniture was developed from styles born on the Continent. They are recorded from the 1720s and were used at the corners of dining tables for self-service when servants were not present. In most cases the tiers, of which three was the most common number, are graduated in size, increasing from top to bottom, and supported on matching stems between each.

In these respects this example is unusual, the larger tier being at the top and the upper support taking the form of a baluster with crisp acanthus carving while below is a plain tapered or 'gun-barrel' stem. It is also uncommon for the raised rims to be carved, especially as here, with different motifs: long and short beads on the top one and rose and ribbon below. The wood used is a hard and dense mahogany which carves well and takes a good polish and it would appear that the maker set about his task with variety in mind. The skilled way in which he carved the tripod base is apparent in the detail, with more acanthus curling from the knurled feet and on the knees where it flicks outwards in a spirited manner. The legs themselves are moulded with panelled sides and sinuous foliage leading to a crown-like central pendant at the bottom of the stem.

Colour Plate 24a. A small Adam period mahogany circular wine cooler or
jardinière, c.1775. The piece is described on p. 252.

Colour Plate 24b. A detail of the jardinière.

A fine Chippendale period mahogany wine cooler

Circa 1765

In his *Works in Architecture,* Robert Adam wrote that the English were "accustomed by habit, or induced by the nature of our climate to indulge more largely in the enjoyment of the bottle" than the French. This would seem to account for the great diversity of types of small container that were made for bottles during the eighteenth century and intended to stand in the dining room, generally under a side table or sideboard, for more immediate requirements. Indeed by the early nineteenth century there were even cabinet-makers who specialised in making nothing else. The terms cellaret and wine cistern or wine cooler are sometimes not used with any clear distinction, including by Sheraton, but generally the former had a lid and was used for storing bottles while the wine cooler, open or closed, was lined and filled with ice for cooling them.

The present example (opposite, left) is a particularly interesting one, being octagonal in shape with a conforming hinged lid rising with concave sides to a fine vase-shaped finial carved with gadrooning. It fits tightly into the rebate of the stand which is carved with egg-and-dart around the edge, tying it in with the carving on the edge of the lid. The rails of the stand are thin and they rest on four most unusually shaped but effective moulded scrolled legs. Typically of this period, the cellaret is banded with wide strips of brass, a lock is almost invariably found, as are carrying handles which, along with the brass castors, underline the portable nature of the piece. Inside it still has its original lead-covered divisions, radiating from a central octagon.

A rare Chippendale period mahogany cellaret

Circa 1760

This example (opposite, right) has slightly flared sides and is square in shape with canted corners. The arrangement of brass bands, carrying handles and the buckle-shaped lifting handle for the lid all follow the same pattern. However, as in many cases, the top is flat and has a moulded edge. Almost all the surviving cellarets and wine coolers are raised little more than a foot from the ground on a stand or with integral legs. It is very unusual to find one on such a high stand as this. The legs are square and splay diagonally from the corners. They are attractively finished off with C-scroll brackets. The small early castors have rollers of leather. Pieces like this were clearly made to be free-standing rather than to fit under a side table. Again the box fits snugly into a rebate in the stand.

A Chippendale period mahogany wine cooler   Circa 1770

Width 29½ins. (75cm) Depth 19¾ins. (50.2cm) Height 23ins. (58.5cm)

Again brass-bound, here to secure the coopered stave construction, this open type of wine cooler developed from the marble or metal cisterns that had been in use in previous centuries. Wooden ones seem to have come in about 1730 and the oval shape was much the most common. They were invariably lined with lead or zinc and generally had a bung or tap in the bottom to drain off surplus water.

The piece has a gadrooned top edge and scrolled mahogany handles. The carving is continued on the stand below a deeply moulded rebate and at the tops of the four cabriole legs finely moulded in the French manner. The curves continue on each side into shaped aprons with central carved clasps, a form sometimes used on seat furniture of the period. (Compare the piece illustrated on p. 62.)

Chippendale, 1762, illus. four rather fanciful "Cisterns" on pl. CLI, one having a carved gadrooned top edge and similar scrolled mahogany handles to this example.

A rare Hepplewhite period mahogany three pillar dining table   Circa 1780

Considering how indispensable it is in every house of any pretension, it is surprising that so little has been written about the dining table and its development. Chippendale and his contemporaries illustrate none in their design books. The most usual type produced in the second half of the eighteenth century resembled two side tables, generally with rounded ends, and sometimes a matching rectangular centre table with hinged flaps or separate leaves all of which clipped together. The disadvantage of this form was the multitude of legs set along the outer edges which both tended to look clumsy, although the tables were normally used covered with cloths, and were awkward to sit at. It was because of this that the pillar dining table was developed. These were and are still the most fashionable and desirable type and are peculiar to this country and later to America.

The table illustrated is a particularly early example, the three bases having the kind of 'gun barrel' stem and cabriole legs that one might expect to find on a table of the Chippendale period. The moulding of the legs, however, points to a rather later date and it is unlikely that pillar dining tables were made earlier than the date of this one. Being made for large eighteenth century dining rooms where they would be laden with elaborate centrepieces and candelabra, the solid mahogany tops often measured up to five feet or even more in depth. In many cases to adapt them to later conditions they have been made narrower. This may well have happened in this case since the wide spread of the bases, each with four legs, would give adequate support to a wider top than it has at present, although there is no doubt that this top is original. The end sections are rounded while the centre is rectangular with a shorter loose leaf resting on swivel brackets and held in place with brass clips between each. Such an arrangement gives the table great versatility of length.

A very fine small Adam period mahogany circular wine cooler or jardinière   Circa 1775

Height 20ins. (50.8cm) Diameter 14ins. (35.5cm)

Also shown as Colour Plates 24a and 24b, pp. 246 and 247. Probably the highest quality jardinière that we have handled, this piece bears all the hallmarks of an Adam design, although no actual comparison is known to exist, and the execution of a major cabinet maker. It retains the gadrooned top edge found on earlier specimens, but the neo-classical vocabulary of trailing husks, acanthus rinceau, paterae and fluting is typical of the most important commissioned work of the period and is carved in impressively bold relief.

There is something of a similar feeling in some of the furniture designed for Osterley Park by Robert Adam much of which was probably made by John Linnell. The leaf-carved and fluted legs on the present piece are particularly early examples of their type. The fact that these features are here combined with the most attractively figured and coloured mahogany adds further to its great achievement.

A pair of gilded mirrors of c.1767 in the Eating Room (illus. in Tomlin, p. 26) display the same robust quality in the husks and the use of acanthus scrolls. The leaf-carved and fluted legs are related to those on the set of six gilded armchairs of c.1777 in the State Bedroom at Osterley (op. cit. p. 64).

An Adam period mahogany serving table   Circa 1780

Width (back) 54ins. (137.2cm) (front) 49ins. (124.5cm)
Depth 26ins. (66cm) Height 34¾ins. (88.2cm)

The side table was particularly fitted to neo-classical design and mahogany examples of this relatively sober and masculine type, often made a few inches higher than most, were well suited for the dining room as serving tables. Like Chippendale period ones before them, they were generally made without drawers. It was probably due to Robert Adam's inspiration that the fashion began of making pedestals, often surmounted by urns *en suite,* to flank the table and so provide space for cutlery, china, wine bottles, etc.

The majority of serving tables are rectangular and large in size like the rooms they went into. This example is both comparatively small and not too deep in proportion and also has an attractive serpentine shape at the front and sides. The fluting of the frieze, the central tablet with an urn and scrolling foliage and the paterae that cap the four legs are all finely detailed and deeply carved. The legs, as often, are square and tapered and the fluting and treatment of the feet are similar to that on the chair on p. 71. The design is improved and lightened by the concave waisting at the tops of the legs, a device found among Adam's drawings.

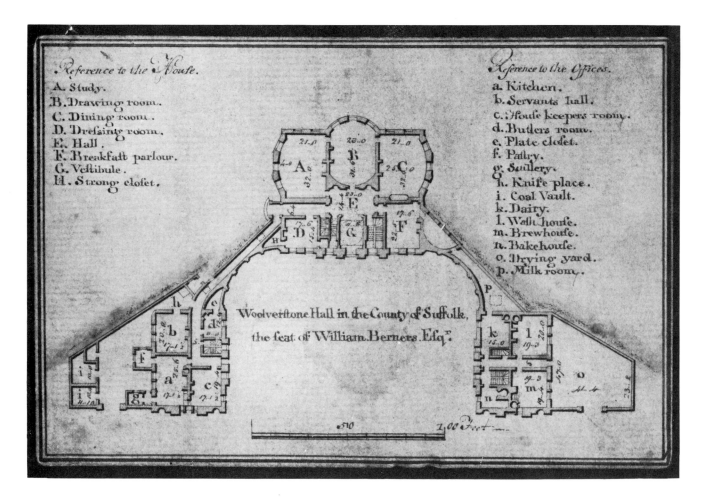

Reference to the House.

A. Study.
B. Drawing room.
C. Dining room.
D. Dressing room.
E. Hall.
F. Breakfast parlour.
G. Vestibule.
H. Strong closet.

Reference to the Offices.

a. Kitchen.
b. Servants hall.
c. House keepers room.
d. Butlers room.
e. Plate closet.
f. Pantry.
g. Scullery.
h. Knife place.
i. Coal Vault.
k. Dairy.
l. Wash house.
m. Brewhouse.
n. Bakehouse.
o. Drying yard.
p. Milk room.

Woolverstone Hall in the County of Suffolk, the seat of William Berners Esqr.

A mahogany serving table designed by Robert Adam

Circa 1776

Width 8ft. 4ins. (254cm) Depth 35½ins. (90.2cm) Height 36½ins. (92.8cm)

This very imposing piece of shaped breakfront form is made in beautiful golden-coloured mahogany. The quality of the central plaque carved with gryphons confronting an urn is emphasised by the restrained way of leaving much of the frieze uncarved although edged with minute mouldings and a band of guilloche. The four legs at the front are again headed with paterae and fluted.

The most unusual feature of the table is its rounded corners at the back. This illustrates well Adam's preference for designing the rooms in the houses in which he and his brother were involved in their entirety. In each case the furniture was individually devised to suit its setting and rounded recesses were frequently used at the ends of rooms.

Several elements present in the table — the gryphons and urn, paterae, fluting and small scale guilloche are found in a drawing by Robert Adam for a casket on stand of 1777. This is reproduced in Ward-Jackson, no. 215. A serving table with several similar features set into a rectangular recess at Woodhall Park, Herts., is illus. in Edwards, vol. III, p. 131, fig. 19.

Provenance: Woolverstone Hall, Suffolk, the seat of the Berners family. The house was designed by the Adam brothers in 1776 and the position of the serving table in its recess may be seen at the bottom of the Dining Room (C) in the plan. Some years after the house was built the use of the Drawing Room (B) and the Dining Room was reversed but the table remained in situ until the Berners family sold the contents of the house in the 1940s.

A fine Adam period mahogany sideboard   Circa 1780

Width 49ins. (124.5cm) Depth 23¾ins. (60.2cm) Height 34½ins. (87.5cm)

The development of the sideboard usually containing a cellaret and other drawers or cupboards as part of its structure may be seen as a natural progression from the serving table and separate pedestals. In 1779 Gillow's were announcing that they were making "a new sort of sideboard table now with drawers etc. in a genteel style to hold bottles". It would appear therefore that this example, being still very much in the carved Adam style, is an early one of its type. It as also of a rare small size and fine quality, the paterae that cap the stop-fluted and fluted legs being sharply carved and the veneers on the drawer fronts splendidly figured and patinated to a rich colour.

The set of original gilt brass buckle-shaped handles are cast with tiny rocaille decoration, an unusual and most attractive feature, as is the finishing off of the sides with cockbeading and handles in keeping with the front. It is clear therefore, that this piece was not intended to stand in an alcove. The doors at the sides are false except for the rear one on the left side, which reveals a cupboard no doubt intended for a chamber pot in the days when it was customary to have these to hand for use during gentlemen's long after-dinner drinking sessions. The right hand side of the sideboard is occupied by a deep lead-lined cellaret drawer, the front of which is panelled to represent three drawers to match symmetrically the three drawers on the left side.

A larger sideboard illus. in Rogers, fig. 188, has a similar pronounced moulding below the frieze and identical legs with paterae cappings and panelled block feet.

A rare Hepplewhite period mahogany dining table   Circa 1785

The markedly individual style of this table shows another attempt at designing a piece that was both stable and comfortable to sit at. There is also the additional advantage in the shelves which might have been used in a similar way to a dumb waiter for additional requirements during a meal. The use of curves in the moulded legs and the serpentine aprons are cleverly contrived. Even the two sides of each triangular platform that face the ends are slightly concave in shape and the rounded ends of the top, which has one leaf clipped in, continue this use of curves. In common with almost all dining tables of the pillar or pedestal type, the presence of castors emphasises their versatile and mobile nature.

A Hepplewhite period mahogany sideboard

Circa 1785

Width 59ins. (150cm) Depth 25ins. (63.5cm) Height 36ins. (91.5cm)

There is something of a similar feeling in the eight unusually tall splay feet that support this piece to those of the previous table. The shaped aprons in between are also alike. As was noted with writing desks, the most desirable and most difficult shape to make is serpentine. In this case the centre drawer is convex while the narrow pedestal ends, each with a deep and a shallower drawer, are concave. The central recess is uncommonly wide and would probably originally have a wine-cooler *en suite* standing under it, although the left hand top drawer is fitted with wooden partitions as a cellaret. The rectangular shape of the recess is softened by the two cusped web-like brackets.

The figured mahogany is faded to a pleasing tone and is crossbanded on the top and edge with tulipwood, which also outlines the drawers, the deep ones with additional oval panels framed with quarter veneering. The Regency brass lion-mask handles are replacements.

One of a pair of Hepplewhite period mahogany serving tables   Circa 1785

Width 70¾ ins. (179.5cm) Depth 29½ ins. (75cm) Height 35¾ ins. (90.8cm)

These tables in mahogany faded to a beautiful honey colour were made especially to fit two curved recesses in a dining room (cf. p. 254). However, the designer has ingeniously compensated for the curved back which is emphasised by a wooden gallery, by shaping the front to give an overall very satisfying kidney shape.

The frieze is skilfully handled with panels of figured veneer mirrored either side of a centre tablet which is of the same classical shape as the example on p. 253. This contains an inlaid oval of mottled figure in a quarter-veneered surround. The slightly projecting plaque and the rectangular panelled cappings to the legs are further distinguished from the rest of the frieze by being edged with faded tulipwood, carefully laid radially, which contrasts with the crossbanding of purpleheart that is used in between. The central plaque incorporates a drawer which is an original and unusual feature: often these were inserted at a later date. The six legs are slender, square tapered and deeply fluted, ending in block feet.

Provenance: The FitzGerald family (the family of the Dukes of Leinster) and made for Halsmead
    House, Prescot, Lancashire, an Adam house demolished in 1936.
Preston House, Preston Candover, Hampshire.

An early Sheraton period mahogany serving table, probably Scottish   Circa 1790

Width 78½ins. (199.5cm) Depth 31ins. (78.8cm)
Height at back 41¾ins. (106cm) Height at front 35ins. (89cm)

The similarity with the previous example of the decorative use of rectangular panels of well-figured veneer and the prominent central plaques with ovals is clear. In this case the panels which are again mirrored either side of the low superstructure, are edged with cockbeading, as are the three frieze drawers below. The panels give access to the interior through two sliding doors. The central ovals and those that cap the front legs and are matched either end above, are recessed and edged with boxwood. The back legs are capped with inlaid oval paterae while the shape is continued in the handles on the frieze drawers.

Other notable features are the mellow faded colour of the piece and the attractive serpentine shaping to both the front and sides. The canting at the front corners allows the square tapered legs to be set diagonally. The legs are all finished with boxwood stringing with large dots at the tops. Serving tables of this particular form with a superstructure at the back were probably made in Scotland; an indication of Scottish manufacture are the drawer linings which are generally of ash or chestnut. In this case they are ash.

A Hepplewhite period mahogany semi-circular sideboard   Circa 1785

Width 60ins. (152.5cm) Depth 28¼ins. (71.8cm) Height 37½ins. (95.2cm)

The simple shaping of this piece is the perfect foil for its outstanding surface. The mahogany is a nut brown colour, with a busy figure which is mirrored either side of the centre, and a splendid patina giving a great range of different tones. The top, like the drawer fronts, is crossbanded and finished with boxwood lines which outline rectangular panels with concave corners, while the elegance of the four square tapered legs inset with wave-moulded panels is enhanced by the unusually tall spade feet.

The triangular drawer above the arched kneehole recess is fitted as a secretaire with a drop front. It is a tribute to the respect paid to the figured veneer that handles have never been fitted.

The form is similar to a pattern in Shearer et al., 1793, pl. 5, fig. 1 which is described as "A circular cellaret sideboard. . .five feet long, the framing fifteen inches deep, two deep drawers, one prepared for the plumber, the other plain, a shallow angle ditto in the middle, a cupboard in each corner, veneer'd front, four plain Marlbro' legs." There are additional options of "a plate drawer. . .a loose cistern for bottles. . .(and) a small ditto to wash glasses in." The Shearer plate shows the piece with handles.

An early Sheraton period mahogany bow-front sideboard Circa 1790

Width 54½ ins. (138.5cm) Depth 26¼ ins. (66.7cm)
Height 35½ ins. (90.2cm) Height with rails 63ins. (160cm)

This sideboard is a good medium size and in fine original condition with a centre drawer flanked by two cellarets of two drawers depth bearing the original stamped brass handles. After 1779, when Maston and Bellamy patented an improved method of die pressing brass in Birmingham, this method of manufacture became increasingly popular for all manner of metal mounts and decoration.

The presence of cockbeading round the drawers, kneehole and bottom edge shows that this somewhat conservative feature carried on right to the end of the century. However, the most interesting aspect of this piece is its retention of a good example of a brass-railed back. Neither of the two sideboards shown in Hepplewhite's *Guide* nor the five in *The Cabinet-Makers' London Book of Prices* display such a feature, but Sheraton's *Drawing Book* shows two, one of which is similar to the present one. He calls them "brass rod used to support large dishes". Their shaping and urn finials makes them a decorative feature which was once found on many more sideboards than it is today, screw marks frequently telling of their subsequent removal. Some examples also supported candle branches which, as Sheraton says, "give a very brilliant effect to the silver ware". He adds that "the branches are each of them fixed in one socket which slides up and down on the same rod to any height, and fixed anywhere by turning a screw." The finely cast scrolled branches on this piece can still be adjusted in this way.

A fine early Sheraton period mahogany serpentine sideboard   Circa 1790

Width 78ins. (198.2cm)

The photograph shows well the superbly figured and faded mahogany, mirrored at either side, with which this is veneered. The drawers are edged with cockbeading and boxwood stringing is much used to outline edges and shaped panels in the stiles. The piece is large and yet the sophisticated serpentine form, the deep shaping of the kneehole which is similar to the previous example, and the comparative shallowness of the drawers and thinness of the square tapered legs remove any sense of bulkiness. In short, the proportions are excellent. The right hand side contains a cellaret the depth of both drawer fronts and on the left is a drawer above a cupboard which has been converted from a deep drawer. This was frequently done in the cause of utility. Sheraton in *Cabinet Dictionary* says that this drawer, which balanced the cellaret, was sometimes meant to hold plate and sometimes lined with lead, to wash glasses in. The handles are later replacements.

A sideboard of similar shape and proportions is illus. in Edwards, vol. III, p. 135, fig. 30.

An early Sheraton period mahogany three-pillar dining table Circa 1790

Length 12ft. 10ins. (391cm) Depth 54¾ins. (139cm) Height 28¼ins. (71.8cm)

Compared with the piece on p. 251 the increased elegance in the pillars of this table is evident. The simple gun-barrel stems are still present and, being short, allow for the long very graceful curves of the legs with their good amount of splay. Each stem has four legs which makes the table more stable than three and means they are less likely to be in the way when sitting at the table. The legs are fluted and end in plain square capped castors instead of plate castors as in the previous example. The top again has round ends with a plain edge and a leaf between each section. The detail shows the unusually fine figure of the tops: a huge expanse of solid timber of such great quality to have been cut from one tree.

Sheraton in the *Dictionary* writes: "The common useful dining-tables are upon pillar and claws, generally four claws to each pillar, with brass castors. A dining-table of this kind may be made to any size, by having a sufficient quantity of pillars and claw parts, for between each of them is a loose flap, fixed by means of iron straps and buttons, so that they are easily taken off and put aside; the beds may be joined to each other with brass fork or strap fastenings."

A Sheraton period mahogany three-pillar dining table   Circa 1790

Length 11ft. 9ins. (368cm) Depth 54ins. (139.5cm) Height 28½ins. (72.5cm)

This is another fine example made in lustrous paler timber of excellent quality. The top has D-shaped ends with its original two leaves and, again, is supported on short gun-barrel stems and graceful legs with a generous splay.

   An interesting feature of this table is that the tops of the two ends swivel round 90 degrees to form side tables which are constructed so that they will stand flush against a wall with satisfactory proportions. The majority of better pillar dining tables were made for convenience with tops that tip up in the manner of tripod tables with an underframing that pivots vertically on a central block at the top of each pillar. However, such an arrangement as is possible with the table illustrated here is most uncommon.

An early Sheraton period mahogany octagonal breakfast table   Circa 1790

Width 45½ ins. (115.5cm) Height 28ins. (71.2cm)

Tables of this sort with circular, oval or occasionally octagonal tops on single pillar bases became popular towards the close of the century. They are usually of a size suitable to seat up to six or eight people for less formal and more intimate meals than the large dining table might have been used for, and in almost every case the tops are hinged on blocks to tip up so that they might be moved to one side of the room when not in use. Small tripod and other tables had been used for tea and supper, generally in the drawing room, for a long while and Chippendale in the *Director* presents designs for 'Breakfast Tables' of Pembroke table form, although these may have been intended mainly for bedrooms. The application of the term to the present type of table is a modern one.

This example is made of attractively faded mahogany, the edge of the top ovolo-moulded and crossbanded with satinwood. As on pillar dining tables the design benefits from a slender gun-barrel stem and four high-swept and elegant splay legs. These have the unusual feature of being faceted towards the top, as are the brass castor caps on the toes.

A Sheraton period rosewood and satinwood oval breakfast table   Circa 1795

Width 57ins. (144.8cm) Depth 49½ ins. (125.8cm) Height 27½ ins. (69.8cm)

The fine colour and figure of the rosewood top of this piece is evident in the photographs. It is veneered in three sections on to mahogany which appears in the edge moulding. As on the previous example the edge here is crossbanded with satinwood which is matched in this case by the rare feature of a solid satinwood pillar and legs. Being a larger size than the previous table, a slightly more solid but still simple pillar is needed for adequate support. The four splay legs are reeded and have brass caps and castors.

A Sheraton period mahogany two-pillar dining table   Circa 1790

Length 88ins. (223.5cm) Depth 54ins. (137.2cm) Height 27½ins. (70cm)

The D-end was another popular shape for the tops of dining tables, in this case being finished off with reeding. The pillars here also illustrate another variation in the use of vase-shaped turning which as a popular form looks back, just as the tapered column does, as far as the Chippendale period. The moulded rings are still small and light and the well-splayed legs plain and elegant. The one loose leaf that the table has is of the period but a later replacement.

An early Sheraton period mahogany serving table

Circa 1790

Width 62½ ins. (158.8cm) Depth 24¼ ins. (61.5cm) Height of table 34½ ins. (87.5cm)

The six long slender fluted and tapering legs and the shallowness of this piece give its proportions particular elegance. This is heightened by the concave centre and the fact that the two flanking drawers are not deepened as cellarets as was the fashion for sideboards. The shape may be compared with examples on pp. 134 and 147. The drawer fronts are veneered with attractively figured timber and edged with very fine reeding which is also used on the top edge and on the concave-sided lozenges that are applied as a decorative feature (cf. p. 191). It is interesting that none of the drawers have ever had locks, the brass handles being of the period but not original to the table. The brass rail above is also a replacement but probably on the original lines, as Sheraton says, to prop up large dishes, although later illustrations sometimes show them used in the manner of curtain rails with the space below hung with material.

A Sheraton period mahogany oval tray   Circa 1790

Width 31ins. (78.8cm) Depth 21ins. (53.4cm)

Few trays that date from before the Chippendale period still survive although they seem to have been much used both for clearing away dinner plates and at tea time. The style followed those of other pieces of furniture so that towards the end of the century oval shapes and marquetry inlay were very popular.

In his *Dictionary* Sheraton states the maximum size of trays to be 32ins. long by 2ft. wide. This example is therefore a particularly large one and a marvellous example of figure and patina. In spite of its size it has not warped as has so often happened with eighteenth century trays, with the resultant loss of original surface through restoration. The decoration is thankfully restrained, being limited to a finely engraved hollywood conch shell in a crossbanded oval of richly grained kingwood, with another similar band round the outside and on the raised outer edge. This leaves a large area of mahogany veneer, quartered and mirrored, which has faded to a superb mellow golden brown, the slight cracks of the medullary rays as they have died out adding to the effect of the swirls of flame-like figure. Few people could surely doubt that the attractiveness of this tray has been greatly enhanced since it was made.

A Sheraton period mahogany oval wine cooler   Circa 1790

Width 22¼ ins. (57.8cm) Depth 17¾ ins. (45cm) Height 28ins. (71.2cm)

The 'cellarets' illustrated in Hepplewhite's *Guide* of 1788 are still the brass-bound type, although by this date examples like this one, veneered on to a sectional carcase, were probably more common. The mahogany veneer in this case is particularly well chosen, pale golden in colour with a watery and almost silken quality. The contrasting crossbanding is in purpleheart and each panel is outlined with boxwood. The lozenge-shaped inlaid escutcheon is typical of the date, although the fine gilt brass Regency lion-mask handles are later replacements. The proportions of the piece are excellent, tapering very slightly and fitting flush on to a stand edged with conforming smaller panels and raised on square tapered legs with just the right amount of splay for balance. The interior has lost its metal lining but retains its drainage bung in the centre of the bottom.

By the time of his Encyclopaedia, *1805, Sheraton writes that cellarets were not so generally used and amongst the higher classes wholly laid aside in favour of the heavy and often ungainly sarcophagus forms of the Regency period.*

A Sheraton period mahogany D-shaped sideboard   Circa 1795

The slightly flattened bow-front shape is very characteristic of Sheraton's designs, and in the last decade of the century, as has been noted on other furniture such as writing tables, the practice of continuing the legs upwards, to interrupt the line of the top edge in the form of engaged columns, was quite common. This vertical emphasis tends to diminish the sense of bulk of a piece of furniture. Here the six legs take the form of particularly well-shaped tapered columns, tightly carved with fine reeding like the top edge, and with capitals well carved with crinkled leaves. The mahogany, and in particular the veneers on the front panels, are excellently matched and figured, to such an extent that, as has been found before, handles have never been added in order not to diminish the effect. There are four drawers, all cockbeaded, including one in the arched kneehole recess and deep ones either side, one of which contains a revolving cellaret.

A Regency period mahogany dumb waiter Circa 1795

Diameter 22ins. (56cm) Height 42ins. (106.5cm)

By the end of the eighteenth century the traditional type of dumb waiter with central turned pillar supports was giving way to more inventive forms. Here the upper of two mahogany tiers is supported on four slender brass rods cast to simulate bamboo. The edges of the tiers are brass bound with finely pierced Greek key fret galleries. The tripod base has reeded splayed legs and a rather unusual form of tapered and reeded column alleviated by a deep concave moulding at its base to balance the proportions.

A practically identical dumb waiter from Inverary Castle, Argyllshire, differing only slightly in the brass edging and marginally broader reeding, is illus. in Rogers, fig. 197.

A Sheraton period mahogany double Cumberland dining table Circa 1795

Length 10ft. 7ins. (323cm) Depth 46¾ins. (119cm) Height 28ins. (71cm)

It is not common to find a table of this type with its two parts intact since often they were split up and adapted to form separate tables. The idea, the first supposedly being made for the Duke of Cumberland (who was commissioning work from Adam, Linnell and others in the 1770s and 1780s), is a development from the double gateleg table, adapted so that the legs spread the weight without obstructing people sitting at it. The four supports to each pedestal swing round on wooden pivot hinges, thereby letting a flap each side fall. Such a device means that this type of table can be reduced to a surprisingly small size. It may also be seen as a forerunner of the Sutherland table. An elegance is maintained by the thinness of the plain tapered columns, the legs joined to them having a hint of a 'knee' developing and ending in brass lion paw feet, both more common features as furniture enters the Regency period. The finely figured top retains its original depth with a slightly convex edge moulding, but the centre leaf which is clipped between the two end sections, although of the period, is not original to the table.

A very similar table is illus. in Edwards, vol. III, p. 222, fig. 31.

274

A Sheraton period mahogany four-pillar dining table Circa 1795

Length 15ft. 8¼ins. (478.5cm) Depth 57ins. (144.8cm) Height 28¾ins. (73cm)

Fine period dining tables of more than three pillars are now rare since so many have been divided into smaller sections. The detail of the top shows that this one is made of quite exceptionally figured timber and that the leaves between each pillar are original and match perfectly. It also retains a greater depth than the smaller tables that have been illustrated which is necessary to achieve satisfactory proportions. The edge of the top is reeded, and the pillars turned with rings, although still not heavily, while the four legs to each pillar have a distinct broadening at the knee and moulding down their top edges. They are capped with brass castors chased with foliage decoration similar to those in the example on p. 152.

An early Regency period mahogany two-pillar dining table

Circa 1805

Length 9ft. 1ins. (277cm) Depth 48ins. (122cm) Height 29ins. (74cm)

This example shows another variation on the pillar type of dining table to give greater length and make it more adaptable. The D-end top has a reeded edge and is supported at the ends by slim ring-turned pillars on three unusually high reeded legs which curve downwards with a certain elegance to square capped castors. Between these are three leaves but, instead of introducing a third pillar to support the centre one, the maker has used two adjustable thin turned legs which take up much less space in storage. They are set well underneath so as not to be in the way of diners.

The idea of using adjustable legs has a certain similarity to an invention of Richard Brown in 1805 an example of which is illus. in Edwards, vol. III, p. 222, fig. 32.

A Regency period mahogany serving table
Circa 1810

Width 91ins. (231cm) Depth at sides 29ins. (73.5cm) Depth at centre 21ins. (53.5cm)

About the turn of the century there seems to have been a certain return in taste to the sideboard table. As Sheraton says in *The Cabinet Dictionary,* 1803, ''the most fashionable sideboards at present are those without cellarets, or any kind of drawer, having massy ornamented legs and moulded frames.'' The view of the top shows an attractively-shaped outline with a concave centre. Of this form Sheraton writes that the hollow front of large sideboards enables the butler to reach across more easily and secures him ''from the jostles of the other servants''!

The quality of workmanship is very high, the top edge and frieze having panels of very close-set thin vertical reeding and a similar herring-bone pattern round the central plaque. The six legs are turned with slightly tapering sections of reeding and end in brass lion's paw feet. Their projecting rounded cappings and the centre plaque have inset mounts finely cast with a palmette motif similar to those on p. 174. Below, the brass cable moulding on the bottom edge continues the close detail of the reeding.

Sheraton in pl. 31 of the Appendix, *illus. a serving table of similar proportions to the present example, with bows either end of the front and a cellaret beneath, though it is straight-fronted between the centre legs.*

A Regency period mahogany patent extending dining table by Morgan & Sanders   Circa 1805

Length 9ft. ¾ in. (276cm) Depth 47 ¾ ins. (121.5cm) Height 29 ½ ins. (75cm)

The first quarter of the nineteenth century saw a great vogue and rivalry in patented mechanical furniture involving tables, beds, chairs and settees, and one of the forerunners in this field was the firm of Morgan & Sanders who were established in 1794 'three doors from the Strand'. They based some of their ideas on a type of dining table patented by Richard Gillow in 1800 and given the name Imperial. This was basically a form whereby the ends could be pulled apart and loose leaves inserted on sliding rails of wood or metal in between. The handsomely engraved brass handle shown in the detail, of which there is one at either end of the table to draw them apart, proclaims the present example to be one of their patents. The clips above these handles release the framework of the table which slides from the centre in a series of telescopic sections. The whole piece is of mellow mahogany, the top having squared ends with rounded corners which was becoming the most usual shape, with reeding on the edge and along the bottom of the frieze. The turned inverted baluster legs are similarly finished and retain a certain elegance in their shaping.

On the Gillow's trade card, illus. in Heal, p. 115, such a table is illus. and described as "forming an elegant sett, to Dine from 4 to 20 persons or any greater Number, the whole Table shuts up into the space of a Large Pembroke Table".

A Regency period mahogany three-pillar dining table   Circa 1820

Length with leaves 13ft. 7ins. (414cm) Length without leaves 8ft. 10½ ins. (270.5cm)
Depth 51ins. (129.5cm) Height 28½ ins. (72.5cm)

Apart from the two leaves which, as is so often the case, are later replacements after the original ones were lost, this table is in its original state and of excellent quality. It is made of that fine mahogany of the date which is dense and heavy with a high natural shine and which carves crisply, although it lacks the figure of the late eighteenth century. The tops are square-ended with rounded corners and the distinctive ovolo moulding that was becoming more common at this time. The turning of the pillars is heavier than on preceding examples and the four splayed legs to each correspond with thick knees and deeply moulded top edges. They end in rather unusual but well carved toes with the kind of scrolls and waterleaf motifs that might have been cast in brass as castor caps.

TABLES

A rare William III period walnut card table   Circa 1700

Width 32½ ins. (82.5cm) Depth (open) 29¼ ins. (74.2cm) Height (open) 27½ ins. (70cm)

Tables made specifically for the playing of cards were first made at the end of the seventeenth century under the prevailing Dutch influence, and this is an early example in particularly fine original condition. It is veneered in mellow walnut which has developed a good varied patina. The top, which has a concave-moulded edge, is hinged and almost circular when open, the flap being supported on two rear legs which swivel out with a gateleg action. Inside it is finished with feathered stringing which is also used to edge the three small frieze drawers which would have contained cards, dice and other gaming equipment. The bottom edge of the frieze is outlined with cockbeading which is again an early use. The five slender turned tapered legs are united with a flat stretcher, waved at the front, with turned finials above the wooden hinges to the gates. The use of pony hoof feet is unusual on English furniture, although the idea is an extremely ancient one, going back to Egyptian and Roman furniture.

There is an identical table at the Victoria and Albert which is illus. in Brackett, p. 91.

An early George I period walnut side table Circa 1715

Width 32¼ ins. (82cm) Depth 19½ ins. (49.5cm) Height 28¾ ins. (73cm)

This table shows well that sophisticated elegance which is occasionally found in the understated detailing of some of the finest English furniture. The walnut is a pale golden colour, on the top quarter-veneered with feathered stringing while the edge has a moulding above crossbanding with subtle re-entrant corners. The three drawers are edged with similar feathered stringing and cockbeading and bear the original brass ring handles. The slender legs are simply tapered with lappets carved at the tops in the manner of seventeenth century cut card work that was used particularly on silver. At the bottom the legs curve elegantly into flattened pad feet.

This kind of small table with a kneehole in the frieze was probably used for both writing and dressing and in various forms remained popular throughout the first half of the eighteenth century.

The type of leg used here so effectively without the curves of the cabriole leg is occasionally found on other furniture such as a card table illus. in Edwards, vol. III, p. 195, fig. 9.

An early George I period oak side table   Circa 1715

Width 34½ins. (87.5cm) Depth 18ins. (45.8cm) Height 27¾ins. (70.5cm)

Making an interesting contrast with the previous piece, this shows none of its refinement; indeed in the eccentric shaping of the frieze there is a sense of overt display, yet it excels in its outstanding colour and patina. The thick veneers of the frieze and top with its wide overhang are of pollard wood which has taken on a splendid natural shine. The piece has several other points of quality, not least the fine shaping of the cabriole legs with cusping at the knees and pad feet. The ovolo moulding of the top edge is matched on the projecting lips of the three drawers which are oak lined with the original brass handles with punched decoration.

An early George I gilt gesso side table attributed to James Moore

Circa 1720

Width 34½ins. (87.5cm) Depth 21ins. (53.5cm) Height 31½ins. (80cm)

James Moore and his partner John Gumley were among the most prominent furniture makers of the early eighteenth century, supplying gilded furniture and mirrors, often in grand baroque style, to the King. In his later work Moore was influenced by the motifs and solidity of Palladian taste and the straight square legs and bold central scallop shell and acanthus motifs of this table are typical. The shallow carving in the gesso takes the form of linked C-scrolls in repeated shaped panels which derives ultimately from French Berainesque strapwork. The legs, which have cusps at the top corners, end in bulbous vase-shaped feet carved with husks, while the curved brackets on the front and sides are edged with ovolo mouldings like the rails and legs.

A similar side table with a carved gesso top and Greek key decoration signed by Moore at Hampton Court Palace, is illus. in Edwards and Jourdain, figs. 24 and 25. The marble top here is not original and, in view of the proportions and the form of the upper mouldings, it is possible that it originally formed the base for a lacquer cabinet. There is a similar example of this at the Victoria and Albert and another stand, now used as a side table, at Petworth House, Sussex.

A fine George I gilt gesso centre table   Circa 1725

This example which has its original carved gesso top is exceptional for the quality of the carving and the graceful shaping of its four cabriole legs. A number of features are again reminiscent of the work of James Moore, but there may have been other makers active in this field of gilded furniture.

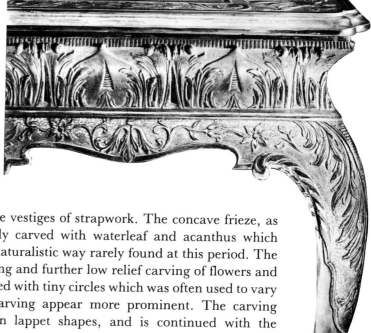

The moulded top with re-entrant corners is decorated with a central acanthus motif surrounded with scallop shells and foliage scrolls and the vestiges of strapwork. The concave frieze, as the detail shows, is particularly crisply carved with waterleaf and acanthus which scrolls over at the top in an extremely naturalistic way rarely found at this period. The aprons on all sides have complex shaping and further low relief carving of flowers and foliage, like the top, on a ground stamped with tiny circles which was often used to vary the texture and thereby makes the carving appear more prominent. The carving extends over the knees of the legs in lappet shapes, and is continued with the impression of scrolling on the pad feet.

A side table supplied to John Meller at Erddig, Clwyd, by Moore in 1726, the year he died, illus. in Edwards and Jourdain, fig. 31, has similar features.

A George I period walnut triangular centre table Circa 1720

Length of side (closed) 31½ ins. (80cm) Max. width (open) 37ins. (94cm) Height 27½ ins. (69.8cm)

This unusual table, like that illustrated on p. 283, displays the effective use of straight turned legs with pad feet. In this case the tops have a little carving and scrolled ears. The table top when closed forms an equilaterial triangle with indented corners and figured veneer crossbanded at the edges with straight-grained walnut. This revolves ingeniously on a central pivot to support three triangular hinged flaps connected with rule joints and also crossbanded at their outer moulded edges. Thus a hexagonal top is formed with an attractive pattern of veneers, the grain running in varying directions.

A fine George II period brass-inlaid mahogany tripod table   Circa 1740

Width 26½ ins. (67.2cm) Height 27½ ins. (69.8cm)

The 1730s saw the introduction of the tripod table, most, except the smallest ones, being made with tops that can be released by a catch to tilt vertically, being pivoted on a block at the top of the stem, and stand out of the way against a wall. Like card tables they were thus intended to be moved about when and as required. In 1733 there is a catalogue entry at the sale of Sir William Stanhope's furniture: "a mahogany scallop'd tea-table on a claw". The term claw was a contemporary one for a tripod base and this description would therefore seem to mean such a table as this (shown opposite as Colour Plate 25), the circular shallow depressions being intended for cups and saucers or supper plates.

Brass inlaid furniture saw a brief fashion at this time, and although examples are not common they are always of fine quality. A number of tripod tables of this kind with between eight and twelve compartments round the top are known, some also with mother-of-pearl inlay, but this is a particularly good one. The hexafoil centre and edges of its compartments are outlined with brass lines and the cusps in between, the tops of the legs and the toes are inlaid with plaques finely engraved with rococo scrollwork. The stem is turned and pestle shaped and well proportioned.

It is impossible to say with certainty who might have made these tables. The rôle of John Channon in this brass inlaid furniture has been discussed on pp. 184-6. The influential German cabinet maker Abraham Roentgen, who worked in England from 1733 to 1738, certainly made pieces of this type, there being an example with rather thin proportions, made after he returned to Germany, at the Landesmuseum, Kassel. While in England he was a journeyman to a cabinet maker named Gern who probably also produced such work, and another known German in London was Frederick Hints who, as well as being a maker of stringed instruments, is recorded in an advertisement of 1738 as being the maker of "Desks and Book-Cases of Mahogany, Tea-Tables, Tea-Chests and Tea-Boards etc. all curiously made and inlaid with fine figures of brass and mother of pearl."

Among the known similar examples one is illus. in Edwards, vol. III, p. 207, fig. 15 (the Duchess of Roxburgh), and another at the Victoria and Albert in the V. and A. Bulletin, April 1966, p. 69, fig. 6. Another type with a triquetra or three-legged base, formerly in the collection of the Earl of Wemyss, Elcho Castle, Perth, was sold by Parke Bernet, New York, 29th April, 1960, lot 504.

Provenance: Sir Alfred Chester Beatty, Kensington Palace Gardens, London.
Walter P. Chrysler, Jun., New York (sale Parke Bernet, 29th April 1960, Lot 229).

Colour Plate 25.

A George I period mahogany tea table

Circa 1725

Width 35ins. (89cm) Depth (open) 34½ ins. (87.5cm) Height 28ins. (71cm)

The rich colour and grain of this early example of mahogany is evident from the flap in the photograph, as is the attractive shaping and rounding of the corners. The form is identical to that of a card table except that the latter were generally lined inside with baize or other cloth. It is likely that many tables without this were made as informal tea or supper tables for the drawing room. On card tables of this type the corner projections generally contained circular shallow depressions which were probably for candlesticks.

As was seen in the example on p. 282, on early card tables the flaps were supported on either one or two swing legs hinged to the back. During the second decade of the century the concertina or folding frame action was developed. This was used on the finest tables through to the Hepplewhite period as it gave greater stability and a symmetry that is much more pleasing to the eye. By releasing a clip the two back legs can be drawn backwards unfolding a hinged continuation of the frieze either side which is locked into place by then drawing forwards a sliding tray underneath. The effect when this is done, with a cabriole leg at each corner and a corresponding frieze on each side, can be seen on p. 300. This tea table also has such an action. The frieze follows the shaping of the top and the finely-drawn cabriole legs are carved with scallop shells and husks with C-scrolls at the sides and forming hips above. They end in ball-and-claw feet. The rounded style and form of the carving is very close to the fashion a few years earlier, for example on the corner chair on p. 35.

A similar walnut card table with a single swing leg action is illus. in V. and A., Tables, *pl. 18.*

An early George II period walnut side table   Circa 1730

Width 35½ ins. (90.2cm) Depth 23¼ ins. (59cm) Height 28ins. (71cm)

This is made from solid walnut of a pale and mellowed colour, particularly on the top which is thin, moulded on the edge and has a considerable overlap. The form and proportions are similar to those of the example on p. 286, including the deep cavetto frieze and astragal moulding below it. Although the taste is more puritan, there are several other features of this piece which give it an unusual character. The four cabriole legs are slender and elegant and although they are not carved, they each have two slight insteps in their length. These are V-shaped, the edges being keeled, as are the club feet in which they terminate. The top sections are edged with C-scrolls which curve round into the aprons which, following the cabriole shape, are convex in profile. At the front and sides these have a restrained lambrequin shaping, the apron at the back being plain.

Provenance: Philip Shelbourne, Esq., Theberton House, Saxmundham, Suffolk.

Colour Plates 26a and 26b. A Chippendale period mahogany urn stand, c.1755, and detail. The piece is described on p. 308.

292

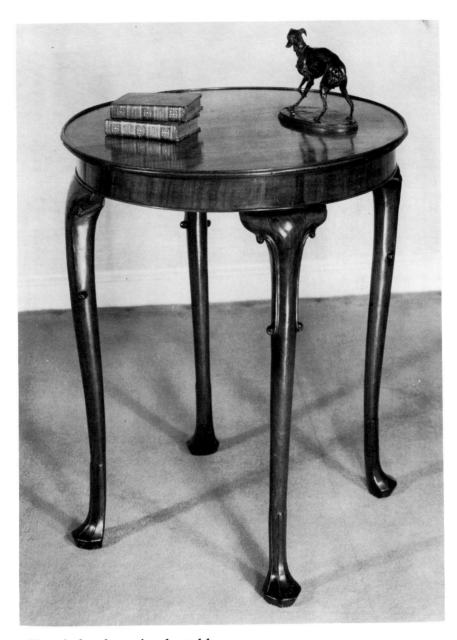

A rare George II period walnut circular table   Circa 1730

Diameter 22½ ins. (57cm) Height 26½ ins. (67.2cm)

It is uncertain whether such attractive small tables as this would have been made with any specific purpose in mind, except perhaps for tea. In this it is the precursor of the tripod table, which was shortly to become the usual way of fashioning circular tables, although rectangular ones often continued to be supported on cabriole legs, as on the last piece. The wood is beautifully faded, the top solid and shallow frieze veneered. The top has a lipped moulded edge with another thin moulding on the bottom edge of the frieze. The four legs are very gently and slightly cabriole in shape narrowed at the top with two C-scrolls below the ears. They end in unusual faceted club feet with alternate raised panels which give the appearance of their being webbed.

Provenance: The late Marjorie Wiggin Prescott, Belle Haven, Greenwich, Connecticut, U.S.A.

A George II period carved and gilded console table   Circa 1745

Width 54ins. (137cm) Depth 28ins. (71cm) Height 34ins. (86cm)

The term console table, as the word implies, originally meant a small side table supported on scrolled brackets, usually linked together by a stretcher. However, it has come to be more generally used for any side table with a marble top which has front supports and is fixed to the wall at the back. This piece is influenced by William Jones' work of 1739, *The Gentleman's or Builder's Companion*, in which some twenty designs for side tables and mirrors were among the earliest published by an English author. The presence here of cabriole legs with hairy paw feet and shells and husks at the knees looks back to earlier types, although, like a number of Jones' designs, the overall feeling is lighter than the solidity of William Kent's work. The carving is very crisply done and the swags which continue at the sides, look forward to the side pendants of mirrors of the 1750s such as that shown on p. 418.

The table has its original moulded Derbyshire fossil marble top.

Pl. 31 of Jones illus. a similar plain frieze, which in this case is finished with a granular textured ground, with swags of flowers and fruit suspended from a centre shell, while pl. 32 again has swags and a gadrooned top edge. The table is discussed and illustrated in Jourdain, 1945, p. 195, (fig. 2).
Provenance: Wentworth Castle, Yorkshire.
Col. Mark Whitwell, The Old Rectory, Stawley, Wellington, Somerset.

A George II period mahogany tripod table   Circa 1750

Diameter 35½ ins. (85cm) Height 28ins. (71cm)

The natural shine on the hard and dense mahogany that was generally used in the solid at this period is evident in this piece, as are the sturdy, well balanced proportions. The finely patinated circular top revolves on the bird cage support beneath. This comprises two squares of wood joined at the corners with turned columns to which the long bearers under the table top are hinged; the top revolves freely on the top of the stem which slots right through the bird cage and is secured with a wedge.

The stem consists of a short fluted section above a squat baluster carved with acanthus with an overhang at the top, and a band of egg-and-dart moulding at the base. The pitting of the ground to give contrasting texture is visible in the detail. The legs have more acanthus at the knees and ball-and-claw feet.

A tripod table at the Victoria and Albert, illus. in Brackett, 1927, p. 221, has an extremely similar stem and base, as does another in Cescinsky, 1937, p. 298.

A rare George II period tripod salver table   Circa 1750

Diameter (open) 26¾ins. (68cm) Height 26¾ins. (68cm)

This table has a most attractive honey colour where the light has bleached it, tending to a darker, redder hue beneath the flaps and at the top of the stem. The identity of the wood, among the wide variety of exotic timbers that were beginning to be imported at the time, is uncertain but it is very hard and heavy with a high natural polish and a grain not unlike that of a mahogany. It is not a wood that would have been easy to carve decoratively.

The top, triangular when closed, is formed of three triangular sections which make an agreeable configuration of grain. This swivels on the stem to support three hinged flaps in the same manner as the triangular table on p. 287. Here the shape, when open, is circular with six shaped notches round the circumference. These were intended to take the feet of a large silver salver carrying a tea or coffee service. Between the tripod legs are niches formed as single flutes and above, the turned baluster stem tapers to a spirally reeded or wrythen knop above a ribbed bell shape.

Two tilt-top tables with the same features are illus. in Edwards, vol. III, p. 164, figs. 1-2. These are at Dunham Massey, Cheshire where the original silver salvers hallmarked for 1741 still exist. Although slightly earlier in date, they display similar treatment of the tripod legs which end in pointed toes.
Another tripod table with three flaps is illus. in Cescinsky, 1911, vol. II, fig. 203 where the type is called very rare.

A Chippendale period mahogany tripod table

Width 23½ins. (59.5cm) Depth 17ins. (43.2cm) Height 27ins. (68.5cm)

It would be difficult to term this eccentrically shaped tilt-top table as anything but clumsy and yet it is not without both charm and interest. The solid mahogany of which it is made has a splendid colour and the view of the attractively shaped top shows its superbly faded patina. The old ink stains have become part of its character and they could only be removed at risk of leaving the surface lifeless and dull. The moulded edge is inlaid with a fine brass line. The stem is moulded alternately convex and concave and leads into an unusual open tripod base made up of opposing curves in an ogee form, with a concave stretcher between, all the top edges being moulded. The feet take the form of rather amusing shoes.

It is uncommon to find a rectangular top on a tripod support, although a drawing of one, also on an ogee base with a stretcher, by John Linnell is illus. in Ward-Jackson, fig. 191. An even more unusual table with a similar base appears in Edwards, vol. III, p. 316, fig. 32, while an octagonal topped tea table on a more refined pierced base was supplied by William Masters to the Duke of Atholl in 1755. It is illus. in Coleridge, fig. 398.

Provenance: The late Marjorie Wiggin Prescott, Belle Haven, Greenwich, Connecticut, U.S.A.

A Chippendale period mahogany tea or china table   Circa 1755

The fashion for tea drinking, in spite of its high cost, spread very quickly to all classes. In 1758 it was stated that "prevalent custom hath introduced it into every cottage". This meant a great increase in the number of small portable tables with tray tops or galleries that were made for the serving of it in drawing rooms. Circular and rectangular shapes are both found.

This example has a shallow moulding round the top edge above a frieze of blind fret. This incorporates a variety of different shapes in what was called chinoiserie taste, although the ogee motifs actually owe more to Middle Eastern influences. Beneath, on all sides, is an edging of gadrooning, with slender cabriole legs at each corner carved with acanthus at the knees and with hairy paw feet which still derive from the ball-and-claw tradition. The crispness of the carving is aided by the hard, dark timber with its natural shine.

Chippendale, 1762, illus. two of similar form to this example, pl. LI, which he calls "tables for holding each a set of China, and may be used as Tea-Tables... Those Tables look very well, when rightly executed."

Exhibition: The C.L. David Collection, Copenhagen.

A Chippendale period mahogany tea or china table   Circa 1760

Width 33½ ins. (85cm) Depth 23½ ins. (59.5cm) Height 28½ ins. (72.5cm)

This is a fine example of a table which came to Norman Adams Ltd. in untouched original state and which needed no restoration save a great deal of waxing to revive its dull, dry surface and bring back its deep natural shine. Such pieces that have so completely escaped the hand of later restorers and French polishers are rare. Its gently complex shaping and splendid proportions are allowed to speak for themselves without the addition of carved detail. The turned baluster gallery is strongly made with astragal mouldings above and below and intermittent ovals as part of the design. It has re-entrant corners and in form is serpentine all round with projections at the centre of each side which are carried down into the shaping of each frieze. The cabriole legs have shaped lappets at the knees much in the manner of cut-card work on silver, as seen in the example on p. 283, and terminate in open scroll feet of an unusual type, although they are not unlike certain examples in the *Director*.

Similar galleries on tripod tables are illus. in Edwards, vol. III, p. 206, figs. 11-12.

Provenance: The Viscountess Walden.

A Chippendale period mahogany card table Circa 1760

Width 35ins. (89cm) Depth (open) 33½ins.
(85cm) Height 27¾ins. (70.5cm)

The ingenious effect of the concertina action of opening card tables,
which was described with reference to the example on p. 288, is well
illustrated here. Some of the hinges and the sliding tray are visible in
the detail. By this time a rectangular shaping of the top and frieze
was the most usual form and depressions for candlesticks and
gaming counters are not found so often. The simplicity of this piece
focuses the attention on the finely patinated surface and the very
graceful cabriole legs with their emphatic hipping at the tops. They
are carved with acanthus and coquillage around cabochon shapes
made up of two C-scrolls, with very slender scrolls down either side
to particularly well-formed French scroll feet finished with foliage on
the toes (cf. p. 43).

A Chippendale period mahogany card table

Circa 1760

Width 35¾ ins. (90.8cm) Depth (open) 35½ ins. (90.2cm) Height 28ins. (71cm)

Like the previous example, this has an interior lined with baize within a crossbanded surround and opens with a concertina action. The edges of the finely figured top are carved with ribbon and rosette above a veneered frieze. Below this the legs display the influence of the fanciful and lightweight Gothic that was so fashionable in certain quarters at the time. Each is formed as a cluster of four slender colonnettes bound with shaft rings in the manner of columns of the Early English period. These are in two tiers with square blocks carved with paterae above and between, and block feet. The cusped scroll brackets continue the Gothic theme.

A delicate stand with very similar treatment to the legs and pierced through, which stability would not allow in this case, is illus. in Brackett, p. 222. Chippendale, 1762, uses the form and shows a section on a side table in pl. LX.

A fine Chippendale period mahogany tripod table   Circa 1765

Width 27¼ins. (69.2cm) Depth 26ins. (66cm) Height 25¾ins. (65.5cm)

The emphasis throughout this piece is on lightness. The wood is a faded golden mahogany, the waved edged tilt-top remarkably thin and the stem very slender with its tapered classical fluted column and three detached colonnettes with a hint of the Gothic, as in the previous example, in the shaft rings. The base is exquisitely shaped as opposing moulded C-scrolls with carved foliage gently trailing over them and a single flute between each leg in the same manner as was noted on the table on p. 296. All this refinement makes an interesting comparison with the not dissimilar shaping of the example on p. 297.

The table has an affinity with designs for 'Claw Tables' in Ince and Mayhew, pl. XIII, where similarly shaped tops on scrolled bases are illustrated. It might be observed that these do not have the central column which may be seen as an adaptation for structural stability which is sometimes lacking in the more fanciful rococo designs in the pattern books of the period. Surprisingly Chippendale included no tripod tea tables in the Director *although bases of this type are found on candle-stands in pls. CXL and CXLVI. A table with a different top but which is otherwise extremely similar, including the square feet, is illus. in Edwards, vol. III, p. 206, fig. 14.*

A fine Chippendale period mahogany tripod table   Circa 1760

Diameter 27¼ ins. (69.2cm) Height 28¼ ins. (71.8cm)

The proportions of this tilt-top table are excellent. The development of fashionable taste during the 1750s is evident if it is compared with the example on p. 295. Even bearing in mind that the latter is a slightly larger table, the treatment of the similar constituent parts shows much greater elegance here. The top is shaped into ten foils with a moulded edge, although these are not made into roundels as was the case on p. 289. The stem is fluted above a baluster, carved with lively acanthus that flicks outwards at the top, on a pitted ground with bands of beading below. The slender legs have generous double curves that curl upwards into French scroll toes. The foliage carved at the knees is brought up to date with a little coquillage at the top and asymmetrical wisps below.

Similarly shaped legs and scrolled toes linked to broad rectangular pads on tripod tables made by Chippendale are illus. in Gilbert, Chippendale, *figs. 469-470.*

A Chippendale period mahogany tripod table   Circa 1755

Width 28ins. (71cm) Height 29ins. (73.5cm)

The octagonal or (as here with alternate sides of different lengths) octangular table was another quite popular variation. In this case the table is particularly well figured with a deep natural shine. The gallery is very delicately pierced with a fret of Gothic inspiration. It is a type which was much imitated during the nineteenth century although, apart from a little restoration, this is in its original state, formed in three ply thickness. The upper part of the slender stem is spirally fluted above a gadrooned moulding and a baluster carved with foliage in a rather stylised fashion on a pitted ground. The plate shows up the splendid hard shine on the cabriole legs which are keeled in section. They have an interlace pattern ending in foliage carved on the knees and Gothic mouchette panels on the sides.

A fine Chippendale period mahogany tripod table   Circa 1765

Width 26½ ins. (67.2cm) Depth 24¼ ins. (61.5cm) Height 28¾ ins. (73cm)

The mahogany of this example is of a different, lighter, colour to the previous table and the surface is very finely faded. The stem is exceptionally slim and yet strong, with fluting above a baluster carved this time with cabochons and coquillage. The base is similar to that on p. 303 with a little more splay, rounded pads and outward scrolling of the toes. These scrolls continue up the sides, dividing at the tops of the legs to curl over above and below. The acanthus carving ends in husks.

The top is of chinoiserie quatrefoil shape and has a most attractive pierced fret gallery in the same taste with four cartouche-shaped hand grips. This is more sturdily made than most such galleries which has meant its survival intact, giving what Chippendale describes in the *Director* as "an aery look". The potential weakness of this fashionable feature on the tops of tables and cabinets was to some extent ameliorated by lamination on the same principal as that applied to modern plywood. Sheraton's description of this in the *Drawing Book* has already been quoted about the example on p. 208.

Although not directly comparable, the proportions of the stem and base are very reminiscent of a tripod table supplied by John Bradburn to Kew Palace in 1767 and illus. in Edwards and Jourdain, fig. 87.

A fine Chippendale period mahogany small tripod table   Circa 1755

Diameter of top 10¾ins. (27.5cm) Height 21ins. (53.2cm)

Small tripod tables of roughly this height were made as stands for tea kettles and their heaters, although no doubt they were placed next to drawing room chairs for other purposes also. Ince and Mayhew and Chippendale both included examples of this type. Being such very attractive and useful objects they were much copied and made up later from less fashionable pieces such as polescreens. The tops were not made to tilt up but generally the finer ones unscrew at the top and bottom of the stem with a wooden thread. An example is illustrated on p. 441.

The table's dignified appearance; with the diameter of the top much less than that across the base, is typical. This meant greater stability and follows the proportions of contemporary wine glasses. The shaped scalloped moulding of the edge, now known by the term pie crust, was also a favourite at the time. The stem is complex with ring turnings, two complementary spirally fluted knops and a ribbed bell shape at the bottom like that in the example on p. 296. The knees of the cabriole legs have once again a covering of carved acanthus and the toes are pointed.

A fine Chippendale period mahogany small tripod table　　　　　　Circa 1760

Diameter of top 12ins. (30.5cm) Height 21¼ins. (54cm)

The keenly-shaped pie-crust top of this example is emphatically dished and has the unusual addition of a rim carved with gadrooning. The stem is fluted and stop-fluted and tapers to a baluster carved with spiral reeding which is finished with an undulating top edge similar to gadrooning. The sturdy base has small panels of flat foliage carving at the top of each leg which ends in a moulded scrolled toes. At the bottom of the stem, in between the legs, are unusual vertical mouldings much in the manner of linenfold carving that was so popular in the sixteenth century. This table, or kettle stand, remains in superb original condition with a finely patinated surface. It is completely free of the meanness of shaping and lack of restraint that tends to result from the later 'carving-up' of such pieces.

A very fine Chippendale period mahogany urn stand

Circa 1755

Width 8¼ ins. (21cm)
Depth 8 ins. (20.2cm)
Height 21¼ ins. (54cm)

The outstanding shaping, carving and patina of this piece can be seen from Colour Plates 26a and 26b, p. 292. The robust moulded scrolls of the base would have supported quite a tall urn on the almost square top, beneath which a slide draws out on which a teapot would have been stood. The acanthus carving on the scrolled toes, knees and stem has a splendid texture with highlights polished by gradual rubbing to a nutty brown colour contrasting with the darker and more matt background. The leaves on the knop of the stem, flicking over at the top, are particularly bold and crisp.

The tapered column has flutes matching those between the legs (cf. the illustrations on pp. 296 and 302), each edged with minute cusping, a most unusual feature. Neither is the variety of the carving spared on the top with bands of beading, fluting and gadrooning beneath a pierced Gothic fret gallery. The gallery is given a final flourish with herring-bone stringing of contrasting holly and ebony round its top edge.

There is a similar fret pattern on the square top of a kettle stand at the Victoria and Albert Museum (illus. Edwards, vol. III, p. 156, fig. 3.).

A rare Chippendale period mahogany kettle stand

Circa 1755

Width 13½ ins. (34.3cm) Depth 13½ ins. (34.3cm) Height 20¾ ins. (52.7cm)

The purpose of this attractive box (shown as Colour Plate 27, opposite) with its integral stand was to shield the flame of the burner that heated the kettle from draughts. For protection the inside is lined with lead. The urn or kettle it contained may have been a silver one for the making of tea or else used in connection with punch or other hot drinks that were popular at the time. The form of the brass carrying handles, which are original, resembles that of the bureau on p. 104.

In common with some other examples, this has a beautifully finished trefoil indentation edged with coquillage in the top edge. This was for the spout or tap.

An example illus. in Macquoid, vol. 3, fig. 226, has a slide below a similar indentation on which to stand a teapot or other receptacle.

Ince and Mayhew illus. some similar examples, pl. XIV, including one with a gadrooned top edge, and Chippendale, 1762, has a rather more elaborate specimen, pl. LV. Of these pieces he writes that they "want no explanation" which implies that the idea was no novelty. Indeed the acanthus carved cabriole legs and pad feet of the stand might point to a slightly earlier date for the present specimen.

Colour Plate 27.

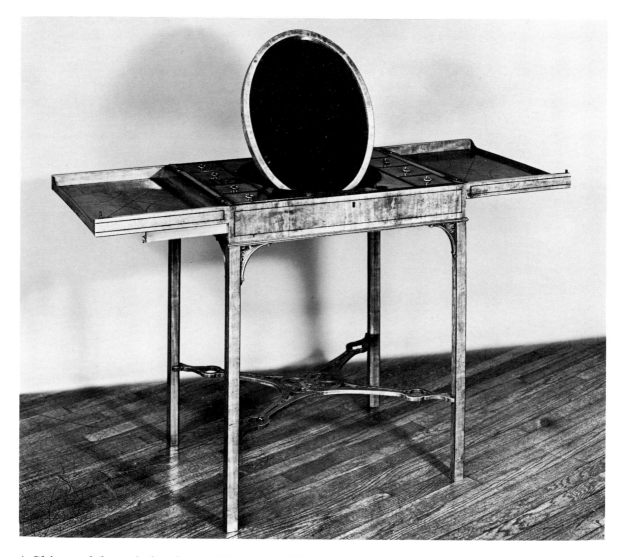

A Chippendale period satinwood dressing table

Circa 1765

This is a piece of fine quality and restraint, veneered in satinwood of excellent colour and patina and very smartly outlined and edged with very thin ebony lines. This form of dressing table, with a divided hinged lid which reveals a fitted interior, in this case of great shallowness, is to be found in contemporary pattern books and remained popular throughout the second half of the century. The flaps of the lid, with geometric line decoration inside, fall back on to pull-out lopers so that they become useful surfaces. The inside is fitted with small compartments, most with lids crossbanded with tulipwood and bearing their original brass buckle handles. In the centre is an oval mirror edged with chequered stringing which rises on an easel support and is detachable — a rare feature. The oval shape is also unusual, most being rectangular.

The table is supported on slender square legs with small brackets filled with coquillage and an elaborate flat stretcher pierced with Gothic foils and mouchettes in the manner of that on a "Breakfast Table" in the *Director*.

Ince and Mayhew illus. quite a similar table, but with a rectangular mirror, on pl. XXXVIII which they call a "Lady's Dressing Table with full apparatus". Chippendale, 1762, pl. LIII, illus. a "Breakfast Table" with a similar stretcher.

Provenance: Sir Guy Sebright, Beechwood Park, Markyate, Hertfordshire.

A fine Adam period mahogany serpentine tea table   Circa 1775

Width 37½ ins. (95.2cm) Depth (open) 37½ ins. (95.2cm) Height 28½ ins. (72.5cm)

The design and quality of this table are of the highest order and it remains in superb condition. As might be expected, it opens with a concertina action, the top edges, which are serpentine at the front and sides to give a consistent shape, being carved with rosette and dart decoration. The friezes have very thin fluting with a naturalistic circular patera in the centre of the front, the shaped bottom edges being outlined with a bold astragal moulding which sweeps most gracefully into the slender cabriole legs. The elegance of these is heightened by the slightly concave mouldings that run down their length to the little scrolled toes with their original castors. At the top are sectors of shell carving and bell flower chains issuing from rosettes.

A point of interest are the rule hinges on the sections of wooden frieze at each side that fold in the concertina action and which are stamped H. Tibats. A number of other fine pieces of case furniture and particularly tables of this kind have been noted with hinges made by this man, who was clearly an important source of iron fittings, probably based in London or Birmingham, during the third quarter of the century.

Several card and tea tables are known which bear comparison, among them one of a pair illus. in Jourdain and Rose, pl. 65 and an identical one of slightly different dimensions in Rogers, fig. 177.

Provenance: The late Thomas Inman.

Colour Plate 28.

A fine and rare Chippendale period carved and gilded console table   Circa 1755

Width of top 13ins. (33cm) Depth of top 10ins. (25.5cm) Height 32ins. (81.2cm)

Although the conception of this piece (shown opposite as Colour Plate 28) fits into the fanciful mould of carvers like Lock and Copland and Thomas Johnson, no parallel to it is known. The mixture of a highly individualistically entwined tree with the more traditional tripod base is most unusual. The rectangular top, its edges carved with gadrooning is inset with a replacement block of marble and supported by the branches that spring from a rockwork base, the asymmetrical trunks gnarled naturalistically in the manner frequently found on rococo mirror frames and bearing sprigs of leaves and flowers. In the centre is perched a bird of the crested and long-beaked chinoiserie ho-ho type. The design, for all its apparent informality, is cleverly contrived to give the top even and adequate support.

The base (detail above) stands in its own right as a splendidly shaped and richly decorated example of the period, deeply carved with lively acanthus, cabochons and coquillage and with long scrolled mouldings down to toes which have the similar bulbous look to them as those on p. 307. The carving in the angles between the legs is applied. The idea of using a tripod as a base for something other than the customary column stem was not unknown, for example in Ince and Mayhew.

When the table was discovered it was covered in thick brown paint. The detail showing this partially stripped off is most interesting. The red grained pine from which the piece is carved is evident, as are the remains of the layers of gesso with which it is coated. Traces of the original gilding were also discovered and this colouring was matched in the restoration.

The table is illus. in Edwards, Shorter Dictionary, *p. 487, fig. 12 and on the cover of* The Connoisseur, *June 1968. Ince and Mayhew included a not dissimilar design to the base under 'Stands for Figures and China Jars', pl. LI.*

A set of four gilded candlestands at Temple Newsam House supplied by James Pascall c.1746 are set on similar rococo tripod bases and a larger console table in the Methuen Collection attributed to Matthias Lock also takes the form of a gnarled tree.

Provenance: Otley, Yorkshire, the birthplace of Thomas Chippendale.

Exhibition: The International Art Treasures Exhibition at the Victoria and Albert Museum, 1962, no. 75.

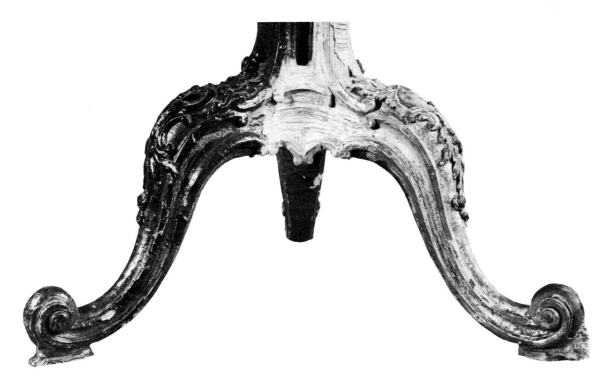

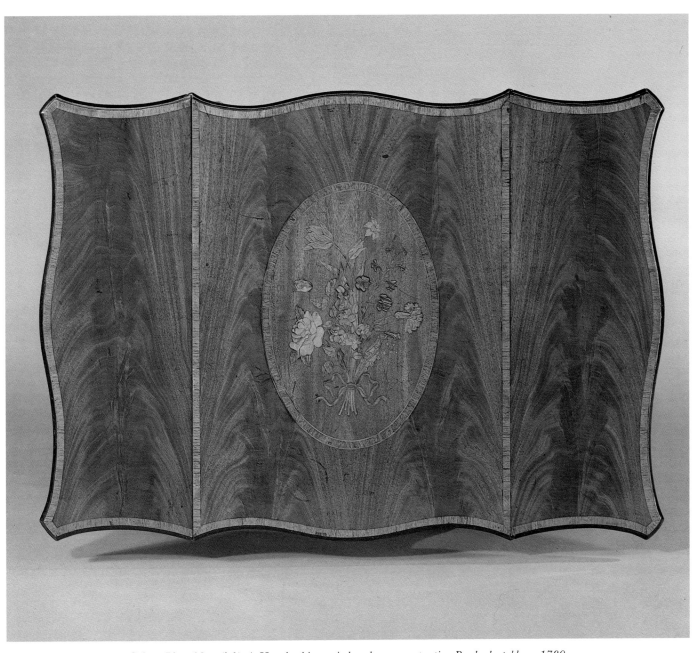

Colour Plate 29a. (left) A Hepplewhite period mahogany serpentine Pembroke table, c.1780.
Colour Plate 29b. (above) Top of the Pembroke table.
The piece is described on p. 319.

One of a pair of Adam period mahogany serpentine card tables Circa 1775

Width 37½ ins. (95.2cm) Depth (open) 37ins. (94cm) Height 28½ ins. (72.5cm)

The shaping and dimensions of this table are similar to that on p. 311 but the decoration is more restrained, leaving the marvellous patination of the wood, particularly on the figured veneered friezes to be enjoyed. The detail of the applied central urn carving shows this very well. The wear on the carving and flat areas is rubbed through to a mellow golden colour while the area around the carving which has not been rubbed varies from a reddish brown to almost black with a toffee-like texture that has built up gradually over two centuries. This is one of the best guides to authenticity in a piece of furniture.

The table has a convex torus moulding on the edge of the top which opens with a swing-leg action. The four moulded cabriole legs, with raised feet instead of castors, are carved at the knees with anthemia and paterae entwined in bellflower chains which are hipped up into the frieze.

The design is similar to a card table at the Victoria and Albert (W1-1927), which also has hipped anthemion carving on the legs and is illus. in V. and A., Tables, 1968, pl. 31.

An Adam period mahogany side table   Circa 1775

Width 37ins. (94cm) Depth 19¼ins. (49cm) Height 31¼ins. (79.5cm)

The presence of a fluted frieze drawer without handles and flanked by paterae is reminiscent of the chest of drawers on p. 377. The moulded top is a simple rectangular shape raised on well proportioned square tapered legs, but fine solid timber is used and there is great quality in the handling and deep carving. In the centre of the drawer is a carved circular patera applied in an unusual fashion as a keyhole escutcheon, while oval paterae with matching beaded borders cap the legs. These corners are slightly stepped out with smaller bands of fluting above recessed panels which are present on all four sides and follow the taper of the legs, being arched at the top and bottom in the manner of flutes. In the centre of each is a further small applied patera. The shaping of the block feet finishes the legs off successfully.

A set of chairs supplied by Chippendale to Harewood House in 1770-1 has similar feet and panelled legs with central paterae and is illus. in Gilbert, Chippendale, *vol. II, fig. 146.*

A fine Hepplewhite period mahogany serpentine Pembroke table   Circa 1780

Width (open) 39 ins. (99cm) Depth 27¼ ins. (69cm) Height 28¼ ins. (72cm)

Also shown as Colour Plates 29a and 29b, pp. 314 and 315. Although of a similar overall form the interpretation here is closer to the French taste than the next example. The shaping of the top is more complex; it is edged with tulipwood crossbanding and ebonised mouldings with superb panels of mahogany curl figured veneer and a central marquetry oval depicting a spray of flowers on a paler mahogany ground. The quality of this is extremely high and the variety of woods chosen contrast very subtly in the manner of that on the escritoire on p. 123.

Again the end friezes follow the serpentine shaping, the drawer being edged with ebony stringing. The pointed shaping of the exquisitely drawn legs, slender and without carving or moulding, is a very French feature, although here they are strongly fashioned from blocks of solid mahogany whereas the French would generally have taken the use of veneer still further and encased them with diagonal strips. The mobile nature of this adaptable piece of furniture is emphasised by its brass cup castors. However it is difficult to imagine that such an accomplished example as this was not intended for the drawing room or boudoir.

A fine Hepplewhite period mahogany serpentine Pembroke table   Circa 1780

Width (closed) 19¾ ins. (50.2cm) Width (open) 40½ ins. (103cm)
Depth 31ins. (78.5cm) Height 27½ ins. (69.8cm)

The Pembroke table in its finest form might justly be termed the most elegant sort of drop-leaf table. Like several other types of furniture which incorporate a proper name, presumably of the designer or a notable person who made an early commission of it, the origin is not precisely known but is thought to have been the Countess of Pembroke. In the *Cabinet Dictionary* Sheraton describes it as ''a kind of breakfast table, from the name of the lady who first gave orders for one of them, and who probably gave the first idea of such a table to the workmen''. The form, with two flaps that rise on hinged brackets, four legs and a drawer at one or occasionally both ends, is first found about the middle of the century and the name Pembrook is found on a trade card of about 1760.

The design of this example barely allows a single straight line and yet its curves are all gentle and flowing, making it a pure example of the English interpretation of French rococo taste. It is in exceptionally fine condition, the solid nut brown mahogany mellowed and deeply patinated as can be seen in the details of the top which is crossbanded with tulipwood outlined with harewood and boxwood stringing within a moulded edge. The frieze follows the serpentine shaping in two dimensions, the single drawer bearing the original lacquered brass handles. The detail of the hipped carving and moulding of the leg also shows the wooden hinge of one of the two fly brackets to each flap, this underframing being made of beech. The cup castors fitted on the raised toes retain their original leather rollers.

Chippendale, 1754, uses the type in pl. XXXIII, where he calls it a 'Breakfast Table', although these generally had a cage for china and other necessities beneath the frieze. He also supplied them with drawers fitted for writing.

The table is illustrated in Apollo, Sept. 1939, *'Tables of the 18th Century' by R.W. Symonds, p. 115, fig. VIII, and* Homes and Gardens, *June 1941, p. 25.*

Provenance: The late Frederick Poke.

A Hepplewhite period mahogany Pembroke table and matching card table   Circa 1785

Card table: Width 36ins. (91.5cm) Depth 18ins. (45.8cm) Height 28½ins. (72.5cm)

These two pieces passed through Norman Adams' hands twelve years apart, coming from different sources but there can be no doubt that they were made by the same hand and quite probably started life together. Another matching rectangular table was also noted at the same time as the Pembroke table. Because of the great movement, particularly of more portable furniture since it was made, it is unusual to be able to record such an assemblage. Interestingly in about 1770 Mrs. Paperdick wrote of furniture removed from the Princess Royal's apartments including two card tables "and a Pembroke table made to match".

The mahogany veneer used in both pieces is an unusual type with a distinctive mottled figure. It is complemented with tulipwood crossbanding and boxwood stringing round the tops and the frieze panels, one end of the Pembroke table being a drawer and the other false, as is found in a majority of cases. Both bear the original squared handles. The shaping of the tops, with instepped quadrant corners, is such that on the card table, when it is opened on a swing leg action, each side is the same length. The legs, with their oval patera cappings, are extremely finely designed and deeply carved.

Although there is no one precise parallel, the elements of upright leaves, octangular sections, husk chains, fluting and toupie feet are all to be found in pls. 2, 6, 9 and 14 of Sheraton's Accompaniment. *In the* Appendix, *pl. II he includes a card table of similar shape, making an interesting suggestion for "managing the tops": "I take it to be the best to rip up dry deal or faulty mahogany, into four inch widths, and joint them up. It matters not whether the pieces are whole lengths provided the jump-joints be crossed."*

Provenance of card table: The late W.D. Thornhill.

An early Sheraton period mahogany occasional table   Circa 1785

Width 26¾ ins. (68cm) Depth 17¾ ins. (45cm) Height 28¼ ins. (71.8cm)

The feeling of this piece is not dissimilar to the last group, with mahogany panels on top and on the frieze bordered with tulipwood crossbanding, here edged with ebony rather than boxwood, and the legs capped with carved paterae. One end is fitted with a drawer. The top and bottom edges of the frieze are moulded, with an unusual use of short fluting in the manner of a dentil cornice beneath the top. Sheraton, p. 17 of the *Appendix,* 1793 tells of the method of adding mouldings to tops veneered on to a pine carcase: ''After the tops are dry, hard mahogany is tongued into the ends of the deal, then slips are glued on the front and back, that the whole may appear solid mahogany.''

The most striking feature of this table is its superbly slender turned and tapered legs, fluted and stop-fluted with turning above and below. It is notable that the brass castors, which are original, are fitted flush to continue the line rather than, as so often, added as if by afterthought.

A Hepplewhite period mahogany oval occasional table by Gillow's of Lancaster   Circa 1785

Width 19ins. (48.2cm) Depth 15¼ins. (38.8cm) Height 29ins. (73.5cm)

This is another of the numerous types of small table that were being produced at this time, often for individual commissions and for purposes which are now uncertain, even if they were specific at the time. Besides an extremely attractive design, it remains in exceptionally original and untouched condition, the nut brown mahogany beautifully mellowed. The oval top, crossbanded with kingwood is hinged to rise revealing a shallow interior. The frieze is outlined with shaped boxwood stringing. The elegance of the slim splayed and tapered legs is enhanced by the lack of turning and the even line of the reeding from the lotus capitals to the toes. They are joined by a scrolled arched stretcher made of very thin struts of wood surmounted by a turned urn finial. The top edge of the frieze is stamped ''GILLOWS LANCASTER''.

N. Goodison and J. Hardy in Furniture History, *1970, pl. 4, illus. one of a pair of gilded tables with marble tops of extremely similar form supplied by Gillow's to Tatton Park, Cheshire in 1795.*

A Hepplewhite period mahogany side table
Circa 1785

Width 48¾ ins. (124cm) Depth 22¾ ins. (57.8cm) Height 33¾ ins. (85.8cm)

The elegant shaping with the serpentine centre cutting away into concave ends gives this piece an impression of shallowness. It is veneered with finely figured and matched mahogany, particularly on the frieze where the effect is satin-like. The top is finished with tulipwood crossbanding while the front has a series of rectangular panels with concave corners, outlined with boxwood stringing at the sides and of satinwood in the centre and capping the legs. The central one retains original painted decoration of classical swags, the fashionable development from the carved mahogany plaque that might have been found a few years earlier on a side or serving table. The six square tapered legs are of purplewood and, like the bottom edge of the frieze, very smartly enhanced with fine contrasting stringing. They terminate in unusual recessed toes.

A pair of early Sheraton period half-round mahogany card tables　　　　Circa 1785

Width 36ins. (91.5cm)　Depth 18ins. (45.8cm)　Height 29ins. (73.5cm)

Half-round and D-shape were the most popular forms for card tables in the last two decades of the century. Most are relatively simple although this pair stands out for its quality. The tops open on a double-swing-leg action that gives better support and symmetry than does a single one. Like the friezes, the tops are left to display panels of splendidly figured mahogany that has faded most handsomely. Round the edges are wide bands of satinwood within mahogany crossbanding and these are etched with a design of intertwined fern and berried foliage. The square tapered legs with thermed or spade feet are, like the crossbanding on the top edges and the bottom of the frieze, of a contrasting, darker mahogany. They are decorated with the popular motifs of chains of bellflower and oval patera cappings, now inlaid rather than carved.

A Hepplewhite period sycamore
urn stand   Circa 1785

Width of top 10½ ins. (26.5cm) square
Height 27¼ ins. (69.2cm)

This is a fine specimen for the quality of the
woods used, the tasteful marquetry and the
attractively waved edge to the gallery. The
intertwined lines and flowerheads, reminiscent of the decoration and ground wood in
the example on p. 202, fit this exactly. In the
centre of the top is a surprisingly naturalistic
rose, very carefully detailed, which would
originally have stood out more brightly
against the mottle background of the
sycamore. The boxwood inlay continues in
the friezes with fluting and stylised circular
paterae which derive from the Japanese
chrysanthemum motif. The slender legs with
spade feet and corner stringing are capped
with pine cones, and have husk trails below
the lower edge moulding.

*Hepplewhite's Guide, pls. 55-6 illus. six designs
dated 1787 for urn tables of varying shapes but all
on splayed square tapered legs with solid galleries
and, as he terms it, "the slide, which draws out to
set the tea-pot on". He adds that they "may be
inlaid of various woods, or painted and
varnished". The Prices of Cabinet Work,
1797, includes further similar designs and it would
appear that this was the standard type at the time.
An identical stand was sold by Christie's at
Godmersham Park, Kent, 6-9 June, 1983 lot 376.*

A rare early Sheraton period mahogany sofa table　　　　　　　Circa 1785

Width 58¼ ins. (148cm) Depth 19¾ ins. (50cm) Height 27½ ins. (70cm)

The sofa table was a development from the Pembroke table that came about towards the end of the century and in which the rising flaps, again on fly brackets, are hinged at the ends, in other words the shorter sides, and they are thus longer and narrower. As the name suggests they were intended to be used in front of a sofa. In the *Dictionary*, Sheraton says that: "The ladies chiefly occupy them to draw, write or read upon". He adds that they "are generally made between 5 and 6 feet long, and from 22 inches to 2 feet broad".

This example is both a very early one of the type, exceptionally shallow by any standards, including Sheraton's and, most unusually, is raised on four legs instead of the central end supports that became normal. The straight grain figure of the top runs along the table and the flaps and is bordered with a narrow crossbanding of tulipwood. A further uncommon feature is the way the flaps are tongued into the top instead of the quadrant rule joints found on almost all Pembroke and sofa tables, the tradition of which goes back to gateleg tables. The frieze is fitted with just one opening drawer, the others being dummies but all are edged with more tulipwood. The square slightly tapered legs are finished with boxwood stringing.

No sofa tables are included in Hepplewhite or Sheraton's Drawing Book, *but in the* Dictionary *Sheraton includes two, pls. 76 and 77, one with a sofa behind.*

A fine Hepplewhite period rectangular mahogany Pembroke table   Circa 1780

Width (open) 37¼ ins. (94.5cm) (closed) 19½ ins. (49.5cm) Depth 26½ ins. (67.5cm) Height 28ins. (71cm)

By the time of Hepplewhite's *Guide* of 1788 it would appear that rectangular and oval shapes were the most fashionable for Pembroke tables. This and the following examples are aptly described by Hepplewhite's words that "they admit of considerable Elegance in the workmanship and ornaments." It would be very difficult to rival the refinement or execution of the marquetry of this piece. It is laid into panels of deep golden satinwood and the utmost care has been taken in the eloquent designs and detailing. In the centre oval of the top a flaming urn is flanked with delicate arabesque scrolls while on the flaps a whole variety of different flowers sprout from the same trailing stems. The panels are each set in quarter veneered mahogany surrounds with a darker mahogany crossbanding and a moulded edge. The drawer fronts continue the urn and arabesque theme which, like the fronds on the example on p. 332, is found in a comparable form on the doors of the Harewood House Library Desk. With one replacement, the cast brass handles are original. The legs are simply square and tapered in the darker mahogany, edged with boxwood and end in shaped feet without castors (cf. p. 326).

Gilbert, Chippendale, *illus. the Harewood Library Desk, vol. II, p. 242. This and the following Pembroke tables follow the general style of pl. 62 of Hepplewhite, 1788.*

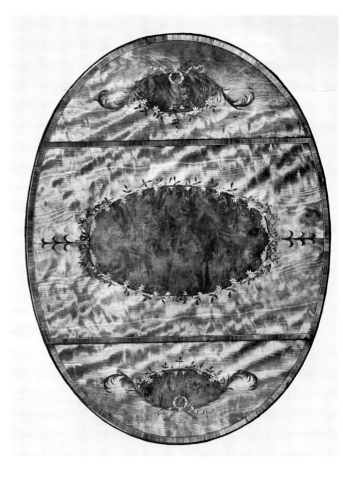

A fine Hepplewhite period oval satinwood Pembroke table

Circa 1780

Width (open) 40¼ ins. (102.2cm) Depth 30¼ ins. (77cm) Height 28¾ ins. (73cm)

Although it lacks mouldings on the drawer and frieze, that around the top is emphasised more than in the example illustrated on p. 335 by being ebonised. This contrasts effectively with the faded tulipwood crossbanding and the glowing yellow of the satinwood veneer with its superb watery figure that resembles moiré silk. The top is inlaid with three ovals of irregularly figured thuja, edged with very naturalistically and minutely detailed leafy shoots with star-like flowers, the panels on the flaps also having ribbon tied palm fronds which are continued on the friezes with fan medallions. Unlike the similar table on p. 335, the square tapered legs edged with ebony are set at an angle to follow the curved shape. They are capped with paterae and have short bellflower chains below.

The decorative use of crossed fronds in marquetry goes back at least to the Harewood House Library Desk of c.1771, and a very similar use on drawer fronts is to be found on library tables made for Alnwick Castle and Osterley Park by John Linnell about the same period, see Hayward and Kirkham, vol. II, pp. 147-8. The quality of the penwork detail on none of these pieces even approaches that on the present piece.

A fine Hepplewhite period semi-elliptical satinwood side table   Circa 1785

Width 48¾ins. (123.8cm) Depth 20¾ins. (52.5cm) Height 31¾ins. (80.5cm)

Also shown as Colour Plates 31a and 31b, p. 345. Like the Pembroke table on p. 330, the top of this has a design of an urn and sinuous arabesque decoration of an exceptional and most delicate type which fits the space exactly without overcrowding it. A variety of different forms of the husk and bellflower motifs is incorporated, including a repeated chain of it inlaid into the crossbanding of purplewood. The edge and frieze panels are banded with tulipwood and decorated with ribbon-tied sprigs of husks which appear yet again in chains down the legs. These are picked out smartly with ebony edging and taper to block feet. The triglyph cappings are shaded (by scorching in hot sand) to appear in their architecturally correct form of concave flutes.

Colour Plate 30a.

A fine Hepplewhite period mahogany Pembroke table   Circa 1785

Width (open) 37¾ins. (96cm) Depth 30¼ins. (76.8cm) Height 28ins. (71cm)

In the table shown above and opposite as Colour Plates 30a and 30b, the restraint of the shaping is matched by the tastefully contained decoration and the whole is of extremely high quality. The original condition of the surface, the mahogany faded to a pale golden colour which borders on that of satinwood, is particularly striking and may be compared with the original red-brown underneath and on the top edges of the drawers, which have had little exposure to light. The figured panels of the top, veneered on to mahogany, are edged with tulipwood crossbanding and an outer border of maple inlaid with an undulating tendril-like pattern, the leaves of which are filled with a dark green composition. In the centre similar decoration is repeated around a large oval patera exquisitely detailed with pen and ink. The flaps have swags of bellflower which hang downwards when they are lowered.

The ends of the table follow the curve of the top and each contains an oak-lined drawer that bears its original turned wooden knobs. The underframing is pine. Capping the legs are small oval patera on a dark ground matching the motif on the top and the legs themselves are delicately fluted and stop-fluted, ending in spade feet.

A Hepplewhite period semi-elliptical satinwood side table Circa 1785

Width 50ins. (127cm) Depth 21ins. (53.5cm) Height 32¼ins. (82cm)

Similar in form and proportions to the examples on p. 333, this illustrates the fashion for combining marquetry and carved decoration in gilded beech or pine rather than mahogany, with similar motifs appearing in each medium. The top is inlaid in a typically Hepplewhite fashion, radiating from a boxwood fan medallion with swags of mistletoe-like foliage and a purplewood arcaded edge with alternate husks and bellflowers within tulipwood crossbanding. The detail of the unrestored top shows well its construction, the parallel lines cracking along the grain of the satinwood veneer indicating the gradual shrinkage of the blocks of wood beneath. The frieze has further fan medallions and foliage swags while the square tapered legs, panelled with concave capitals, are carved with thin bands of guilloche and bellflower trails above the fluting.

Provenance: The late Mrs. M.J.L. Holder, Brighton, lady-in-waiting to H.R.H. the late Princess Louise, Duchess of Argyll.

A rare pair of Adam period small gilded and painted tables

Circa 1785

Width 17½ins. (44.5cm) Depth 17ins. (43.2cm) Height 29ins. (73.5cm)

Few lightweight and elegant tables (also shown as Colour Plates 32a and 32b, p. 348) of this kind, still very much in the Adam style, survive, and this makes them of particular interest. The design of the curved square legs joined with concave-sided platform stretchers is most attractive and gives adequate stability. The carved square paterae on the stretchers, like the trails of bellflower and beads and small paterae on the scrolled toes, are applied to the beechwood framing.

Although the gilding has been renewed, the painted decoration of the tops, which are of mahogany, is original. This takes the form of most effective chequered marbling. It is interesting how the treatment of this differs between the two, one being predominently black and blue-green with a central square panel depicting putti *en grisaille* against a pink background, the other very multi-coloured, the central plaque left empty. This was probably because something with a square base, perhaps a candelabrum, was intended to stand on this table and not the other.

The legs and stretchers have an affinity with a work table at Osterley Park, illus. in Edwards, vol. III, p. 322, fig. 4.

Provenance: The Earls of Dysart, Ham House, Richmond, Surrey. The tables bear labels with the family arms and the inscription 'Ham D'. They may possibly be the same as "A pair of handsome wood stands with figures" listed in the North Drawing Room in 1844 and 1884. An old photograph shows one of them in that room. It seems therefore that they might have been one of the few eighteenth century additions made by the 5th Earl to this remarkably unaltered seventeenth century interior.

Stobo Castle, Peeblesshire, Scotland. The tables were not included in the bequest of Ham House to the National Trust by Sir Lyonel and Cecil Tollemache in 1948.

One of a rare pair of Adam period gilded and painted corner tables   Circa 1780

Radius 18ins. (45.8cm) Height 36½ins. (92.8cm)

This pair of graceful small tables, again with square central panels on the tops, retain their original ivory painted decoration on the black ground, the inspiration for this clearly coming from the so-called Etruscan fashion. A French designer named Dugourc claimed to have employed this before 1770 but it was probably Robert Adam who first did so on any scale from 1775 when he provided furniture for Derby House and Osterley Park. The style was derived from the motifs on vases of the 4th and 3rd centuries B.C. which were reaching Northern Europe from Italy at the time and although thought to be Etruscan were, in fact, Graeco-Roman, while the form of rinceau and some other motifs are Pompeian or later still, not least the leaves and flowerheads in the borders.

The edges of the tops are carved with hollow guilloche, while there is another form at the tops of the fluted tapered legs, similar to that on p. 336. The legs have tall feet with upright leaf decoration and are joined with platform stretchers with deeply concave and fluted front edges, which continue the painted decoration.

The use of a black ground, as in red figure pottery, was archaeologically correct and Adam designed a chair for Lord Stanley in this manner. However the closest parallel is a Pembroke table in the Etruscan room at Osterley Park, illus. in Tomlin p. 82. This has very similar delicate anthemia and other decoration painted in ivory on black with gilded edges. An inventory of 1782 lists it as having been made by Clay, probably Henry Clay who specialised in japanned goods made of papier mâché and who is recorded by Georg Christoph Lichtenberg in 1775 as producing a variety of goods "black with orange figures in the style of Etruscan vasès". One of the tables is illus. in colour in The Connoisseur, *June 1963.*

One of a pair of early Sheraton period painted satinwood pier tables   Circa 1785

Width 34½ ins. (87.5cm)
Depth 17½ ins. (44.5cm). Height 34ins. (86.5cm)

Also shown as Colour Plate 33, p. 357. The elegant outline with the combination of convex and concave surfaces is a development from the example on p. 326, with the serpentine shape finally lost. The proportions, with the square tapered legs, are excellent. The top is edged with tulipwood crossbanding and borders of foliage on a grey ground. In the centre is an oval well painted with a vase of flowers *en grisaille*, suspended amid vine festoons with swags of flowers below. Tulipwood is again employed round the frieze panels and on the cappings to the legs, with further pastel decoration of laurel garlands, drapery swags, husk trails and, in the centre, a medallion which looks much more contemporary than classical. The painting is shown above in its unrestored state and in the colour plate restored.

One of a similar but larger pair of tables is illus. in Cescinsky, 1911, vol. III, p. 302. Like the present pair, these have undecorated strips of satinwood left along the back edges. These would probably have accommodated the pier glasses that hung above them. As with many commodes made in the second half of the century, this overhang, in this case some 2ins., allows the back edge to touch the wall over the dado. Another similar table is included in Harris, p. 91.

One of a fine pair of Adam period carved and gilded pier tables with painted tops   Circa 1785

Width 37½ins. (95.2cm) Depth 15¼ins. (38.8cm) Height 35ins. (89cm)

From the end of the 1770s with Robert Adam at the forefront, the taste for painted decoration grew with immigrant painters such as Kauffmann, Cipriani and Zucchi having considerable influence, particularly on the use of classically inspired panels of figures. Apart from its aesthetic introduction of colour it proved to be a cheaper method of decoration than marquetry of equivalent quality and would not fade.

The quality of the painting is particularly good and in its original untouched state. The top is veneered in satinwood and painted with extremely naturalistic swags of flowers with a circular medallion *en grisaille* of Britannia flanked by cornucopias in a semicircle of upright leaves and a border of oak sprigs entwined with ribbon. The D-shaped outline, sometimes as here with the added refinements of inset corners, was a popular one, the first published designs being Sheraton's. The decoration is most attractively edged with realistic pearls set against a black background.

The frieze has foliage carving and a central oval classical medallion which, like the beaded edging here and on the stretcher, echo the painting on the top. The subject matter of this painting and that of the carved medallion differ on the other table of the pair. The tapered fluted legs have capitals whose extraordinary form of Ionic attenuation is about as distant from the classical order as that on some Elizabethan refectory tables and bed posts. At the bottom they are encased in plumes and joined with a flat concave-shaped stretcher finely carved with a guilloche pattern like the previous tables and a domed acanthus centre piece.

The form of these tables is similar to a pier table included in Sheraton, Appendix, *pl. 4, which in turn is like a piece shown* in situ *in pls. 51 and 61 of the* Drawing Book *proper. Of this Sheraton says: "As pier tables are merely for ornament under a glass, they are generally made very light, and the style of finishing them is rich and elegant. . . The frames are commonly gold, or white and burnished gold. Stretching-rails have of late been introduced. . . with good effect, as they take off the long appearance of the legs, and make the under part appear more furnished". Such stretchers were in fact in use as early as the 1760s. See also the notes on p. 342. The tables were discussed in* The Connoisseur, June *1967.*

One of a pair of early Sheraton period painted satinwood pier tables   Circa 1790

Width 35½ ins. (90cm) Depth 16½ ins. (42cm) Height 35ins. (89cm)

Here painted decoration is used throughout and very effectively against the golden yellow of the background. A comparison with p. 340 shows a remarkable similarity in the shape and handling of the tops which are clearly painted most skilfully by a closely related hand, and based on perhaps the same contemporary print or design. The ribbon hung swags contain many of the same colourful flowers and the ribbon entwined border, here on all sides and on a dark background, is edged with just the same close set pearls.

The table is supported on slender square tapered legs smartly outlined with black and white lines. These project slightly from the frieze with its foliate arcading and palmette design and are capped with confronting busts above trailing leaves and berries, all carried out in pastel shades. The feet are very slightly shaped and marked off from the legs with banding as is often found on such tables towards the end of the century.

Pier tables, as console tables, were usually made in pairs to stand between the windows of drawing rooms or saloons, generally beneath mirrors in which the decoration of the tops would be reflected.

A pair of side tables in the Lady Lever Art Gallery, illus. Fastnedge, pl. 28, have tops and lower tiers of the same outline and very similar decoration. The same hand is evident also in another pair sold in the Chrysler sale (Parke-Bernet, New York, May 6-7, 1960, lots 529-30), which are extremely similar to the illustration on p. 340 but with carved swags beneath the frieze. There is another, single, pier table from the same group in the Victoria and Albert Museum. They are all edged with kingwood crossbanding.

Exhibition: The Art Treasures Exhibition, 1932.

343

An early Sheraton period half round side table painted by E. Grant   Circa 1790

Width 38½ ins. (98cm)

Although Grant was by no means the most accomplished artist of his day, he has produced here a very charming work and signed it boldly in script 'Delineavit et Pinxit' at the back edge, which is a very rare feature. On an ivory coloured ground, worked up with clouds and gesticulating classical women, is an oval panel representing Art in the typical Italianate idiom of the day. Above it is a rather odd flourish of pea pods and tendrils which continue in the broad border fecund with flowers and fruits, painted in pale colours on a black ground. Below the brass bound edge of the top, the frieze and legs of the table are painted black, another late eighteenth century and Regency fashion, and decorated in gold with vine branches and trails. The square tapered legs, capped with paterae, are outlined in gold and elegantly curved outwards at the bottom to tall spade feet (cf. p. 151).

Colour Plate 31a. Detail of the satinwood side table shown below.

Colour Plate 31b. A Hepplewhite period semi-elliptical satinwood side table, c.1785. The piece is described on p. 333.

An early Sheraton period plane tree occasional table   Circa 1790

Width 21¾ins. (55.2cm) Depth 15¾ins. (40cm) Height 30ins. (76.2cm)

The use of London plane is occasionally, although rarely, found on small items of furniture made towards the end of the eighteenth century. Its distinctive lacy grain, formed by an unusual development of broad, close-set rays evenly distributed as darker flecks, is clearly visible on the frieze and underframing in the photograph. Its liability to warp prevented its use for delicate or larger scale purposes, although it is a wood traditionally employed in the interior fitting of London Underground carriages.

Besides the plane veneer with its fine ebony edging, a variety of other more exotic woods are incorporated. The top is inlaid with a chequered parquetry design of contrasting colours surrounded by an intricate border of circles and tulipwood crossbanding with a minute line of chequered stringing at the very edge. In spite of the fact that the border of the front frieze runs right to the outside edges, the drawer, which has its original brass handles, only extends as far as the stiles. Another unusual feature is the cross stretcher of square section which tapers, like the legs, away from the centre with its small turned dish which may have been intended for some ornamental object.

An almost identical table is illus. in Cescinsky, 1937, p. 367.

A Sheraton period set or quartetto of padouk wood tables   Circa 1790

Width of largest 18½ ins. (47cm) Depth 11¾ ins. (29.8cm) Height 29½ ins. (75cm)

Sets of tables which diminish progressively in size so that they slide inside one another were an ingenious, neat and space saving invention. They were generally made in threes which Sheraton calls trio tables, and fours or quartettos. Robert Southey the poet describes them as ''a nest of tables for the ladies. . . You would take them for play-things, from their slenderness and size, if you did not see how useful they find them for their work''. They were also used as occasional tables in drawing rooms, as George Smith in his *Household Furniture,* 1808 says, to ''prevent the company rising from their seats, when taking refreshments''.

The unusual use of heavy padouk wood (see p. 351) in the construction of these tables gives some stability to a form which by its nature tends towards flimsiness. The surface has faded to an attractive golden colour, while the tops are inlaid with ebony lines and have a slightly raised outline of the same wood.

A set is illus. in pl. 75 in Sheraton's Dictionary, *of which the slender ring-turned legs, the splayed feet and slat stretchers are found on a number of examples including the present one.*

Colour Plate 32a. The tops of the tables shown below.

Colour Plate 32b. A rare pair of Adam period small gilded and painted tables, c.1785. These pieces are described on p. 337.

An early Sheraton period rosewood games table   Circa 1790

Width 35¾ins. (91cm) Depth 22¾ins. (57.8cm) Height 28ins. (71cm)

This fine quality piece is made in the same form as some contemporary writing tables and sofa tables, and the simple elegance of the end supports with the wide sweep of their splayed legs is very similar to the example on p. 160. The rounded rectangular shape of the top also has this simplicity, with no handles or mounts and the plainest of box castors, while such decoration that there is is very much on the surface of the wood. This is veneer of rosewood of particularly striking contrast, especially on the top where the sun has bleached the lighter parts to a creamy colour, while the dark grain stands out even more than it would have originally. This is shown in the detail of the sliding centre section which is reversible and inlaid with a chess board on the underside which has not been exposed so much to the light. Beneath this is a well for playing backgammon, the centre drawer fronts in the friezes being false. Flanking these false fronts are two small cedar-lined drawers which open to front and back, so that chess men and other gaming equipment inside could be reached from either side. Throughout, each panel of rosewood is bordered with boxwood stringing.

A Sheraton period sabicu and yew wood sofa table   Circa 1795

Width (open) 59ins. (150cm) (closed) 36½ins. (92.8cm)
Depth 26ins. (66cm) Height 28ins. (71cm)

Again, this table has the early simplicity of the twin end supports and the high rectangular stretcher that make sofa tables so appealing. It also incorporates some unusual woods, most of all on the top which is veneered in sabicu laid in six narrow strips, the grain of which is mirrored in the corresponding section at each end. Its colour is an attractive gold and a similar type to that on the bureau on p. 103. The top is crossbanded with contrasting purplewood with a reeded edge. The veneer on the frieze and underframing is a faded yew wood, with its characteristically irregular burr figure, edged with ebony stringing. Except in a few unusually deep examples, sofa tables normally have two drawers in one side and two matching false fronts the other which is the case here. The brass knobs are later replacements but the lion's paw castors are original.

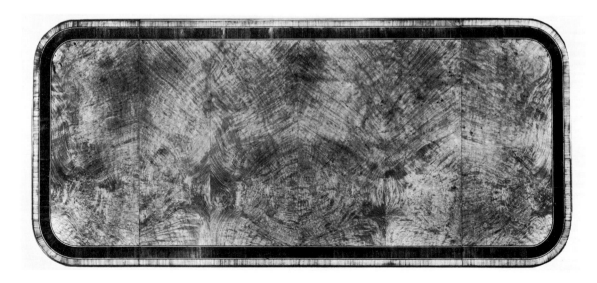

An unusual Sheraton period padouk wood sofa table   Circa 1790

Width (open) 60¼ ins. (153cm) (closed) 37¾ ins. (96cm)
Depth 24¼ ins. (61.5cm) Height 28¾ ins. (73cm)

Various features of this table would suggest that it was made in the Far East to an English design. Although the wood was grown in Burma and off its coast in the Andaman Islands and a certain amount imported to the West and used in furniture made here (see p. 347), the construction of the drawer linings shows Oriental characteristics. Of the three drawers on the side shown (the other side has two false drawer fronts), the flanking ones have inscribed on the undersides in black ink Chinese characters for left and right.

The reddish-brown colouring of the padouk is faded to a pale golden brown, the rounded rectangular top having a thin crossbanding of satinwood, of the East Indian variety, while elsewhere panels are outlined with ebony stringing. The friezes on both sides have the unusual and attractive feature of kneehole recesses in the centre, the high-set stretcher bar also curving upwards. The brass knobs are later additions. The end supports are well-shaped and finely finished with recessed panels and brass castor caps cast with foliage.

One of a pair of Sheraton period mahogany sofa tables   Circa 1795

Width (open) 60ins. (152.5cm) (closed) 35½ ins. (90.2cm)
Depth 24ins. (61cm) Height 28½ ins. (72.5cm)

The twin slender reeded columns are another, more unusual, form of support for sofa tables, reminiscent of those of quartetto tables (cf. p. 347). They rest on bases composed of splayed legs joined by further reeded bars and applied with roundels. The curve of the legs is well balanced by the vaguely French double curve of the stretcher, similarly outlined with ebony stringing and centred by a cuboid block. The mahogany has a fine faded colour, the edge of the top reeded to harmonise with that below, and crossbanded with kingwood, while the drawer fronts have ebony edging. These are false on one side and lined with oak and cedar on the other. They retain their original sheet brass knobs, a feature which is especially unusual on sofa tables where, partially because of the dummy drawers, the originals have often been pulled off and lost. As has been noted before, in a number of cases handles have also been put on later where originally there were none.

One of this pair is illus. in Jourdain, 1948, fig. 100.

Provenance: The Earls of Shaftesbury, St. Giles House, Dorset.

A rare Sheraton period oak drinking table   Circa 1795

Another original form of table that made an appearance at the end of the eighteenth century was of this rounded semi-horseshoe shape. These were normally made to stand in front of a fire for men to drink at after dinner and had a system of brass rods and sliding coasters on the inside. This example shows no sign of having had this which might imply that a separate circular or oval bottle stand was used. It is also unusual in being made in two similar sections which clip together, increasing its versatility. It is possible that it was made to stand in an alcove against a wall.

Oak, especially with a marked grain, was coming back into popularity and used particularly in veneer. Here, in the solid, the surface has a most attractive faded golden colour with a high polish, crossbanded on the top with yew wood and with a boldly reeded edge. The tripod bases are slender with finely ring-turned vase-shaped stems and reeded splayed legs. These are capped with their original pointed shell-shaped castors.

An early Regency period mahogany sofa table   Circa 1805

Length (open) 59ins. (150cm) (closed) 34½ins. (87.5cm)
Depth 26ins. (66cm) Height 28½ins. (72.5cm)

The pillar support that proved so popular on dining and breakfast tables at this time is also found in the Regency period on some sofa, Pembroke and card tables. Here the column is turned with ebonised rings and the four legs, with an ample splay to steady the top, are of the early graceful type without the later protuberances at the top. They end in simple square castor caps and, like the top and frieze, are outlined with ebony stringing. As the detail shows the top is veneered in very finely flame-figured mahogany. The friezes have similar veneer on two drawer fronts and two false ones, none of them having handles but opening by grips beneath the edge. Between are inlaid brass fleur-de-lis motifs.

A Regency period rosewood work and games table　　　　　　　　Circa 1805

Width 29ins. (73.5cm)　Depth 16½ins. (42cm)　Height 30½ins. (77.5cm)

This neat and multipurpose piece is another example of the taste for compactness and ingenuity of the period. As in the case of patent dining tables, a number of firms were each trying to improve on and outshine their rivals. Sheraton devotes quite a lot of space to work tables in the *Dictionary*, and on p. 292 discusses the type with a silk bag beneath, ''used by ladies to work at, in which bag they deposit their fancy needlework. The work bags... are suspended to a frame which draws forward in which frame is a lock which shoots its bolt up into the outer edge of the rail of the top''. He also makes an interesting observation about the relative regard for woods: ''The edges should be of brass and the ground of black rose-wood when they are required to be elegant otherwise they may be very neatly made of mahogany''. The faded rosewood here is indeed finely finished with brass inlay and pierced galleries and a variety of mouldings at the top.

At each end of the top are two semicircular galleried compartments with hinged lids. The square centre section rises on an adjustable support as a reading slope. This part also slides right out on runners to reveal a backgammon board beneath. A lower slide draws forward as a work surface and this, too, can be removed, reversed and fitted into the grooves on top as a chess board. There is also a shallow drawer. The table is supported on twin scrolls of inverted lyre shape inlaid with roundels of brass and black composition, a Regency development from the patera. These are joined by a platform stretcher and raised on splayed feet with hairy paw castor caps.

A very similar table is illus. in Edwards, vol. III, p. 323, fig. 11. This has the same two-tier stretcher, edged with boxwood.

A fine Regency period rosewood circular centre table   Circa 1810

Diameter 48ins. (122cm) Height 28¾ins. (73cm)

The design of this piece follows one piece by Thomas Hope already mentioned in connection with the example on p. 168. It was a Regency trend to introduce on many tables a frieze which sometimes can be deep and heavy. Here there is a shallow one with moulded brass edging which balances the concave-sided triangular plinth base. The proportions of the conforming pedestal are much thinner than the Hope original and the overall appearance is very successful and as sophisticated as the detailing. The top is veneered with beautifully patinated rosewood with a wide band of inlaid brass scrollwork round the outside. The inspiration for this was the return to favour at this time of Boulle marquetry (cf. p. 170). Both the Boulle and contra-Boulle (panels of brass with the detailing in wood) techniques are used here in work of great quality.

The curve of the pedestal is emphasised with brass and ebony outlines with a brass moulding of leaf tips round the bottom edge. There is a further band of inlaid foliage edging on the top surface of the base, while the bold winged paw feet are finely cast in solid brass and add fitting grandeur to the piece.

Colour Plate 33. The top of a Sheraton period painted satinwood pier table, c.1790. The piece is described on p. 339.

A fine Regency period rosewood sofa table   Circa 1805

Width 59½ ins. (151cm) Depth 23ins. (58&5cm) Height 27½ ins. (72.5cm)

Besides being narrow, this table has great elegance and quality which combines some of the best features of the Regency style without any of the later heaviness. The faded rosewood top is crossbanded with ebony and five concentric outlines of brass stringing of varying thicknesses with another on the edge. Ebony is exceptionally difficult to work, its hard, brittle nature being seen in the photograph in the fine surface splits caused in drying. On English furniture some other close-grained wood such as pearwood stained black was often used instead. The friezes, with two mahogany-lined drawers and two false drawers, are again finished with brass lines and knobs which are original.

The table stands on twin end supports in the form of lyres (cf. p. 169) finely curved with ivory knobs at the tops and ending in turned ebonised bosses, as do the splay feet which scroll downwards into boldly cast hairy paw castor caps. Every side is veneered with cross-grained rosewood and inlaid with brass stringing, including the slender arched stretcher which is partially turned and partially square in section. One other most unusual and unexpected feature, visible only when the flaps are raised, is the charming painted motif of crossed arrows tied with a ribbon, above the lyres at either end.

A Regency period burr elm rectangular centre table Circa 1815

Width 56¼ ins. (143cm) Depth 28ins. (71cm) Height 29ins. (73.5cm)

Elm, like oak, returned to fashion for its attractive irregular burr figure, often, as here, contrasted with ebonised mouldings and details. This imposing piece of fine colour is very much in the archaeologically weighty style that George Smith made popular through his *Designs for Household Furniture,* published in 1808. The large S-scrolls and anthemia on the end supports are reminiscent of a design of his for a dressing table, as are the small scrolled consoles inside that support the cross arch. The plinths on which the ends stand are fitted with castors and ring-turned bosses in keeping with the many on the uprights above.

Edwards, vol. III, p. 233, fig. 29, illus. George Smith's design (dated 1805) and a piece based on it.

COMMODES AND CHESTS

A fine Queen Anne period walnut bachelor's chest

Circa 1705

Width 30½ ins. (77.5cm) Depth 13¾ ins. (35cm) Height 30¼ ins. (76.8cm)

The term bachelor's chest is probably not contemporary but has come to be used for this type of small and very shallow chest of drawers where the top is hinged with an elbow hinge at the front so that it folds forwards to rest on pull-out lopers. This was probably intended for writing at, although this example, unusually, has a pull-out slide immediately beneath it also. Original pieces of this type are rare and much copied and to find one in such untouched condition is exceptional. The details show its outstanding figure, colour and patina; the build up of minute scratches, blemishes and marks that give every inch of the surface interest and character.

The top is crossbanded all round with walnut with an inset feathered border, and this same high quality is maintained on the inside surface. The sides likewise have wide strips of crossbanding at the front and back edges and the well-proportioned graduated drawers are all oak-lined and feather-banded at the edge, within a beading on the carcase. They bear their original brass handles and escutcheons with punched decoration. One other feature of extreme rarity is the presence of four original squat cabriole legs with pad feet instead of the more usual bracket feet.

Symonds, 1946, fig. 46 shows a walnut chest with similar feet.

A fine small George I period walnut chest of drawers   Circa 1720

Width 29¾ins. (75.5cm) Depth 19½ins. (49.5cm) Height 33¾ins. (85.8cm)

Although not a bachelor's chest the same comments of condition, glowing colour and deep patina are as true here as for the previous piece (see also Colour Plate 34, p. 376). The pierced handles and escutcheons, which are all original except one, and the graduated drawers which have fine feather-banding inset from their cockbeaded edges, show the main developments of style since the other was made. The top is quarter-veneered and feather-banded also and the sides, made in the solid, are each cut from the same thickness of walnut. There is a framed brushing slide made, like the drawer linings, of almost silvery oak that has dried out naturally without oil or polish and with minimal shrinkage cracks precisely where they would be expected. The bracket feet, although they have had a degree of restoration, were also made of solid walnut. This piece is also discussed in the section on patina, pp. 18-20.

A rare George I period walnut miniature chest of drawers   Circa 1720

Width 15¾ ins. (40cm) Depth 8¾ ins. (22.2cm) Height 12¼ ins.(31cm)

As was the case with the bureau bookcase on p. 178, this is a piece where the proportions of the individual parts are in keeping with the whole. It has a good faded colour and several points of quality including a crossbanded top and feather banding on the oak-lined drawers. It is an early example like the previous chest of the use of cockbeading on the drawer edges and also of a flush rather than an overhanging top. Yet the small brass knobs and oval escutcheon plates which, like the carrying handles on the sides, are all original, are what might have been expected in the Queen Anne period. The chest stands on neat bracket feet with simple cusp shaping.

A George I period burr elm chest-on-stand   Circa 1725

See also Colour Plate 35, p. 378. Again an unusually good example of its date for surface and patina, this shows extremely well the "lustrous colour" and "tenor of the grain, and toughness" of elm that John Evelyn noted in his *Sylva*. The highly erratic grain patterns and irregular surface which gives it such great character are visible in the illustration.

The piece is made, as was usual with this type of furniture, in two sections, the top in the form of a chest of graduated drawers with a cavetto cornice, fitting behind a moulding in the top edge of the base. The base has two further tiers of drawers instead of the more usual one, the side drawers in the lower tier slightly deeper to fit the intricate shaping of the apron which is echoed at the sides. The drawers are all outlined with crossbanding and bear their original brass handles and escutcheons (except one replacement) with complex piercing. The whole is given a rather noble appearance by being supported on four cabriole legs with unusually formed trefoil feet. It is worth noting that very few of these pieces retain their original legs.

A similar form of base on a walnut example is illus. in Cescinsky, 1937, p. 185.

A George I period walnut tallboy   Circa 1720

Width 42ins. (106.5cm) Depth 21ins. (53.2cm) Height 72ins. (183cm)

Also shown as Colour Plate 36, p. 380. The chest-on-chest was a natural development from the chest-on-stand, giving extra storage space, generally being made for clothing in the bedroom, rather than for the drawing room. It appeared about 1700, although the term tallboy would seem to date from the late eighteenth century, appearing in the Gillow Cost Books of 1784. At this period, most had a straight top and cavetto cornice, the row of dentils here being an early use in furniture of a classical motif derived from the Ionic and Corinthian orders of architecture. The fluted canted corners, rarely found on the top and bottom as here, are also drawn from classical pilasters. It was usual to have three small drawers at the top, presumably to give ease of removal for access since the contents would be out of most people's reach *in situ*.

Below are three graduated drawers in each section, which as in the last case were made separately to allow transportation. The drawers are crossbanded, bordered with feather banding and edged with a projecting ovolo lip, a form found particularly in the second and third decades of the century. All the drawers have very good quality oak linings with concave quadrant mouldings at the sides which, although an early use, are original as are the pierced handles and escutcheons with their unusual flat tops. The photograph shows well the method of applying mouldings at the time in crossbanded sections. As might be expected these have tended to warp very slightly over the years.

For all the quality of the cabinet work the chief glory of this piece is its superb colour: straight-grained walnut with crossbanding on the sides and burr on the front and even on the base and bracket feet, faded to a delicate golden, almost honey, colour.

An early George I period walnut secretaire tallboy Circa 1715

Width 40¼ins. (102.2cm) Depth 20¾ins. (52.5cm) Height 75ins. (190.5cm)

The design of this piece (opposite, left) is very similar to the previous one, the long drawer fronts here each being veneered with three sections of well-selected burr veneer within feather-banding, crossbanding and a projecting moulded lip. On the lowest the divisions are marked with further banding and in the centre there is an arched niche inlaid with a sunburst of holly and ebony, an idea adopted from Holland and found on some of the highest quality tallboys of the period. Unlike the previous example, the lower half has four graduated drawers, the uppermost of which is fitted with pigeon holes and drawers as a shallow secretaire. This pulls forward, the front being released by two hooks and eyes, and let down on two hinges, a much more primitive system than the later spring catches and quadrants.

The swan-neck handles and escutcheons are replacements probably put on later in the century, the marks of the original plates being particularly clear on the bottom drawer.

A secretaire tallboy of very similar type is illus. in Edwards, vol. I, p. 140, fig. 39, and another tallboy, in vol. II, p. 42, fig. 34, has fluted canted corners, also on the top section only, which curve to a point at the bottom in just the same way as they do on this piece.

A small Chippendale period mahogany chest of drawers Circa 1760

Width 31½ins. (80cm) Depth 20ins. (50.8cm) Height 32ins. (81.2cm)

As chests of drawers began to be made of mahogany rather than walnut the chief decorative features were generally the shaping of the feet, the front corners which often continued to be chamfered, and, as developments in metalwork progressed, more elaborate handles and escutcheons. This piece (opposite, right) has all these features of quality, as well as a beautifully faded surface to the wood of which it is made. The four drawers, which always give a better balance than three, are well graduated with a brushing slide above and flanked by angles enriched with chinoiserie blind fret. The four ogee bracket feet are boldly shaped and the handles and escutcheons finely chiselled. The bottom two grips are period replacements. There is a noticeable similarity in proportions, feet and handle grips with the bureau on p. 103.

A Chippendale period mahogany serpentine dressing chest   Circa 1760

Width 46ins. (117cm) Depth 23½ins. (59.5cm) Height 33½ins. (85cm)

Here again signs of foreign influence may be seen to be creeping into a solid, peculiarly English style chest of drawers. The serpentine shaping of the French commode, here used in a very mild form, was much more difficult and expensive to produce than the straight front, but brought a greater elegance which fashion among wealthier patrons demanded. At the sides only the moulded top was given a half serpentine shape, the carcase being straight, which is found in most cases. The canted angles continue down into shaped bracket feet and are carved with very restrained but neat foliate console scrolls at the top. The graduated drawers retain their original simple swan-neck handles and are veneered in fiddle-back mahogany. The top one is fitted with lidded compartments, divisions and stoppered glass bottles with a central rectangular mirror that rises on an adjustable easel support. It is remarkable that this has survived in such perfect condition. This chest would almost certainly have been made for a man, the small ladies' dressing tables of the time generally affording rather fewer fittings.

A Chippendale period mahogany serpentine chest of drawers Circa 1765

Width 53ins. (134.5cm) Depth 25¾ins. (65.5cm) Height 34½ins. (87.5cm)

The proportions and shaping of this chest are almost identical to the previous example including the original brass swan-neck handles. The drawer fronts are veneered with a lighter and more dramatically figured type of mahogany which is laid on each in two mirrored sections. However, the most interesting and extremely unusual feature is the naturalistic inlay on the canted corners. This takes the form of a sinuous shoot bearing leaves, berries and flowers intertwined with rushes, sprouting from a rockwork base. The inspiration is clearly similar to that seen on certain rococo mirrors (e.g. p. 428) but it is also an early example of the return to fashion of marquetry decoration.

A not dissimilar motif in carving is used in a like manner by Ince and Mayhew, pl. XLIII. This 'Commode Chest of Drawers', incidentally, is the only such piece in that work, the term 'chest of drawers' hardly appearing in Chippendale's Director *either. Seeking as they were to be in the forefront of fashion, such pieces had become subordinated to the more obviously French commode.*

A fine Chippendale period mahogany serpentine commode Circa 1760

Width 44½ins. (113cm) Depth 20ins. (50.8cm) Height 33ins. (84cm)

The term commode is a French one and the piece developed there in the early years of the eighteenth century, being defined in 1718 as "une grande table avec des grands tiroirs" (a large table with deep drawers). With the fashion for French elegance in England from the middle of the century it became very popular here and the "French commode table" as Chippendale termed it, featured prominently in trade catalogues, often being the principal piece of furniture in a drawing room. Here, however, there are clear signs of greater English conservatism. Despite the serpentine front, the doors are simply panelled with corner rosettes and a gadrooned moulding to show off expanses of superb figured mahogany. The ends are similarly panelled, with fine brass rococo carrying handles the like of which were not attempted on the front.

The carving of the aprons and four elegant cabriole legs, with a shell, acanthus and C-scrolls down to the scrolled feet, is very finely carried out, yet even here the French elaboration of Chippendale's designs that continues carving right up the angles is not present, the shaping being much more anglicised and the piece made in two sections. The majority of commodes at this period displayed drawers, the use of cupboard doors, as in this specimen, generally being more popular later in the century, although the interior here is taken up with four finely-made drawers with their original brass buckle handles. Their fronts are cockbeaded and the illustration above shows the typically redder mahogany, drier and more matt in its surface which has not been exposed to patination and waxing like the outside (see also p. 21).

The shallow proportions of this piece, its short carcase with a carved apron and tall legs follow quite closely the shape of a group of commodes based on pls. LXIV and LXV of Chippendale 1762. Cescinsky, 1937, illus. two of these on p. 273. Restraint similar to that demonstrated on this piece is seen on a commode that has the same hatched lattice ground in the apron, illus. in Jourdain and Rose, pl. 108.

A fine small Chippendale period mahogany serpentine commode Circa 1760

Width 35½ ins. (90cm) Depth 22ins. (56cm) Height 32½ ins. (82.5cm)

Of excellent proportions and mildly serpentine at front and sides, this is another piece that shows the very best of anglicised style and to that extent it is rather unlike contemporary published designs. The mahogany which is straight-grained vertically has mellowed to a deep nut-brown colour. The top edge is carved with gadrooning and intermittent rosettes and leaves while the front corners below are re-entrant, an unusual and un-French feature at a time when the fashion was to make corners canted or keeled. The three oak-lined drawers retain their original fire gilded escutcheons and handles cast with rococo scrollwork, C-scrolls and coquillage around central cabochons. They are particularly well chosen, since just the same motifs are used in the carving of the aprons and on the knees of the four well-shaped tall cabriole legs which end in finely scrolled toes. The back legs have an ingenious twist to them, so that the detailing of the knees is shifted a little to one side to be more visible when the piece is standing against a wall.

A slightly larger commode from the same workshop is illus. in Jourdain and Rose, fig. 108. This has identical shaping, including the re-entrant corners, vertical figuring and carving on the aprons and feet.

374

Colour Plate 34. A small George I period walnut chest of drawers, c.1720.
The piece is described on p. 364.

A rare shallow Adam period mahogany chest of drawers Circa 1770

Width 40½ ins. (103cm) Depth 13¼ ins. (33.5cm) Height 34¼ ins. (87cm)

The unusual proportions and form of this piece would imply that it might have been made as part of a specific decorative scheme. There is a drawer in the frieze which has a fluted front and is separated by a moulding from three similarly oak-lined graduated drawers below. All the horizontal mouldings are ebonised. The front corners project slightly and are canted with fluting between paterae carved in the frieze and, uncommonly, on the plinth base. The finely chased brass handles are original, although a little earlier in style.

This model of handle, with asymmetrical rococo plates and grips of two C-scrolls with foliage in the centre, may be noted on a number of pieces of furniture of the Chippendale period including a pair of commodes by Chippendale at Goldsborough Hall, Yorks. (Gilbert, Chippendale, figs. 226 and 270). Like several other common types, they would probably have been purchased from the same founder's stock.

Colour Plate 35. A George I period burr elm chest-on-stand, c.1725. The piece is described on p. 366.

One of a fine pair of Chippendale period mahogany bedside cupboards   Circa 1765

Width 18ins. (45.8cm) Height 28ins. (71cm)

The pierced scroll aprons and very slender square tapered legs, chamfered on the inside, give an effective feeling of lightness. This is heightened by the breaking of the straight line in the knurled feet with their attractive foliage carving which flicks outwards at the top. The cupboard itself has moulded edges to the top and oval panels on three sides, edged with astragal mouldings and surrounded with quartered veneer with carved rosettes at each corner. The panels are superbly veneered with figured mahogany, the front one retaining its original finely wrought buckle-shaped handle, cleverly devised with a rosette back plate to be placed in the centre as part of the design. The stiles and cappings to the legs have recessed panels showing chinoiserie influence.

The proportions and much of the inspiration of this pair is taken from a design for a night table by William Ince in Ince and Mayhew, pl. XXXIII.

Provenance: The Arthur Leidesdorf Collection.

Colour Plate 36. A George I period walnut tallboy, c.1720. The piece is described on p. 367.

A Chippendale period mahogany breakfront cabinet   Circa 1770

Width 42ins. (106.5cm) Depth 20ins. (51cm) Height 32ins. (81.2cm)

The conception of this and the next piece is not dissimilar: the slightly breakfront centre, the narrow side doors with shaped rectangular panelling and the plinth base; it is interesting to compare the many ways in which the next piece excels, the more so since this is a fine and unusual piece in its own way. The veneer of the panels and cockbeaded drawer fronts has a superb flame figure which is mirrored on the doors, and a patina which varies splendidly from light to dark. The cast brass handles are all original. There are three frieze drawers above a moulding that echoes that of the top edge, and another drawer and a double one below, the latter perhaps intended as a cellaret.

A more direct comparison of shape may be made with a lacquer commode provided by Chippendale for Harewood House c.1770-2, illus. in Gilbert, Chippendale, *vol. II, fig. 218.*

A fine Chippendale period mahogany commode attributed to John Bradburn or William Vile

Circa 1765

Width 65½ ins. (166.5cm) Depth 26¾ ins. (68cm) Height 34½ ins. (87.5cm)

The quality of the cabinet work of this piece is outstanding and the subtle serpentine shaping of its breakfront centre section compounds the technical achievement. Beneath the top edge, which is finished with a brass moulding, are four doors each enclosing, in a similar English manner to the example on p. 372, graduated red cedar-lined drawers which retain their original swan-neck handles. The side doors have shaped rectangular panels edged with bead and reel with flower heads at the corners, while the centre ones have a single large circular moulding of twisted ribbon and flower with distinctive acanthus clasps and subsidiary segmental panels. The ends are similarly panelled with ovals. Each panel is surrounded with crossbanding and contains superbly matched figured veneer. The commode, which like that on p. 372, has no brasses or handles on the front, is raised on a plinth base and has all its front corners rounded.

The attribution to John Bradburn is based on similarities with "a neat mohogany press for Linnen with 4 wood doors" of which the base only survives, which he invoiced for £84. 10. 0 to Buckingham House in 1770, where it still remains. It is illus. with the present piece in Coleridge, figs. 388-9 and also in H. Clifford-Smith, p. 279, pl. 65. There is an even closer link in the oval shapes and acanthus clasps to the work of William Vile for whom Bradburn worked before setting up his own business with William France in 1764, in which year he also succeeded as Royal Cabinet Maker to George III on Vile's retirement (see Coleridge, figs. 3, 9-11, 16, etc.). A pair of commodes, illus. in Jourdain and Rose, fig. 118 and another, serpentine, one of a pair, illus. amongst other places in Edwards, vol. II, p. 112, fig. 5, are undeniably by the same hand, having precisely the same centres. Vile retired through ill health and died in 1767 so that it is difficult to be certain about the precise authorship of this group. Even John Linnell was employing a similar motif at this time, see Hayward and Kirkham, figs. 16-18, 20, as perhaps was Benjamin Goodison, see Coleridge, fig. 369.

A Chippendale period mahogany bedside cupboard   Circa 1770

Width 21¼ ins. (54cm) Depth 18½ ins. (47cm)
Height 31¼ ins. (79.5cm)

Compared with p. 379 this is a more usual, but nevertheless good quality, example of a bedside cupboard or 'night table' as it was generally known at this time. This type, where the front legs are fixed to move forwards to support the bottom drawer which contained a framed chamber pot (concealed by the shaped apron), remained popular for a long period. The complex shaping of the wooden gallery with pierced grips is a usual feature, with two doors below enclosing a cupboard. These are particularly well made in this case with figured panels in shaped moulded surrounds crossbanded with mahogany of very striking grain.

Ince and Mayhew do not give such a design, neither did Chippendale include any furniture of this kind in the Director, *but he was providing similar examples to clients, for example "a large Mahogany night Table and Necessary Stool with a Stone pan £2. 15. 0" to Mersham le Hatch in 1767, illus. in Gilbert,* Chippendale, *vol. II, fig. 455.*

A fine Chippendale period mahogany breakfront clothes press   Circa 1770

Width 80ins. (203cm) Depth 24ins. (61cm) Height 98ins. (249cm)

Access to tallboys was often inconvenient, and numerous designs for clothes presses are given in the pattern books of Chippendale and his contemporaries, these having cupboards containing shelves or trays that slid forwards on runners above a lower section of drawers. Through most of the eighteenth century this method of storing clothes seems to have been more popular than hanging wardrobes with hooks, although larger examples such as this one often combined the two with hanging space in the wing sections. In this case the cabinet maker adopted the unusual strategy of making the narrow flanking doors and drawers beneath them dummies and giving access with single full-length doors in each side.

In the construction and detailing of the piece, nothing was sacrificed to quality, as the close-up shows. The pediment is a fanciful confection of double scrolls enclosing paterae and bellflower trails centred on an oval plaque with lozenge hatching similar to that on the apron on the piece on p. 373. The side finials display just a hint of chinoiserie. The cornice is a complex affair, again superbly carved and detailed with waterleaf, arched fluting and ogee machicolation which shows up well, as does the pediment carving, on a ground of contrasting satinwood. The doors have splendidly matched and mirrored panels of figured mahogany edged with satinwood within shaped rectangular astragal mouldings with circular boxwood paterae at the corners. Even these are inlaid with enormous care. The drawers below are again mirror figured and have all their original brass handles and interestingly-shaped ivory escutcheons. The press is in remarkably untouched condition throughout, apart from the loss of its sliding trays in the interests of later fashionable convenience.

Provenance: H.R.H. the late Queen Mary, Marlborough House, London.

A very fine small Chippendale period mahogany commode in the French style   Circa 1760

Width 41½ ins. (105.5cm) Depth 21½ ins. (54.5cm) Height 32½ ins. (82.5cm)

The French influence shown in recent pieces has been very much subordinated to English traditions, with consciously uncomplicated surfaces and carving in wood rather than metal mounts; handles, where they exist at all, being comparatively simple. Here the whole conception captures much more of the fanciful spirit of the rococo style and yet the interpretation, which is extremely successful on this small scale, is very much that of an English craftsman.

The cabinet work is of the highest order, the fact that the piece has survived in such fine condition without the need for repair which would harm its deep patina, bearing witness to this. The veneers of beautifully figured mahogany are laid all over in the Continental form of a geometrical parquetry of lozenge shapes on to a pine carcase. The use of pine instead of mahogany might have made easier the shaping of the bombé front and sides, but it is still exquisitely carried out. The linings of the drawers are mahogany, another sign of quality, and curved to follow the three dimensional shape, the sides of the commode being fully serpentine. The broad crossbanding which is used on the top and sides and quartered in a radiating fashion on the drawer fronts, like the band of feathering round the top and cockbeading on the drawers, are rather conservative and English features. In the same way the fact that the top is veneered and not marble, as would have been found on a French commode, shows the desire to conform to the less formal and more homogeneous English taste. Practically no commodes made in England during the eighteenth century had marble tops.

The ormolu mounts are also superbly wrought, the keeled front corners having protective strips the whole way down to the toes in the French manner and the handles and escutcheons in full rococo taste, the former being provided with special stops. Yet none of the mounts overpower the design and they are sufficiently restricted to let the very lively surface speak for itself.

E.T. Joy, 'An English Commode in the French taste', The Connoisseur, *May 1971.*

Provenance: The late Marjorie Wiggin Prescott, Belle Haven, Greenwich, Connecticut, U.S.A.

Exhibition: The Ashmolean Museum, Oxford, 1963-1970.

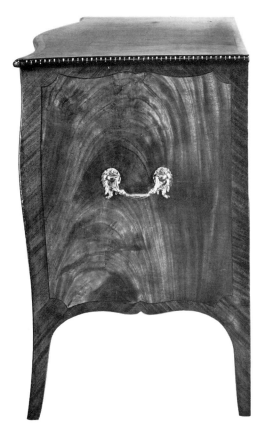

A fine Hepplewhite period mahogany commode in the French taste   Circa 1775

Width 46ins. (116.5cm) Depth 20½ins. (58.5cm) Height 32ins. (81.5cm)

The large gilt handles on the front of this commode (shown above and in Colour Plate 37 opposite) are cast in an up-to-date classical manner with swags of husks hung from ribbon-tied paterae, although the carrying handles on the sides are still typical of the 1760s (cf. p. 102). There are no other metal mounts and this piece displays marked English restraint in certain other ways: its shaping is serpentine only at the front and mildly bombé, as is shown by the very gentle curves of the keeled corners, which is perhaps consistent with the development towards neo-classicism. However, the proportions are very pleasing, being shallow, and the tall splayed legs remove any feeling of heaviness.

On the front, full and effective use is made of the paler golden coloured mahogany that was now coming in, particularly from Honduras. It has a beautifully selected curl figure that is permitted to carry through the carcase between the oak-lined drawers. Around the edges and the shaped panels of similar veneer on the sides are bands of slightly redder mahogany laid diagonally. The top is crossbanded with satinwood and again displays the double-arched mahogany figuring. The drawer fronts and corners are edged, like the other panels, with ebonised stringing while the top edge moulding is also painted black with a most unusual decoration of white dots and dashes. This is difficult to parallel and might imply the hand of a top quality provincial maker of which there were a number at the time working, for example, in Yorkshire whence this commode is known to have come.

This piece makes an interesting comparison with full-blown commodes of similar type and of certain London manufacture such as one belonging to the Duke of Norfolk, illus. in Coleridge, fig. 234. Here the veneering of the drawer fronts, the shaping of the aprons and the top, and the general proportions are all comparable but the richer decoration and shaping of the other are quite evident. A very similar commode with identical handles on the drawers was included in the CINOA International Art Treasures Exhibition at the V. and A., 1962 (no. 81).

Colour Plate 37.

389

A Hepplewhite period marquetry semi-elliptical commode   Circa 1780

Width 52ins. (132cm) Depth 19½ins. (49.5cm) Height 35ins. (89cm)

As has often been noted with cabinet furniture, it is the pieces of shallow dimensions that tend to look proportionally most satisfactory. This one is no exception (shown above and in Colour Plate 38 opposite). It displays the fashion for marquetry surface decoration which had by now eclipsed carved mahogany on commodes, and its rounded outline, except for slight curves into the projecting stiles, is symptomatic of a move to the more classical shapes rather than the rococo-derived serpentine. In order to obtain uninterrupted surfaces, commodes were now almost always made with doors, although sometimes there were drawers in the friezes. In this respect this example is most unusual, having a hinged top rising to reveal an arrangement of fitted toiletry compartments, which would imply use in a boudoir rather than a drawing room. There are few fine commodes with such a feature.

The frieze is inlaid with a swag motif and the three panels below, the centre one of which forms a door enclosing a cupboard, have a design of palmettes and strips of satinwood and harewood radiating from central ovals. The use of these and other contrasting woods is striking. The top follows the same pattern, which lends itself well to the shape. Marquetry was ousting the use of brass mounts and these are here restricted to wreathed urns at the tops of each stile and foliate caps to the square tapered legs.

An ormolu mounted commode with a hinged top operating in the same manner was sold by Christie's at Wateringbury Place, Kent on 31st May, 1978, lot 138.

Provenance: The Duke of Richmond and Gordon, Goodwood House, Sussex.
E.R. Brigham, Esq., Wetton Hall, Brough, Yorkshire.

Colour Plate 38.

A Hepplewhite period small satinwood semi-elliptical commode   Circa 1785

Width 39½ ins. (100.5cm) Depth 18ins. (45.8cm) Height 31½ ins. (80cm)

Hepplewhite's *Guide* includes only one design, dated 1787, for a commode. This is of rounded form and has several features in common with the example shown opposite in Colour Plates 39a and 39b. Of it he writes "This piece of furniture is adapted for a drawing-room; within are shelves which answer the use of a closet or cupboard — may have one principal door in the front, or one at each end...The pannels may be of satin wood, plain, or inlaid; the top and also the border round the front, should be inlaid". A wide variety of woods are employed in the inlay of this piece, but it is very neatly and tastefully contrived so that, just as Hepplewhite uses uncluttered panels of figured wood in his example, large areas of warm figured satinwood are left, with great effect.

The top is inlaid with a fan medallion, which was so fitting to the oval shapes popular at the time, with a neat border of ribbon swags and flowerheads on a dark ground. The frieze has more swags, of bellflower, at the sides and of drapery suspended from an urn on a contrasting ebony plaque on the centre drawer. The central cupboard door and side panels are edged with tulipwood and have matching circular medallions of a satyr's head and urns on a very strikingly figured ground. The stiles are capped with paterae and have bands of darker wood which taper through the lower astragal moulding into slender square legs. The mouldings are of purpleheart. The only mounts on the piece are the chased foliate toe caps which are comparable to those on the previous example.

Hepplewhite's Guide, *1788, illus. the design for a commode on pl. 78. The border decoration is a rather superior version of that shown on pl. 54 of Sheraton's* Drawing Book.

Hayward and Kirkham, fig. 120, attribute to John Linnell a small commode of similar shape and refined decoration based on small circular medallions.

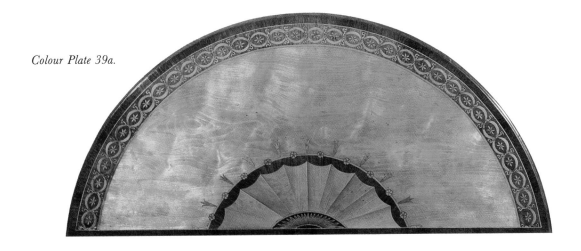

Colour Plate 39a.

Colour Plate 39b.

A fine Chippendale period mahogany commode in the French taste attributed to Pierre Langlois

Circa 1768

Width 51ins. (129.5cm) Depth 22ins. (56cm) Height 33ins. (84cm)

The fine bombé shaping of the front of this commode is used as a vehicle for the display of two huge expanses of attractively coloured straight-grained mahogany veneer laid in an unusual diagonal fashion. The moulded-edged top with lobed front corners is similarly treated. The doors are left to speak for themselves with two rococo keyhole escutcheons as the only ornament. They are similarly veneered inside, a finish of higher quality than might be expected on a French commode, and enclose four short above three long drawers, all of which retain their original swan-neck handles. The sides of the piece are straight and also shallow which is beneficial to the overall proportions since the uninterrupted front gives rather an appearance of heaviness in the photograph. The keeled corners are boldly shaped and mounted throughout their length with mouldings cast with twining flowerheads, foliage and scrolled toes which conceal castors.

These corner mounts and the general form of this piece are identical to a number of other commodes of the period which are generally associated with Pierre Langlois the *émigré* Frenchman who was so influential in integrating the French taste in this country.

The work of Langlois was discussed in detail by P. Thornton and W. Rieder in a series of articles in The Connoisseur, *Dec. 1971 – May 1972, during which (Apr. 1972, p. 265, fig. 18) a closely comparable commode was ascribed to him. This has a pagoda-inspired gadrooned top edge, shaped rear stiles, grooves for sliding shelves inside and minor differences in the apron and corner mounts including feet which are true sabots. It was formerly with the present commode at Cannon Hall, Yorks., where it is known that John Spencer, having made extensive alterations between 1765 and 1768, patronised several fashionable cabinet makers including John Cobb. This type of corner mount is thought to have been commissioned from Langlois' son-in-law Dominique Jean, although Gilbert,* Chippendale, *illus. identical ones on a commode at Nostell Priory that he attributes to Chippendale (vol. II, fig. 227). Another similar commode from the collection of the Duke of Norfolk was sold at Christie's, 1st June 1961, lot 118. This had the rare feature of silver plated foliate mounts.*

Provenance: The late Mrs. Spencer-Stanhope, Cannon Hall, Cawthorne, Yorkshire, and Banks Hall, nr. Bradford, Yorkshire.
The late Marjorie Wiggin Prescott, Belle Haven, Greenwich, Connecticut, U.S.A.

One of a fine pair of Chippendale period marquetry commode in the French taste attributed to Pierre Langlois Circa 1770

Width (back) 53½ins. (136cm) (front) 41¾ins. (106cm)
Depth 21ins. (53.5cm) Height 32½ins. (82.5cm)

The proportions of this are very similar to those of the previous example, all such pieces being of the general shape typical of Parisian commodes of the 1750s. That such French productions were being imported directly is shown, along with a comment characteristic of English taste, in a letter written by the Earl of March to Paris in 1766: "Pray don't let the commode be too much ornamented. J'aime le grand simple comme le Prince: but as it will be a principal piece at the end of the room, between the windows, it must be handsome so as to be an object."

Langlois followed these French styles closely, but at the same time incorporated in most cases such traditionally English features as wooden rather than marble tops, deal rather than oak carcases, dust boards between the drawers which were not often used in France until later, and the finishing of the interiors that were generally superior to French ones. Although it is dangerous to make attributions on the basis of comparisons of individual characteristics, a number of these are compelling. The angle mounts are identical to those on the previous commode and the apron mounts and brass bands round the top edges typical of Langlois' work. There are a number of commodes discussed in the Thornton and Rieder articles (see p. 394) with this same unusual light and dark striped diagonal crossbanding, either of laburnum or a particular species of rosewood. The effect is reminiscent of the idiosyncratic work in laburnum and broomwood by George Sandeman of Perth and has no parallel in the French rococo repertoire. On some examples, such as a pair of commodes at West Wycombe Park, the banding frames rectangular panels, as here, and on others it is merely found on the top edge moulding.

The trellis pattern in these panels is derived from a type of decoration used in France and has already been seen in another variation on pp. 196 and 202. The diagonals are interwoven with florets veined in ink at the intersections. On the doors the decoration is laid into a ground of plane tree, the angle of the photograph showing well the lacy grain which leads to its sometimes being termed lacewood. Its use is unusual on furniture (cf. p. 346). The overall effect, with the bold lattice-work and diagonal banding on the doors running in the opposite direction to that on the carcase and the whole design being repeated on the top, is extremely skilfully contrived and handled.

A Hepplewhite period tulipwood and marquetry commode   Circa 1785

The D-shape or "elliptic sweep" as Sheraton called it, became more popular in the 1780s for a variety of cabinets and tables. In the piece shown opposite as Colour Plate 40, the shape, as so often happens, is set between two square stiles which, like the corresponding ones at the back, stand slightly proud at the sides and end in short square tapered legs. Metal mounts are completely absent, the two frieze drawers and cupboard doors being opened using keys. The drawers are almost concealed in the decoration of boxwood or holly inlaid fluting. Below them is an astragal moulding, which is matched on the bottom edge of the commode and the retaining moulding on the right hand door, while the edge of the top is unmoulded with an unusual inlay of dots.

The doors are veneered with tulipwood, as are the sides and the stiles, and have crossbandings of kingwood. It is uncommon to find such a large expanse of tulipwood, which was usually imported from Brazil in small billets. Its attractive pinkish hue and red grain, which frequently bleach out to almost white, are still quite apparent. In the centre of each door is a large marquetry oval patera very finely detailed with engraving and suspended from a crinkled ribbon bow in a surround of sparsely arranged husks. A further small medallion hangs below.

Exhibition: C.I.N.O.A. International Art Treasures Exhibition, Victoria and Albert Museum, 1962, no. 76.

Colour Plate 40.

A Hepplewhite period mahogany serpentine commode   Circa 1780

Width 62ins. (157.5cm) Depth 23ins. (58.5cm) Height 31¼ins. (79.5cm)

The shallow proportions and unusual form whereby the sides splay outwards sharply from the front to back make this a particularly satisfying piece. The shape allows full appreciation of the graceful use of serpentine curves which are elegantly complemented by the tall splay feet. The mahogany veneer is not highly figured but has a fine mellow colour with an almost watery texture; it is neatly picked out with boxwood stringing round the drawer fronts, top and side panels and a little crossbanding on the canted angles. The four graduated drawers retain their original cast brass ring handles with centre paterae. The sides are fitted as cupboard doors enclosing shelves.

Shearer et al. gives a similar design dated 1788, p. 9 and pl. 20, fig. 2, which he calls "A Serpentine dressing chest, with ogee ends. . .three feet long in front, and five at back". This is also comparable in its handles and treatment of the angles but much inferior in its straight tapered feet. Earlier pieces made in this same splayed serpentine fashion are illus. in Macquoid, vol. 4, pl. II, and Edwards, vol. II, p. 119, fig. 23.

A fine early Sheraton period shallow side cabinet   Circa 1785

Width 60ins. (152.5cm) Depth 17ins. (43.2cm) Height 36ins. (91.5cm)

Once again a wealth of different woods are employed in giving this piece fine and varied colour and texture. The top, like the front, is divided into three sections marked by engaged satinwood columns. The main panels, with narrow ovals on the lower doors and one in the centre of the top, all superbly figured and laid mirror fashion, are of sabicu or horseflesh mahogany (cf. pp. 103 and 350) in surrounds of contrasting pale bird's-eye maple with purplewood lines between. The four door panels are recessed which allows for a degree of movement and, along with the fact that sabicu is a very stable timber, this accounts for their remarkably uncracked and unwarped condition. The mouldings round them are of ebony, while kingwood and tulipwood are used for the other crossbandings. The sides of the cabinet are veneered in satinwood.

In contrast, all the decoration on the front columns, the fluting and oak leaves, is painted on in the fashionable manner in the original green and pink colours. The frieze, which is marked off with crossbanding even across the columns, contains one long and two short drawers lined with red cedar, a sign of the quality which is already evident in the rest of the piece. Similarly, the doors are constructed of mahogany and even the back boards of the cabinet are of panelled construction. The brass handles and toupie feet are later replacements, although both are very much in keeping.

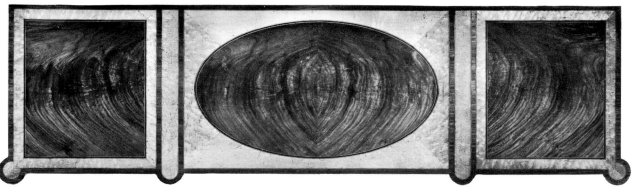

Colour Plate 41. A pair of Regency period simulated calamander wood chiffoniers, c. 1810.
The pieces are described on p. 410.

An early Sheraton period shallow satinwood serpentine commode Circa 1785

Width 51ins. (130cm) Depth (centre) 18½ins. (47cm) (end) 10ins. (26cm) Height 34½ins. (88cm)

Even at this period the serpentine front with all its elegance is still to be found. It is not difficult to draw comparisons with the previous piece, in the shallow proportions and the division into three sections of two short and one long frieze drawer, in this case oak-lined, above oval panelled cupboards. The predominant wood here is satinwood, quartered round the ovals and contrastingly outlined with narrow bands of amaranth (purplewood). Behind the gilded brass grilles which are replacements, each oval retains an original board on which is painted in shades of green a very skilful simulation of pleated silk. Real 'green silk fluting' was recommended by Sheraton for cabinet doors and is seen in a number of his plates. The square tapered feet, outlined like the stiles with amaranth and carved with beading, are original.

Sheraton published a design for a commode with a similar bowed centre and painted oval panels in the Appendix, *pl. LXVI. He makes the rather surprising statement that "the internal part is merely plain shelves, as these pieces are never intended for use but for ornament". A satinwood commode illus. in* Fanfare for Europe, The British Art Market, *1973, p. 184, is of this same form with painted silk panels. It combines painted satinwood engaged columns comparable to those on the previous piece and also introduces panels on the flanking doors the shape of those on the next piece.*

A Sheraton period rosewood breakfront side cabinet Circa 1790

Width 45¼ ins. (115cm) Depth 18½ ins. (47cm) Height 33¾ ins. (85.5cm)

The quality of this unusual and useful piece of drawing room furniture, which combines cupboards and open bookshelves, is once again easy to see. The contrasting woods employed here are rosewood and darker amaranth, with boxwood stringing throughout heightening the smart appearance. The top, like the frieze drawer fronts, is crossbanded with inset corners, and the panels in the doors below, which are unusually echoed at the sides as well, follow a similar shaping. These have rosewood quartered crossbanding round them and they are set, except at the back edge, between simple slender amaranth engaged columns that run into inverted baluster feet. This rare use of the violet coloured wood in the solid displays its hard texture and smooth, lustrous surface. The breakfront section contains a frieze drawer and three shelves, while the flanking drawers are false and part of the fronts of full length cupboards. Behind the original brass grilles are further examples of wooden panels, again original, painted to represent pleated silk, this time of a creamy brown colour.

One of a pair of Regency mahogany bow front chests of drawers   Circa 1800

Width 51¼ ins. (130.2cm) Depth 22¾ ins. ʿ57.8cm) Height 36¼ ins. (92cm)

The chests of drawers made towards the end of the eighteenth century were generally fairly plain affairs, as may be seen in Hepplewhite's, Shearer's and Sheraton's designs. If they were not straight-fronted they usually had a shallow bow, whether concave or convex as here. Besides the rarity of surviving as a pair these pieces are of unusually high quality. Each contains three red cedar-lined drawers with splendidly matched figured mahogany fronts inlaid with ebony lines and double wing motifs. The brass knobs, stamped with lions' heads, are original. At the front angles project engaged columns inlaid with stop-fluting of ebony and mahogany which end in feet turned with ebonised rings. The treatment here is reminiscent of the bookcase on p. 235.

A Sheraton period mahogany
whatnot cabinet   Circa 1790

Width 18½ ins. (47cm)
Depth 14½ ins. (36.8cm)
Height 60ins. (152.5cm)

The rather inelegant but descriptive term whatnot, being the English equivalent of the French *étagère,* is first recorded about 1790 in the records of Gillow's to describe a tall stand with tiered shelves for the display of ornaments, books and other small items. The object was presumably too much of a novelty to appear in any of Sheraton's works. This example is therefore a particularly early one with three thin reeded shelves above a cabinet base. Some later ones are found fitted with one or two drawers, usually at the bottom, but the arrangement seen here is rare. The drawer front and cupboard doors in the base are veneered with well-figured mahogany and edged with ebony lines above four splay feet, while the corner uprights above have the attractive feature of scrolled tops with applied turned bosses.

An early Regency period mahogany chiffonier   Circa 1805

Width 32¼ ins. (82cm) Depth 15¾ ins. (40cm) Height 60ins. (152.5cm)

Although of the Regency period, the detailing of this piece is still delicate and light in its scale, as are its proportions. The top section of various shelves has an unusual wooden reeded three-quarter gallery, and brass rods and bold S-scroll supports each side. The S-scrolls are inlaid with brass motifs and ebony lines and finished with gilded carved whorls. Quality is shown in the back boards of mahogany panelling. The cabinet section contains a shallow drawer, fitted for writing and with a baized slide, above two cupboard doors of finely matched mahogany with recessed shaped rectangular panels. All these have fine double ebony outlining. The stiles, like the top edge, are decorated with dainty brass beading. Inside the cupboard are two small drawers at the top. It is interesting to compare the perfect matt gilding of the lion-mask ring handles on these with the naturally polished similar ones on the outside drawer. The typically Regency lion theme is carried on in the brass paw feet on the short sabre type legs which match those supporting the S-scrolls above.

One of a pair of Regency period black lacquer commodes Circa 1810

Considerable imagination is displayed in the design of this commode which shows both the boldness of the Greek Revival and the return to fashion of chinoiserie taste as was so firmly expressed at Brighton Pavilion. The gilt lacquer panels in the concave ends have a notably Western feeling to them and are surrounded with interlace of Norse inspiration and English-looking flowers. There is another small panel in the centre beneath the doors. The doors themselves, which enclose cupboards, are backed with pleated silk and have the original brass grilles in an elliptical pattern that was fashionable at the time.

At the front and back corners are gilded reeded columns, tapering architecturally the wrong way but used in the manner of Greek terms, the tops carved with rams' heads and festoons while the bases, which stand on projecting brackets carved with upright leaves, are carved with cloven hooves. In spite of these strong verticals, there is considerable horizontal emphasis in the gilded reeded divisions below the doors and in the squared edge of the white marble top. The influence for the use of marble is probably now more directly classical than French. The commodes stand on quadrant bracket feet and are in very well preserved condition.

A pair of Regency period simulated calamander wood chiffoniers   Circa 1810

Width 24ins. (61cm) Depth 9¼ ins. (23.5cm) Height 48½ ins. (123.2cm)

As well as being small in size, these cabinets (also shown as Colour Plate 41, p. 402) are finely shaped and proportioned and have their original painted decoration. The more striking the grain that woods of the rosewood family had at this period, the more desirable they seem to have been. Furthermore, the practice of painting on the dark grain was widespread, both to enhance rosewood with less contrast and to simulate it on other woods such as mahogany, beech or, as here, pine. The whole of the surface is stained and grained beneath the cream painted decoration. The use of pine in this context is by no means symptomatic of inferior quality, indeed the quality here is very high, even the centre drawers being lined with red cedar.

The cabinets have several of the elements of detail that were made popular by Thomas Hope in his *Household Furniture and Interior Decoration,* 1807: the terms either side of the doors with their gilded wood sphinx heads and feet, the quadrant bracket feet painted with anthemia, and some of the motifs in the decoration elsewhere. Yet there is none of the rather stiff and formal feeling of Hope's work, the elements blending in with such niceties as recessed panels in the terms, the concave-fronted base and the attractive shaping of the sides of the graduated shelves above, outlined with painted lines. There are even brass castors concealed behind the feet. The cupboard doors have rectangular panels with instepped corners filled with brass lattice work and backed with silk, the shape being repeated on the sides.

MIRRORS

**A rare Queen Anne period
green lacquer pier glass**   Circa 1705

Width 22ins. (56cm) Height 60ins. (152.5cm)

Mirrors of glass do not seem to have been made in this country until early in the seventeenth century and the use of the more traditional polished metal plates continued well past the Restoration. It was not until this time that the inherent problem of producing pieces of glass of any size thick enough to stand grinding was overcome. The 2nd Duke of Buckingham set up a glass-house at Vauxhall about 1663 which made great advances, but it was only rarely until well into the eighteenth century that plates were produced over about 3 or 4 ft. long. Thus, when the architectural emphasis on height which came from Holland towards the end of the seventeenth century was reflected in fashionable furnishings, it became usual for mirrors to contain two separate plates. Sometimes these had a decorative strip concealing the join or else, as here, the two plates were just butted together. These plates have their original shaped bevelled edges, very shallow and almost concave in section, having been cut probably by hand on a piece of glass only some ³⁄₁₆in. thick; modern glass being up to double this thickness. The glass also has the typical dark colour and rust pitting on its unevenly ground back.

This mirror would have been made to hang on a narrow pier between two tall windows above a table. It is framed, like many of the period, in pine, with a convex cushion moulding shaped with scrolls at the top beneath a flat cresting, pierced with a little stylised foliage. The whole is japanned with gilded chinoiserie decoration in a relatively symmetrical manner. The great majority of japanned or lacquered examples were carried out in black. The dark bottle green used here is very rare.

A similar, but slightly later pair of mirrors, but with a black ground to the decoration, is illus. in Symonds, 1929, fig. 227.

One of a pair of early George I gilt gesso mirrors

Circa 1715

While the tall pier glasses were still fashionable, smaller mirrors were being made, often in pairs, to hang elsewhere in rooms. They normally had a pair of brass or occasionally glass candle holders which slotted into brackets at the bottom so that the candlelight would be reflected in the glass and light given off much increased. The brackets here are incorporated into the design, the arms being original where so many have since been lost. The mirror plate is rectangular, alleviated with slight indents at the top corners. It is not bevelled, the frame taking over the whole decorative rôle, with moulded surrounds of ogee section decorated with foliage scrolls. The scallop shell below and female mask and plumes above are typical motifs of the date but all the carved decoration is of particular quality and vigour, crisply incised, and in the case of the plumes and flanking pediment scrolls and flowerheads, deeply cut. In terms of development the overall shape with its interesting but orderly scrolled outline is particularly attractive before the architectural elements become more dominant and rigid. The detail illustrates the minute all-over crackling of the gesso and original gilding, burnished on the highlights and matt on the ground.

An early George II gilt gesso mirror   Circa 1735

As with the height of pier glasses early in the century, mirrors of this period more than any other piece of furniture were influenced by architectural design. This is not surprising as they were actually attached to walls and could be given similar treatment to windows, doorways and overmantel panelling. In William Jones's *The Gentlemens and Builders Companion* of 1739, mirrors and associated console tables are the only items of furniture included. Thus an elaborate, usually scrolled, pediment with a central cartouche, above an emphatic cornice and a rectangular plate in a shaped architrave surround, became the fashionable form.

The example shown opposite, left, is a good one with deep undercutting of the acanthus foliage on the entablature and at the bottom. The plate is framed with bead moulding, shallow carved decoration and a shouldered surround of egg-and-dart. The sides are edged with lively foliage hanging from consoles and similar to that carved on the pediment scrolls. The mirror has lost its candle arms although the brackets remain.

A rare George II period mirror in a carved mahogany frame   Circa 1750
Width 26ins. (66cm) Height 50ins. (127cm)

On the architectural mirrors of the 1730s and 1740s a balance was sometimes struck between gilding the mouldings and carving, and veneering the other parts in walnut or mahogany. However, on the mirror shown opposite, right, the only gilding is on the border round the bevelled plate and to find such delicate piercing and carving in mahogany rather than gilded pine on a mirror, is most unusual. In style it bears a certain similarity to a gilded mirror at The Vyne, Hampshire, in that it retains vestiges of architectural formality in the top scrolls with a sheaf-like cresting and in the moulded, almost rectangular surround to the plate and the side pendants. Yet the vigour and fine details of the rococo taste are evident. For the most part the foliage, C-scrolls and coquillage are carved quite symmetrically but the applied motif below the cresting shows a deliberate move away from this.

A similar gilded mirror at The Vyne, Hants., is illus. in Edwards, vol. II, p. 338, fig. 69.

A Chippendale period carved and gilded rectangular mirror   Circa 1755

Width 28ins. (71cm) Height 56½ins. (143.5cm)

The mirror shown opposite, left, is of great sophistication and restraint. It displays various influences that were current at the time although its conception is still almost symmetrical. The coquillage and foliage scrolls at the bottom corners are clearly rococo, while the slender side pillars with their plume capitals divide off small sections of mirror plate with shaft rings in a Gothic manner. Finally the splendid sweep of acanthus, pierced with Gothic mouchettes, that forms the canopied cresting, has a Chinese pagoda-like quality. Its foliate dome is repeated at the bottom of the mirror where it caps a substantial rotunda on a rockwork base, very much of the type used for fashionable garden temples of the period.

A Chippendale period carved and gilded rectangular mirror   Circa 1755

Width 23ins. (58.5cm) Height 47ins. (119.5cm)

The use of pinewood for mirror frames where, unlike other forms of furniture, there was hardly any need for load-bearing or functional considerations, lent itself superbly to displays of every sort of rococo virtuosity which were hardly possible in mahogany. The most successful examples are often those which exhibit a degree of restraint in that the various elements relate to each other and there is a sense of containment. Most of the contemporary pattern books display confections of the most extravagant kind in which structure is completely subordinate to decoration. This example (shown opposite, right) manages to avoid such over-exuberance. There is a much lighter feeling than on any previous example and even the lines of the mirror plate are broken with C-scrolls and foliage, rendering bevelling superfluous.

The mirror has a certain relationship in form to one illus. in Edwards, vol. II, p. 339, fig. 73. The earlier features of floral pendants at the sides and 'ears' at the corners of the plate are still just discernible in the finely carved and pierced frames of each.

416

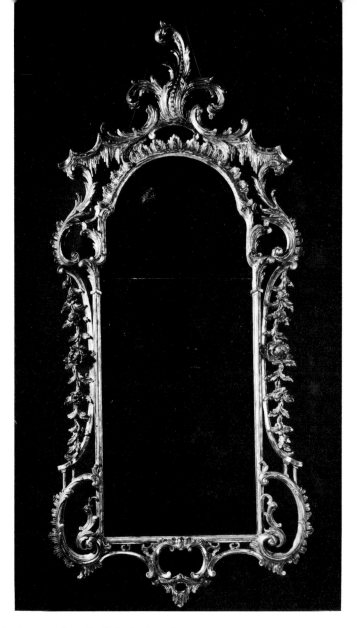

A Chippendale period carved and gilded pier glass   Circa 1755

Width 33ins. (84cm) Height 71½ ins. (181.5cm)

In spite of the fact that many of the technical problems of producing mirror plates had long been overcome, mirrors remained among the most expensive and prized items of furniture. This was partially because of the high cost of producing and silvering the glass satisfactorily and also the reimposition of an excise on mirror plates in 1740. For example, in 1769 Chippendale procured for the Earl of Mansfield at Kenwood two plates 74 by 44 inches at a cost of £69 10s. each, while the charge for the frames was only £16. Like many others at this time, these plates were probably imported from France. Consequently it seems to have been a not uncommon practice for earlier plates to be reused in new frames to bring them up to date. Bills at Petworth in Sussex show this kind of updating of furniture in the rococo style by the firm of Norman and Whittle, while even the Royal accounts have evidence of it in the case of mirrors.

A similar situation is probably the case here, since the shaping and proportions of the two abutting plates are very much of the Queen Anne period and may be compared with the example on p. 412, while the frame is emphatically rococo with several features in common with the previous example. The bold acanthus cresting and pendant flowers are particularly similar and here, added to the vocabulary, are the grottoesque icicles at the top and the slim pseudo-perspective angular columns that edge the lower plate, both of which are often encountered at this period.

A Chippendale period carved and gilded rectangular mirror   Circa 1760

Width 30½ins. (77.5cm) Height 58ins. (147.5cm)

The successful fusion of Western and Oriental motifs is well illustrated in this example. The design combines a light delicacy with a spiky liveliness that is far from overpowering. Thin gnarled tree trunks with leaf sprays loosely based on oak foliage writhe up the sides from rockwork bases, which in turn are linked to a central acanthus motif with C-scrolls. At the top is a finely carved pagoda-like building in which sits a Chinese figure on more rockwork. He is flanked with scrolls and foliage and trellis-work rising to plume-like leaf sprays.

Even at this period the treatment of mirrors still sometimes followed interior decoration and many elements of the cresting of this mirror and particularly the fine sweep of the acanthus canopy, and the similar one on p. 417, are to be found, for example, in Lightfoot's astonishing chinoiserie wood carving at Claydon House, Buckinghamshire.

A Chippendale period carved and gilded oval mirror   Circa 1760

Width 25ins. (63.5cm) Height 55½ins. (141cm)

The use of an heraldic crest on a mirror of this period is most unusual, although they are found occasionally on the cartouche crestings of mirrors made earlier in the century. The boldly carved gryphon's head must have been the crest of whoever commissioned the mirror to be made, although since several families made use of a similar motif, it is now impossible to tell who it might have been.

Mirrors of oval shape became popular from the middle of the century and designs for them are found in all the pattern books of this period. The curves lend themselves particularly well to all round flowing rococo decoration and obviate the need to negotiate corners. Here the frame is composed of foliage scrolls curling in every direction and yet forming a satisfying overall pattern with, either side of the cresting, rather singular icicle ornaments. The presence of the small figures of two hounds and a duck at the base of the mirror points to the influence of the carver Thomas Johnson who published his book *One Hundred and Fifty New Designs* in 1758 which included numerous similar figures, animal and human. The double C-scroll balustrade at the top of the mirror is another motif found in these designs.

A fine Chippendale period carved and gilded oval mirror Circa 1760

Width 31ins. (78.5cm) Height 53ins. (134.5cm)

Many of the motifs previously noted are again present here including a border of coquillage, acanthus scrolls and oak trees sprouting from rockwork bases. The trees have Chinese ho-ho birds perched on their branches. The cresting again takes the form of a fanciful building, approached in an almost baroque manner up steps with balustrading similar to that in the previous example, and topped with a foliate canopy of the type noted in the example on p. 419. Besides its very attractive design, the mirror excels in its carving. In places this is as much as 3½ ins. deep, superbly interlaced and undercut and finished with great crispness: a work of great skill.

On this, like most of the mirrors of the period, much of the gilding has had to be renewed. It is rare for any to survive in perfectly original state, especially in the lower areas which were within reach of maids as they cleaned. Even in the eighteenth century, Royal accounts show not infrequent repair and regilding of mirrors. In the same way it is usually impossible to say whether an old plate is original or not since, as the silvering became spotted and fogged with rust and damp, many were either renewed or resilvered.

A fine Ch'ien Lung period Chinese mirror painting in its original Chippendale period carved and gilded frame Circa 1760

Width 37½ins. (95.2cm) Height 59ins. (150cm)
Width of painting 23¼ins. (59cm) Height of painting 35¼ins. (89.5cm)

Some of the most exquisite survivals of the mid-eighteenth century are Chinese mirror paintings. It is a technique that has never been mastered with anything like the same skill or quality in the West. It would appear that mirror plates were shipped especially to the East for this reverse painting to be carried out and the results set often in carved and gilded frames for use in rooms decorated in the popular chinoiserie taste. This frame was clearly made specifically for the purpose with its internal moulded rectangle and subsidiary glass plates round the outside, with restrained edging foliage scrolls. It is interesting, however, that this, like many other examples, has no hint of chinoiserie decoration in its carving.

The painting, still in fine condition and with its splendid soft colouring of reds, blues, browns and greens very fresh, is carried out with utmost delicacy and feeling. It depicts an aristocratic young lady, her dress embroidered with the Imperial dragon (implying she is a member of the Emperor's family), with her attendant and an old man fishing in a romantic landscape. The minute detailing such as the birds and ducks is typical of the very finest work of this kind. The rockwork on which the fisherman sits and the gnarled tree trunk behind him are very similar in treatment to the carving of some of the recent mirrors discussed.

The piece was illus. on the front cover of The Connoisseur, *June 1973.*

One of a fine pair of Chippendale period carved and gilded girandoles Circa 1760

Overall width 28ins. (71cm) Height 44ins. (111.8cm)

The term girandole, which derives from an Italian term for a firework, was generally adopted in the mid-eighteenth century for this kind of elaborately carved wall sconce in French rococo taste. The notion of glittering light came from the fact that they generally have two scrolled candle arms which reflect light in both the gilded carving and the mirror plate back. The mirrors in the example shown opposite, right, are original although, in common with many, the carving is so exuberant that they are almost eclipsed by it. The highly asymmetrical composition of writhing foliage scrolls, coquillage and icicles is extremely finely carved and deeply cut, the introduction of architectural elements like the slender pagoda-topped structure being quite usual. The candle arms which are modelled on metal frames end in thin foliate gilt brass candle holders.

Designs for these fantastic creations appear in most of the contemporary pattern books with a wealth of variation and not dissimilar tall confections to these may be found in Chippendale, 1762, pl. CLXXVII, as well as in Ince and Mayhew and amongst Thomas Johnson's designs.

A fine Chippendale period rococo chimney piece

There are many examples in contemporary pattern books of overmantel mirrors carved in wood together in one design with the mantelpiece below them, but elaborate survivals like this one are rare. Chippendale gives his approbation in that a carver might ''give full scope to his capacity in the execution of these designs''.

The detail shows the superb quality of the carved pine and also how the wood, which would originally have been gilded, has been stripped at a later date. The mantelpiece is particularly elegantly wrought with bold curves and foliage curling over as brackets for the mantelshelf. Above, the scrolls and coquillage continue leading up to an oval plate surrounded with branches of oak bearing a wealth of clustered leaves and acorns, at the top of which perches a marvellously conceived eagle confronting the hound below. An old photograph of the mirror *in situ* shows further oak foliage above the eagle and a dead dog hanging from its beak. It is interesting to ponder whether this was lost by accident or design!

Some of the carved motifs, in particular the hound looking up to the eagle on the cresting, are probably taken from Chippendale, 1762, pls. CLXXXI and CLXXXII, and are also reminiscent of some of Thomas Johnson's designs.

Provenance: The Kemys-Tyntes family, Halswell Park, Somerset.

One of a pair of Chippendale period carved and gilded girandoles   Circa 1765

Width 26½ ins. (67.5cm) Height 44ins. (111.8cm)

Girandoles were probably always made in pairs and carving of such asymmetrical character as this has more meaning when the two complementary pieces are seen together. Nevertheless the design here, pierced through round the mirror plate rather than backed by it, is ingenious in conception and execution and very light in its effect. It incorporates, beneath the spirited acanthus cresting, a variety of foliage and flowers including bruised rushes framing the perspective pseudo-columns already noted on p. 418. The brass foliate candle holders at the end of the twisted branches are replacements.

A fine Chippendale period carved and gilded pier glass   Circa 1765

Width 60ins. (152.5cm) Height 9ft. 6ins. (290cm)

Still very much rococo in its handling, this mirror is typical of quite a large number of huge examples that were being commissioned, apparently regardless of cost, for the largest houses in the land during the 1760s. The carving of its foliage scrolls and naturalistic flowers and fruit is extremely crisply and richly done; typically, the division into plates of a manageable size is brought into part of the design, the band of berries and flowerheads across the centre concealing such a join.

There are several features of similarity with the work of John Linnell. A pier glass at Hopetoun House, Midlothian, illus. in Hayward and Kirkham, vol. II, fig. 210, has similar proportions with scrolls at the bottom corners and the same attractive way that sprays of flowers trail across the outer mirrored borders (cf. p. 423, left). It has a lower border of classical Vitruvian scroll where the present example has gadrooning and Linnell's drawing on which it is based, fig. 209, shows that it was intended to stand above a fully neo-classical pier table. Another feature used by Linnell more than his contemporaries is the cresting of a basket overflowing with flowers (e.g. figs. 186-8).

A Chippendale period carved and gilded oval mirror   Circa 1765

Width 27ins. (68.5cm) Height 39ins. (99cm)

This frame is of notably greater simplicity than recent examples, and yet it is extremely graceful. It is formed of two palm branches naturalistically intertwined and ribbon-tied at the top and bottom of the plate, their tips touching again off centre above this as an almost circular cresting. Foliage springs out in a lively fashion with small sprays of flowers and fig-like fruit appearing sporadically.

The treatment is similar, including the heels at the base of the branches, to that of some much larger mirrors designed by Robert Adam for Kedleston, Derbyshire, and two drawings of mirrors incorporating the same intertwined form by John Linnell are illus. in Hayward and Kirkham, vol. II, figs. 195 and 196. It may also be compared with one illus. in Fanfare for Europe, The British Art Market, *p. 156.*

A fine Chippendale period carved and gilded overmantel mirror   Circa 1765

Width 52ins. (132cm) Height 46ins. (117cm)

The adventurous but symmetrical design that gives this mirror such a satisfying appearance marks the transition between rococo extravagance and the return of classical order. Besides the tight foliage scrolls which still flick outwards to give an irregular outline, a number of new classical motifs are apparent. The fine and elegant scroll supports at the bottom corners divide and end in rinceau curls from which chins of bellflowers trail, while the cresting is topped with a large pierced anthemion. The two styles are most skilfully combined and set around a central oval which divides off numerous small sections of mirror glass.

The overall taste of this piece and some of the details are similar to an overmantel mirror made for Ramsbury Manor, Wilts., which is illus. in Edwards, vol. II, p. 348, fig. 100, while a slightly later drawing of similar form by John Linnell is reproduced in Hayward and Kirkham, vol. II, fig. 301.

Exhibition: C.I.N.O.A. International Art Treasures Exhibition, Victoria and Albert Museum, 1962, no. 135.

A Chippendale/Adam period carved and gilded oval mirror   Circa 1770

Width 32ins. (81.2cm) Height 53½ins. (136cm)

This is another example of the successful fusion of Chippendale period form, here of an oval mirror framed with fronds, with the more up-to-date vocabulary of the day. The plate is bordered with guilloche decoration above an anthemion and rosette motif from which curl leafy shoots, some of the foliage flicking over realistically, rising to a cresting which incorporates more rosettes and acanthus linking the fronds together. This is topped with a spray of wheat ears, fashioned on metal stems. The effect is comparable to the plumes of earlier days (cf. p. 413).

One of a pair of Adam period carved and gilded pier glasses   Circa 1775

Width 44¾ ins. (113.5cm) Height 67¼ ins. (171cm)

Along with classical mouldings and ornament, the Adam period saw the reappearance of rectangular outlines often, as here, shouldered in a similar manner to the example on p. 415 (left). Proportions increased in height and, although this example does have two bevelled plates framed with a beaded border, it was unusual for the central plate to be divided any more. Though prices seem to have remained extremely high, about this time a new process for casting mirror glass instead of blowing it was adopted from France and this made the production of huge pieces easier. The use of bevelling, which was unnecessary on complex rococo mirrors, is frequently found again.

The detailing of this mirror is restrained and very crisply carried out, including the outer mouldings which are carved with what the Linnells called 'water leaf and raffle tongue', raffle being a common contemporary term for acanthus. Outside this are fine acanthus scrolls on the lower half while, mounted on the border of glass within, are circular paterae, the upper ones suspending husk swags which, by crossing the mouldings, neatly tie the upper rectangular plates into the design. At the bottom is a spray of plumes and a semi-patera.

A comparison to this mirror may be made with several elements in an overmantel at the Victoria and Albert, illus. in Edwards, vol. II, p. 353, fig. 110.

A pair of small Adam period carved and gilded oval mirrors   Circa 1775

Width 15ins. (38cm) Height 38ins. (96.5cm)

In this fine pair of mirrors with trailing chains of bellflower there is a great feeling of lightness and delicacy in keeping with their size. The mouldings of beading and guilloche are thin and, as is found in some of Adam's later work, form concentric inner frames, glazed in between and joined to the outer with carved paterae with the same effect as the chair back on p. 66. Paterae are also used to space the bellflower chains from the frames. The chains hang from unusual trumpet-shaped crestings topped with anthemia from which hang lambrequins, a motif common in the late seventeenth century but not at this period (cf. p. 55). Below these are charming plaques of cherubs against painted green backgrounds within wreaths, the foliage of which is picked up at the bottom of the mirrors with pendant bellflowers to balance the whole concept in a remarkably successful manner.

An Adam period carved and gilded girandole

The double-framed oval mirror and the bracket beneath still have very much an Adam appearance, but much of the surround has a new fragile delicacy that could not have been achieved so effectively, if at all, in carved wood. This is due to new techniques that were adopted in answer to fashion, of making a framework for delicate scrolls and swags of metal wire on which the details were fixed, moulded in a special composition of resin, whiting and size before being gilded. Sometimes details were also fashioned in soft lead or pewter. Thus the spray of wheat ears rising from the urn (cf. p. 430), the very thin trails of leaves, the graceful scrolls beneath the plate and even the candle arms are made in this manner. The brass candle holders are later replacements.

The combination of an oval glass with a prominent horizontal bracket beneath from which candle branches sprout is one that originates amongst Adam's designs; e.g. The Works in Architecture, *1774, vol. I, no. 2, pl. VIII. An example with similarities to the present one is illus. in Musgrave, fig. 162. Hepplewhite, gives one design of 1787 on the same lines with similar trails above in pl. 115, but generally, in his and Sheraton's works, girandoles had become no more than wall sconces without mirrors.*

Sheraton, Drawing Book, *p. 416, writes of the soft lead or plaster detailing: "Persons unacquainted with the manufacturing part. . . may apprehend them to be slight and easily broken; but this objection vanishes, when it is considered that the scrolls are made of strong wire, and the ornaments cemented to them."*

Colour Plate 42.

A rare Ch'ien Lung period Chinese mirror painting in its original carved and gilded frame

Circa 1780

Width 36¼ins. (92cm) Height 24ins. (61cm)

This painting of great quality depicts a view across the river Thames to Radnor House, Twickenham, the home of the Pleydell-Bouverie family, Earls of Radnor. At this time extremely close copies were made from prints or drawings that were sent out to Canton as commissions and an engraving of this scene is recorded. It is interesting to see how influenced the owner of the house was by the chinoiserie style which was at this period not in the mainstream of fashion. This is shown in. the extraordinary mixture of lattice-work glazing bars in many of the windows, the timbering of the bridge to the left and the garden buildings, especially the substantial pagoda-like structure in the foreground.

The frame displays classical rather than Oriental influence, with a plain rectangular outline and carving of gadrooning and beading with guilloche and pierced rosettes in between.

A mirror painting of the same scene is illus. in Jourdain and Soane Jenyns, fig. 65.

Colour Plate 43.

One of a pair of Adam period carved and gilded oval mirrors Circa 1775

Width 20ins. (50.8cm) Height 50¼ins. (127.5cm)

Of similar form to the mirrors on p. 432, the elegant simplicity and slenderness of this design is very evident and again the workshop drawings of John Linnell provide close comparisons. The moulded frames carved with bands of beading, fluting and waterleaf, the urns above and ribbon bows from which trail long chains of bellflower round the edge of the mirror to foliage at the base, are all to be found in these drawings. All these motifs were probably however in quite current usage. The intricate crinkling of the bows is particularly finely represented. At the top and bottom of the frame the curled acanthus is still a vestige of the foliate canopies of which several examples were noted on earlier pieces.

See Hayward and Kirkham, vol. II, figs. 197-8, for comparisons of Linnell's drawings. The firm of Gillow's was still making frames of a similar style in 1788. The drawing and costing for one of varnished mahogany part gilt is reproduced in Cescinsky, 1911, vol. III, fig. 386.

A Sheraton period mahogany cheval mirror   Circa 1790

Width 23¼ ins. (59cm) Height 54ins. (137.2cm)

Cheval or full length mirrors became popular in the last decade of the century when there was also an increase in the production of toilet mirrors, probably simply as a result of vanity. They were known also as 'horse dressing glasses', but whether this derives from the four-legged frame or from a pulley or horse in the mechanism, is uncertain. In the *Cabinet Dictionary,* 1803, Sheraton describes them under 'Horse' as "a kind of tall dressing glass suspended by two pillars and claws" that "may when hung by two centre screws, be turned back or forward to suit the person who dresses at them. The standards are sometimes glued up hollow to admit a weight on each side equal to the glass and frame, by which means the glass is raised to any height the same as a sash window is."

The elegance and quality of this piece is exceptional, with much decorative use of boxwood lines and crossbanding, including delicate feather banding of mahogany on the uprights. The urn finials and stretcher are finely turned and the sweep of the legs, which end in scroll toes and tiny cylindrical feet, is particularly graceful.

Sheraton, Drawing Book, *gives a design and description in pl. XVII where, as in the present example, the weights are suspended on webbing to which is glued veneer as a tambour to conceal it neatly.*

A Sheraton period carved and gilded rectangular mirror   Circa 1790

Width 23ins. (58.5cm) Height 51½ins. (131cm)

Towards the end of the century there are comparatively few designs extant for hanging mirrors. Perhaps, partially because of a rise in the rate of excise on mirrors relative to their size, the trend was towards smaller ones. Hepplewhite's *Guide,* gives three plates dated 1787 of rectangular pier glasses stating that this shape is ''most in fashion at this time'', Sheraton's *Drawing Book* gives none and his *Cabinet Dictionary* mentions only the new fashion of convex mirrors. As is usually the case with convex mirrors, the concave pedimented top of the mirror above is surmounted by an eagle with wings spread. From its beak hang fine metal chains following the concave line to urn acroteria. These urns are of a fluted type typical of the period (cf. p. 433). Beneath are elongated reeded columns, with upright leaf capitals, which frame the rectangular plate, a frieze of naturalistic foliage sprays, and a band of waterleaf at the base. Such a return to architectural formulae, albeit in this attenuated manner, is frequently found at this date.

The pediment is hatched with a lattice design and has inset in the centre an oval of *verre églomisé,* or glass worked on the reverse side with gold leaf and oil paint which was then protected with varnish. This technique had come from the Continent in the late seventeenth century and is found on the border of some Queen Anne period mirrors. It was now returning briefly to fashion and Sheraton discusses it in some detail in the *Cabinet Dictionary* where he calls it ''back painting'', the same term as had been used for Chinese mirror painting.

MISCELLANEOUS

A fine George II period carved pine wood stand
Circa 1740

Height 57½ ins. (146cm)

Solidly carved stands were very much a feature of large Palladian houses in the second quarter of the century, being used to support candelabra, vases or statuettes. Some of these were derived from ancient Greek terms incorporating human busts or, as here, were adaptations using figures in a more baroque manner. This piece is made in three sections, the vase at the top, the boy and dolphin, and the pedestal base each of which fit together with pegs into a very skilfully conceived whole. Again, in the very classical vein which William Kent influenced so profoundly, the surface is stained dark to simulate bronze. The motifs, including acanthus, egg-and-dart, husks and large scale fluting, are all very typical of the date, as is the scale pattern used on the dolphin. All are carved boldly and by a very capable hand.

A Chippendale period mahogany torchère

Circa 1765

The refinement of this piece contrasts with the previous one. The conception is clearly an extension of the tripod table with a deeply dished circular top supported on a slender fluted column and tripod base. At the bottom of the column is a ring of guilloche and a section of long carved leaves while the top of the base is neatly edged with gadrooning. The base itself, with its elegant moulded legs ending in toes that scroll outwards and broad rectangular pads, is reminiscent of that on the table on p. 305 (bottom).

In common with the best small tripod tables and kettle stands, the top and base were made to unscrew. The original wooden threads are visible in the photograph and it is a tribute to the fine original state of the piece that these still grip tightly and have never been tampered with. As so many tripod tables have been made up from polescreens and other pieces married together, such a feature gives a valuable degree of assurance of authenticity.

A similar pair of torchères with almost identical toes was supplied by Chippendale to Ninian Home for Paxton House, Berwick-on-Tweed in 1774 for £3. 6s., see Gilbert, Chippendale, *vol. II, fig. 385.*

441

A Chippendale period mahogany reading stand   Circa 1760

Width of top 24ins. (61cm) Depth 17ins. (43.2cm) Height (min.) 30ins. (76.2cm)

Another variation on the use of tripods was the reading stand with a rectangular top which was hinged to rise on an adjustable easel support. The book ledge is held in place by two pegs and is removable so that when the top is laid flat the piece forms a not ill-proportioned tripod table. The baluster stem is brass-bound at the top and contains a stout centre core that rises on a ratchet system and can be screwed up securely with a nut in the required position. The legs are each formed as two opposing scrolls, with acanthus carving on the upper one and moulding below curling into scrolled toes on rectangular pads. This shaping is the reverse of that on the table on p. 302. The sides of the top scrolls have recessed panels and, like the piece on p. 302, there are single flutes between each leg. The stand, which by its nature is portable, retains its original small leather castors. It seems to have been quite usual at this period to read standing up.

Ince and Mayhew give a design of this type which they call a reading or music desk, pl. XXVI.

A set of Chippendale period mahogany hanging shelves   Circa 1760

Width 30½ ins. (77.5cm) Depth 8½ ins. (21.5cm) Height 35¼ ins. (89.5cm)

Lightweight hanging shelves were a good subject for the display of chinoiserie and less often Gothic pierced fretwork and motifs. Both Chippendale and Ince and Mayhew have a number of such designs showing considerable fanciful elaborations, some said to be for books and some for displaying china. The taste of this set is distinctly chinoiserie, with blind fret on the drawer fronts and sides and a pierced lattice pattern in the side supports. The three moulded shelves are attractively graduated in both height and depth with scrolled brackets at the bottom matched by smaller scrolls at the top. This fretwork, both in its design and its solid rounded form, is reminiscent of the back of the Cockpen armchair on p. 57. The three shallow drawers have fine mahogany linings and bear their original brass ring handles.

Provenance: The late Marjorie Wiggin Prescott, Belle Haven, Connecticut, U.S.A.

A small set of Chippendale period mahogany shelves   Circa 1760

Width 13¼ ins. (33.5cm)
Depth 7½ ins. (19cm)
Height 44¼ ins. (112.5cm)

These exceptionally narrow shelves are constructed of fine quality mahogany and have the unusual dual purpose of hanging on a wall or standing on a table against a wall. Again the base contains drawers bearing their original small ring handles. There is no back board. Below are waved aprons forming short bracket feet at the corners. The sides of the four shelves are pierced in square section with Chinese motifs based on the quatrefoil motif, the uprights rising to spade-shaped finials.

Provenance: Herbert Rothbarth, Checkenden Court, Checkenden, Reading, Berkshire.
The late Marjorie Wiggin Prescott, Belle Haven, Connecticut, U.S.A.

One of a small pair of Chippendale period carved and gilded brackets   Circa 1760

Width 8¾ins. (22.2cm) Depth 7¼ins. (18.5cm) Height 13ins. (33cm)

Like mirrors on a smaller scale, brackets gave a good deal of scope for rococo and chinoiserie enthusiasm. Smaller ones were commonly made in pairs so that the asymmetrical features could be balanced when they were hung on a wall. The contemporary design books give many examples, Chippendale terming them ''Brackets for Busts'', and Ince and Mayhew ''Brackets for Candles or Busts''. They were also often used for porcelain figures and vases. Thomas Johnson offers a selection with his customary penchant for animal, bird and human figures. The displayed eagles here face one another supporting rounded shelves edged with coquillage and perching on C-scrolls and foliage.

A bracket of the same sort of design is illus. in Edwards, vol. I, p. 119, fig. 12.

One of a rare pair of Chippendale period carved and gilded candelabra   Circa 1760

Width 17ins. (43.2cm) Height 20ins. (50.8cm)

Unlike the fragile details on later pieces which were modelled with wire and composition, at this period the twisting branches and leaves were carved from wood and it is most unusual for such delicacy to have survived on pieces which, by their portable nature, are more susceptible to damage than those which could be hung on walls. The style of the gnarled tree and branches rising from the rockwork base embellished with C-scrolls is much like that found on a number of mirrors and girandoles (such as those on pp. 421 and 426). The two candle arms end in gilt brass foliate holders, while on a further branch in the centre perches a parrot-like bird. The pair are very nearly mirror images of one another allowing for all the minor discrepancies that are the hallmarks of, and give so much charm to, hand-carved work.

Provenance: Sir Mark Pleydell, Bt., Coleshill House, Berkshire, where they are recorded on the mantelpiece in the library before 1889.
The 2nd Earl of Radnor.
The late Miss M.E. Pleydell-Bouverie.
The late Marjorie Wiggin Prescott, Belle Haven, Greenwich, Connecticut, U.S.A.

An Adam period carved and gilded wall bracket   Circa 1775

Of similar feeling to the next piece, the rams' heads and hoof feet here are connected by three extremely slender curved and moulded supports, linked at the centre with a band of fluting. The centre lion's head is a variation and has, behind it, an added flared support in the manner of fan vaulting. The shelf is of shaped semi-circular outline, edged with waterleaf carving and decorated on the underside with unusual radiating crinkling like pleated silk. At the base is a breakfront panelled plinth applied with paterae.

The overall form is similar to that of a console table derived from an early eighteenth century French and English type which Adam developed for example in a design for a ''Table-frame for Sir Laurence Dundas Baronet'' of 1765, which was executed in two versions probably by Samuel Norman. One is illus. in Edwards, vol. III, p. 296, fig. 63. The lesser pressures of weight on the bracket facilitate a more elegant and successful design in comparison. Another supplied by Chippendale to Harewood House in 1769 is shown on the same page.

One of an outstanding pair of Adam period carved pine and limewood torchères with contemporary candelabra

Circa 1775

Height of torchère 56¾ ins. (144cm) Height of candelabra 21½ ins. (54.5cm)

Stripped at a later date to the natural wood, these would have originally been, as Sheraton writes of candle stands, "sometimes...finished in white and gold, and sometimes all gold, to suit the other furniture". Nevertheless nothing of the imposing quality of superbly sensitive carving has been lost. Again quoting Sheraton, *Drawing Book,* p. 416, candle stands "are used in drawing-rooms, for the convenience of affording light to such parts of the room where it would neither be ornamental nor easy to introduce any other kind". This form, based on Greek and Roman bronze tripods for incense burning, was one that was much favoured by Robert Adam. The rams' heads are taken from classical models, although the idea of turning them to face inwards at the ends of scrolls, leaf carved to resemble horns, is ingenious, the shape being the basis of the Ionic capital. Continuing the theme, cloven hooves appear on the concave triangular plinth base.

The detail shows the great skill of the carver, particularly in the layered foliage. A very similar, possibly the same, hand was responsible for the pair of two branch candelabra which are carved with tall scrolling leaves of just the same type. These reached us through a different source but they may have started life together with the torchères.

There are not dissimilar examples of torchère engraved in Adam, *particularly in vol. III, 1822, pl. VIII, which were designed for the Marquis of Bute at Luton Hoo in 1772. A pair of gilded tripod candle stands almost certainly by him at Osterley Park, Tomlin, p. 46, make use of similar decoration such as beading on the curved uprights, fluting, acanthus, Vitruvian scrolls and waterleaf. An identical gilded torchère is illus. in Musgrave, fig. 147.*

Exhibition: National Museum of Wales, Cardiff.

One of a pair of early Sheraton period carved and gilded wall sconces   Circa 1790

This a fine example of that very fragile taste of the end of the eighteenth century which Sheraton shows on sconces that he calls girandoles in the *Accompaniment to the Drawing Book.* The style, with its thinly-drawn scrolls and long crinkled feather-like leaves, owes much to Roman and Renaissance grotesque decoration which Robert Adam brought back into fashion. The method of construction of the more delicate parts using wire and composition, has already been discussed with reference to the example on p. 433. The introduction of a displayed eagle as a cresting and brass chains, here suspending carved tassels, is also very typical of this time (cf. p. 438). The eagle motif continued as a popular one for mirrors through the Regency period but at this stage the emphasis was on lightness. The slender centre upright is treated in a variety of ways, tapering and fluted in the lower half to end in a pine cone finial. From its centre three candle arms, which retain their original gilt metal holders and drip pans, scroll downwards, while corresponding curls scroll under and over above like rinceau, terminating in matching paterae.

See Sheraton, Accompaniment, *pl. 4, for similar examples of girandoles (sconces).*

Provenance: Lord Burnham, Hall Barn, Beaconsfield, Buckinghamshire.

An early Hepplewhite period mahogany wash stand   Circa 1775

Width 15½ ins. (39.5cm) Depth 14¾ ins. (37.5cm) Height 32ins. (81.2cm)

The wash stand as a distinct piece of furniture appeared about the middle of the eighteenth century, generally either on a tripod or four-legged base. It had a circular hole in the top in which a basin was inserted, and below usually one or two drawers, and a circular platform for an ewer of water. As Sheraton says in the *Cabinet Dictionary,* 1803, the stretcher should not be less than 13ins. from the underside of the drawer "to allow sufficient height for the bottle". In the last quarter of the century much ingenuity was exercised in concealing the purpose of wash stands, but the earlier ones tend to stand for what they are and are often treated with much elegance.

This is a particularly good example and its dark patinated surface is evident in the photograph. By the nature of their use such pieces tended to suffer a lot of water damage so that a surface in fine condition is unusual. The serpentine moulded top has, besides the basin rim, two other depressions, probably for soap. Beneath is an attractively shaped apron and four moulded supports that rise from a shelf with a drawer that bears its original buckle handle. The slender cabriole legs, graceful and keeled in section in the French manner, curve downwards from a second, differently shaped, apron and are joined by stretchers that rise to the centre platform.

A rare Sheraton period mahogany double Canterbury   Circa 1790

Width 33ins. (83.8cm) Depth 12¼ins. (31cm) Height 20½ins. (52cm)

The Canterbury was another apparently eponymous piece of furniture devised towards the end of the century. Sheraton's *Cabinet Dictionary,* 1803, notes that the term "has of late years been applied to some pieces of cabinet work, because, as the story goes, the bishop of that see first gave orders for these pieces". He adds that the term was used both for a supper tray to stand by a table like a dumb waiter and for "a small music stand, with two or three hollow topped partitions, framed in light slips of mahogany, about three inches apart from each other, and about 8 inches deep, for holding music books. These sometimes have a small drawer. The legs are made of 1⅛ mahogany, turned or plain, tapered, with castors, and are adapted to run in under a piano-forte".

The Canterbury illustrated here follows the same lines with certain adaptations. Because of its unusual length it has not been fitted with castors but with brass carrying handles at each end. The three dividers are slatted, while the sides have turned tapered column supports which balance the legs by tapering the other way. There are two drawers with fiddle-back mahogany fronts and scribed edges. The brass handles are replacements, as on most Canterburies, having probably originally been fitted with turned wooden knobs.

A sketch and estimate, £1 8s., for a 'Japan'd satinwood' example of the single type appears in the Gillow Estimate and Sketch Books for 1793 and is illus. in Fastnedge, pl. 92.

Colour Plate 44. A pair of early Regency period polescreens, c.1800.
The screens are described on p. 462.

An unusual set of Sheraton period satinwood bed steps   Circa 1790

Width 16ins. (40.5cm) Depth 28¾ins. (73cm) Height 32ins. (81.2cm)

These narrow and fine quality steps are a neat compromise between a bedside cupboard and steps to get into a high bed. They are made in three tiers with a low galleried top, the upper tier being a pot cupboard opened by an ingenious catch operated by the pin inside the keyhole. The door is flanked by slender columns turned in rosewood. Below are two treads, relined with leather, and a mahogany-lined drawer retaining its original brass handle. The upper panels of satinwood on the front and sides and the edges of each tier are crossbanded with tulipwood with very thin lines of boxwood and harewood. The steps are supported on four turned tapered feet.

An unusual small set of Sheraton period turned mahogany library steps   Circa 1800

Width 16ins. (40.5cm) Depth 16ins. (40.5cm) Height 30ins. (76.2cm)

The form of these two-tread steps with their diagonally placed guard-rails at the top is not dissimilar to some of the elaborately turned chairs that were made in the seventeenth century and earlier. The art of turning on a lathe is a very ancient one, reel and bobbin turning, as this type is known, being developed particularly in oak in the second half of the seventeenth century. Its revival here in mahogany is uncommon but nevertheless most attractive, especially patinated to a beautiful colour as it is. The design fits extremely well the need for simple yet strong construction.

Provenance: The late Mrs. Marjorie Wiggin Prescott, Belle Haven, Greenwich, Connecticut, U.S.A.

Colour Plate 45. A pair of ormolu-mounted Blue John and white marble perfume burners, c.1774.
The pieces are described on p. 477.

A Sheraton period mahogany metamorphic library steps/table attributed to Francis Hervé

Circa 1790

Table: Width 22ins. (56cm) Depth 40ins. (102cm) Height 33¾ins. (86cm)
Steps: Depth 62ins. (157.5cm) Height 91ins. (231cm)

Another field in which much ingenuity was exercised during the second half of the eighteenth century was that of library steps with numerous designs to transform them into tables, chairs and stools. In the *Appendix to the Drawing Book,* 1793, Sheraton gives two such designs, one being on similar lines to the present example (shown overleaf). He says that it was "taken from steps that have been made by Mr. Campbell, Upholster to the Prince of Wales. They were first made for the King, and highly approved of by him, as every way answering the intended purpose. There are other kinds of library steps which I have seen, made by other persons, but, in my opinion, these must have the decided preference, both as to simplicity and firmness when they are set up. The steps may be put up in half a minute, and the whole may be taken down and enclosed within the table frame in about the same time."

The brass button on the side, which releases the top, is visible in the photograph. The hinged top folds right over, having the lower three treads fixed on its underside. When closed these fit between the upper treads, which themselves rise on an easel support, the chamfered hand rails and supports unfolding ingeniously and latching into place. The whole is made of fine solid mahogany and remains in excellent original condition, including the plate castors.

In discussing his second model for steps, Sheraton makes an interesting observation on the patenting of designs which reflects on the many different types of dining table which appeared early in the nineteenth century (see p. 278). Both models, he says, "have obtained a patent; yet any part being materially altered, will evade the act, though the whole be nearly the same." This is clearly what Francis Hervé did. He is recorded as active between 1783 and 1796 at 32 Lower John Street, Tottenham Court Road and was a well-known cabinet maker in his day providing furniture for Althorp and over £3,000 worth to the Prince of Wales at Carlton House, where, as Sheraton noted, Robert Campbell, the patentee of his first design for folding library steps was also employed.

Sheraton, Appendix, illus. these designs on pl. V. A set of metamorphic steps bearing Hervé's inscribed label and almost exactly matching these are at the Victoria and Albert. Another, unlabelled, from Heveningham Hall, Suffolk, is illus. in Edwards, vol. II, p. 290, fig. 13.

A metamorphic library steps/table described on p. 457.

A Regency period mahogany metamorphic library steps/chair attributed to Morgan and Sanders and sold by Thomas Weeks

Circa 1810

Width 21¾ins. (55.2cm) Height of chair 35¾ins. (91cm) Height of steps 29ins. (73.5cm)

In July 1811 Ackermann's *Repository* published an illustration of a 'Library Chair' of precisely this type, made by Morgan and Sanders of Catherine St., Strand, see p. 278. They claim it to be "the best and handsomest article ever yet invented, where two complete pieces of furniture are combined in one — an elegant and truly comfortable armchair and a set of library steps". The mechanism is extremely simple, the chair being hinged at the front seat rail so that when it is released by pressing brass buttons each side it folds forward to form four treads, the top ones supported on the wide curved top rail. The whole is made of fine faded mahogany with figured veneer on the top rail and reeding on its border, on the scrolled arms, uprights, seat rails and sabre legs. The seat is caned and the inserts on the treads have been releathered.

The brass catch on one side is inscribed with the name of Thomas Weeks, Titchborne Street, London. Weeks established an eccentric sounding museum of 'mechanical curiosities' at 3-4 Titchborne Street in about 1797. Attached to it was a shop where it seems the public could purchase examples of the variety of furniture and ornaments on display. He probably commissioned work from several London firms, among which were these steps/chairs from Morgan and Sanders. Sheraton throws a little light on such practices when he says, of evading the patent on the steps discussed in the last plate: "those masters...who do not think it worth their while to be at the trouble of introducing any essential alteration in them may have these steps from Mr. Robert Campbell and Son, Mary-le-bone Street, London, with a sufficient allowance for selling them again."

A library steps/chair in the library at Trinity College, Oxford, illus. in Edwards, vol. II, p. 291, is identical except that it is not fitted with catches.

A fine pair of Sheraton period globes on mahogany stands   Circa 1790

Diameter 17ins. (43.2cm) Height 39ins. (99cm)

With parts of the world still being charted there was a great interest in cartography during the eighteenth century and many libraries had revolving globes mounted on stands which turned them into both functional and decorative pieces. The globes were usually made in pairs, one depicting the earth's surface and one the heavens, with paper covers which were stuck on to wooden spheres. When new discoveries were made globes could be brought up to date with a new cover, which was probably so in the present case. Both are inscribed by W. & S. Jones, Holborn, London, the celestial on the right being dated 1800 and the terrestrial 1802, while the stands, which are eminent examples of elegant design, may well date from at least ten years earlier. Their proportions and form are not dissimilar to the table on p. 325. The globes themselves are not large and they rest in rings edged with boxwood stringing, each supported on three very slender reeded tapered legs joined by a finely moulded arched stretcher. This is topped by an original urn finial which balances the one in the centre of the globe support above. The brass castors with flush sockets are original.

A pair of early Regency period globes on mahogany stands   Circa 1800

Diameter 24ins. (61cm) Height 41ins. (104cm)

Because its form was both attractive and functional in supporting the framework, the tripod base remained traditional for globes for a long time. These are made from particularly fine tight-grained mahogany and display several tendencies of the period with reeding on the edge of the horizon circles, complex but by no means heavy turning on the stems, and graceful ogee legs ending in spade feet and plate castors. The stands and the globes remain in excellent condition. As in the previous example the terrestrial globe has probably been recovered since it is dated 1807 while the celestial one is 1800. Both are inscribed as made by W. and J.M. Bardin and supplied by A. Wellington, Crown Court, Soho, London.

A rare pair of early Regency period polescreen/tables

Circa 1800

Width of tops 13ins. (33cm) Depth of tops 16½ins. (42cm) Height 28ins. (72.5cm)

With open fires normally as the only source of heating in houses, screens of various types were much used to protect people sitting nearby from the direct heat, particularly since a lot of easily melted wax was used in the making of cosmetics. The last twenty years of the eighteenth century saw a wide variety of polescreens often of elegant proportions and usually on tripod bases with small screens adjustable in height. The unusual type illustrated here and as Colour Plate 44, p. 453, where the screens are hinged to blocks at the tops of the stems and can be fixed in a horizontal position by means of catches in the manner of tilt-top tripod tables, is yet another tribute to the ingenuity of the age. The proportions work most successfully.

The octangular tops retain their original decoration of confronting classical chariots in the heavens, finely painted *en grisaille* within a blue border. The edges are cockbeaded. The bases are very slender and well formed with baluster stems carved with rope twist and a gentle sweep into the tall tripod splay legs which rest on ball feet. It is notable that the direction of the rope twist is opposite in each case. The gilding which contrasts with the black paint has been restored.

A not dissimilar screen, which has apparently been converted into a table later, is at Temple Newsam House, Leeds, see Gilbert, Furniture at Temple Newsam, *etc., vol. II, no. 318.*

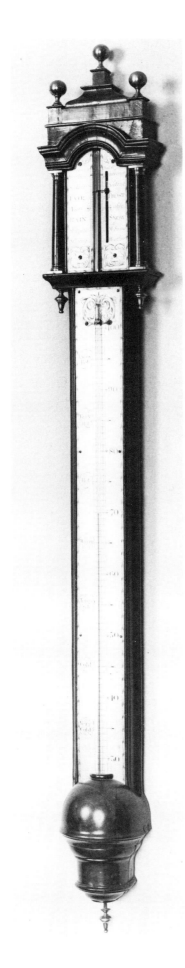

A Queen Anne period walnut stick barometer

Circa 1710

Height 41½ ins. (105.5cm)

Initially barometers were developed by leading clockmakers, so it is not surprising that the form on which many barometers, such as this one, were based was that of a longcase clock. This has a particularly elaborate and finely moulded hood section with an arched cornice and three original ball finials on top. The silvered brass plates are finely engraved, with barometer scale and pointer at the top flanked by wooden pillars with brass capitals and bases and a thermometer mounted on the trunk. The side edges are moulded and the turned cistern cover at the bottom is original.

This type of barometer, developed towards the end of the seventeenth century, relies on the pressure of the atmosphere on a column of mercury in a sealed tube rising from a cistern at the base. It was improved upon about 1700 by the introduction of a screw device which, when tightened, prevented the infiltration of air into the tube and made the barometer portable. This is the purpose of the brass finial beneath the cistern.

Many barometers at this date, unlike later ones, are unsigned. Such is the case here, although its quality and style are similar to the work of one of the best known makers of his day, and perhaps the first to specialise in the manufacture of barometers, John Patrick. He worked at Jewin St. and later Ship St., Old Bailey, London between about 1686 and 1720.

An advertisement of Patrick's meteorological instruments dating from c.1710 and illus. in Goodison, 1969, pl. 8, shows some similar examples. Another similar anonymous specimen is included in Edwards vol. I, p. 27, fig. 4.

A fine Chippendale period mahogany striking bracket clock
by Edward Houlgrave, London
Circa 1765

Width 12¼ ins. (31cm) Depth 7¾ ins. (19.8cm) Height 20½ ins. (52cm)

As a furniture dealer Norman Adams chose clocks not so much for their rare movements but for the quality of the cases. All too often fine walnut and mahogany cases have been spoilt by over-restoration and over-cleaning. This example retains a deeply patinated surface and also the unusual feature of beautifully formed urn-shaped finials carved in wood instead of the more normal brass. This is true also of the other areas of carving: the acanthus cresting to the bell top, the pendant oak foliage and blind fret on the chamfered corners, the pierced fret panels as well as the mouldings of ribbon and stick, bead, and dart. The pierced floral spandrels, along with the moulded ogee bracket feet and carrying handles either side, are, however, made of brass.

The arched silvered face applied with gilded rococo spandrels is signed E. Evargluoh, London. Houlgrave is recorded as a watchmaker in Liverpool in 1764 about which time he was made bankrupt, moved to London and thereafter signed his name in reverse.

See Baillie, p. 159.

A Chippendale period mahogany and walnut striking longcase clock by Thomas Helm, Ormskirk Circa 1765

Width 22ins. (56cm)
Depth 9¼ins. (23.5cm)
Height 87½ins. (222cm)

This very shallow and well-proportioned clock has a fine mellow patina and displays many points of quality which are surprisingly often found on provincially-made cases. Only perhaps the mixture of timbers mark it as not a London-made piece. The mouldings of the broken pediment and those between the trunk and plinth are particularly deeply and well shaped, as are the four small ogee bracket feet on which it stands. The friezes at the top and bottom of the hood have chinoiserie inspired blind fret, showing the influence of contemporary fashionable pattern books. The four slender fluted Doric columns, with wooden capitals and bases, continue a tradition that goes far back into the seventeenth century; they are matched by engaged quarter columns, again with wooden capitals and bases, at the angles of the trunk. The corners of the plinth are chamfered and flank a shaped square fielded panel of mirrored walnut.

The face follows the traditional type with gilded pierced spandrels, silvered chapter and seconds rings and a calendar aperture. It is signed Helm, Ormskirk. He is recorded as working in 1761 and as repairing the town clock in Ormskirk, Lancashire, in 1770.

See Baillie, p. 149; Britten, p. 680.

465

A Hepplewhite period mahogany repeating bracket clock by Robert Underwood, London

Circa 1780

The bell-topped rectangular form remained the most popular for bracket clocks through most of the eighteenth century. This is another example, plainer than the previous bracket clock, but in a case veneered with beautifully coloured and figured mahogany and in unusually original condition. The brass spandrels, still rococo in feeling, are finely cast, and the carrying handle, pine cone finials and squat ogee bracket feet are also brass. The arched face is silvered and shows the tendency by this date towards a more simplified form without a superimposed chapter ring or further applied spandrels. The detail shows the back plate charmingly engraved with a patera, foliage scrolls and a female bust wearing a coolie hat.

R obert Underwood was a member of a family of clockmakers working in the City of London. The name is recorded at Noble Street, near St. Pauls 1769-1808, and at 3 Falcon Street 1769-1810.

See Baillie, p. 321; Britten, p. 760.

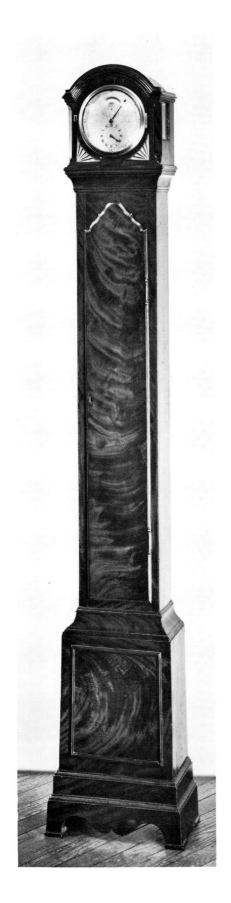

A rare Hepplewhite period small mahogany longcase clock by Willam Bull, Stratford, London   Circa 1785

Width 12½ ins. (31.8cm)
Depth 7ins. (17.8cm)
Height 66½ ins. (169cm)

In *The Longcase Clock* (p. 438), Tom Robinson terms a clock with a height of less than 6ft. a 'grandmother clock' and says that "with very few exceptions those now in existence were produced in the last hundred years". The height restricts the fall of the weights so that a normal eight-day movement has difficulty in running its full time and a normal pendulum would strike the sides of the narrow trunk. To overcome this, this clock incorporates a very rare three wheel, two pinion movement. The case is extremely slender and veneered in beautifully figured and coloured mahogany with a moulded arched top and inlaid fan spandrels below a brass bezel that surrounds the circular silvered face. The plinth is subtly tapered to increase stability with a double skirting, the lower one shaped at the front.

Britten records only two other movements of this type, one by James Ferguson the celebrated astronomer and the other by John Smeaton who probably designed it in collaboration with Dr. Franklin. Bull is recorded in Baillie, p. 45, as working between 1770 and 1804, two bracket clocks made by him being illus. in Cescinsky and Webster.

Provenance: The late Mr. Bernard Baruch.

Exhibition: The Metropolitan Museum of Art, New York, loaned by Mr. Baruch.

A fine Sheraton period balloon bracket clock by Benjamin Vulliamy, London, and bracket

Circa 1795

Width 13ins. (33cm) Height of clock 24ins. (61cm) Total height 40ins. (102cm)

The elegantly waisted balloon shape was favoured by some clockmakers towards the end of the century. This case is of extremely good quality, as befits a clock by a member of one of the most important family of makers of the time. Like the flared bracket, which is original, it is veneered with patinated satinwood and crossbanded with kingwood edged with boxwood and ebony stringing. On to this a Medusa head on the front and foliage sprays and swags at the sides are finely painted in cream *en grisaille,* giving a convincing three-dimensional *trompe-l'oeil* effect. The mouldings of the base are likewise painted with bands of waterleaf, bead and ribbon, and inlaid fluting interspersed with painted paterae. The cresting, topped with an urn, also has foliage decoration. Around the enamelled face the bezel is of brass, as are the ogee bracket feet and the pine cone finial at the bottom of the bracket.

The movement is signed by Benjamin Vulliamy (fl.1775-1820) who inherited his father Justin's workshop in Pall Mall (see p. 470) and in consequence the royal appointment to King George III.

The Bank of England has a mantel clock, the movement also by Vulliamy, the case of which is similarly veneered and painted with a Medusa head, swags and tall leaves, probably by the same hand. At the same institution is a most unusual balloon pedestal clock, the movement of which dates from about 1820 (by Brockbank and Atkins), but the case is earlier and the balloon top handled in an almost identical fashion to the present one with different painted detail. These are illus. in Edwards vol. II, pp. 102-3, figs. 64 and 68. Also in this group are a balloon clock which Norman Adams Ltd. has handled, the movement this time by Upjohn of Bond St. and another sold by Christie's at Godmersham Park, June 6-9, lot 212, the movement again by Vulliamy. It would appear that these were the product of a highly skilled clock casemaker who supplied a number of different London clockmakers.

Provenance: Mrs. Dudley Cory-Wright.
The late Mrs. Marjorie Wiggin Prescott, Belle Haven, Greenwich, Connecticut, U.S.A.

A rare Chippendale period mahogany wheel barometer attributed to Justin Vulliamy, Pall Mall, London Circa 1770

Width 11¼ins. (29cm) Depth 3¾ins. (9.5cm) Height 49ins. (124.5cm)

The principle of the wheel barometer was invented soon after the Restoration by Robert Hooke but it was not developed as a substitute for the stick barometer until the middle of the eighteenth century. The idea was to transmit the movement of mercury in a tube to a pointer on a dial by means of a glass float, pulley and counterweight system, thereby allowing the taking of more accurate readings on an enlarged scale. The fact that by the close of the eighteenth century the form had become much the most popular one for barometers is, however, due less to seeking after accuracy than to the appeal of the elegant shapes that were developed for the cases.

In this example the influence of the clockmaker's craft is evident, both internally and externally in the circular brass face with its finely pitted surface and the applied silvered scale rings and gilt rococo spandrels set in a square frame. The large dial allows readings of up to ⅟₃₀₀in., and during one revolution the small dial moves through 120 degrees. The detail of the movement shows the presence of finely adjusted friction rings to steady the pointer and, in the other detail, the two recording hands which mark the extremes to which the pointer has moved since the last reading was taken. Although it is not signed, the attribution is made on the basis of two barometers clearly from the same workshop, both of which are recorded as being made by Vulliamy (fl.1730-c.1790). One of these at Nostell Priory, Yorkshire, was supplied by Chippendale in 1769 for £25, although the design of the case was not his. The case of the other, in the Royal Library at Windsor Castle, is clearly from the same workshop as the present example, although it has added elaboration. Both are of the same form, made from fine quality mahogany with fielded panelled doors above and below mounted with hygrometers and thermometers respectively. At the top and bottom is finely carved acanthus foliage, that at the top having lost its finial in this case. This carving is strikingly similar to work produced by William Vile and John Bradburn whose many royal commissions make an attribution to the latter quite likely (cf. p. 382).

See Goodison, N., 'Clockmaker and Cabinet-Maker', Furniture History, *1966, p. 18, pl. XVI; Goodison N., 'A Clockmaker's Barometer',* The Connoisseur, *June 1975, p. 138.*

A rare Hepplewhite period mahogany wheel barometer by John Whitehurst, Derby
Circa 1785

Diameter 14ins. (35.5cm)
Height 42¾ins. (108.5cm)

This development of the wheel barometer, which in shape is more like a banjo than most later pieces so called, is distinctive of the work of Whitehurst. The silvered dial is engraved with precision and has a very fine steel pointer and recording hand which is operated by a knob at the right hand side. The case is made of hard and dark mahogany, deeply patinated and crisply carved. The stem of semi-circular section, which is hollowed out behind to house the tube, takes the form of a classical column shaped with distinct entasis, and a capital of fluting and acanthus. The finial above is probably a replacement for an original urn, this feature being missing from most examples in this group of barometers. The bezel and moulded frame round the plate are elaborately carved with various forms of beading and foliage, the bezel on a number of other examples being left undecorated apart from the pearl beaded edge. Finally, to break the rather severe classical lines, acanthus scrolls are applied at the foot of the column.

John Whitehurst the Younger, 1761-1834 continued in his uncle's business at 22 Irongate, Derby, after the latter moved to London in 1775.

See Goodison, 1969, pp. 261-2 and a similar example on pl. 158; another in the Irwin Untermyer Collection is illus. in Hackenbroch, fig. 36; another from the Leidesdorf Collection was sold by Sotheby's 27-8 June, 1974, lot 158.

A fine Adam period cut glass chandelier   Circa 1785

Width 30ins. (76.2cm) Height 44ins. (111.8cm)

Chandeliers are notoriously difficult to photograph but the effect achieved here shows up extremely well the dramatic effect of light on the shallow cutting and faceting and the attractive grey tone of the finest eighteenth century lead glass. This example is both small and very well proportioned without the ostentatious exuberance which sometimes hides the structure in a mass of trailing droplets and scrolling arms.

A number of aspects tie in its style with that of contemporary furniture. The effect of neo-classical taste is evident in the urn shape in the stem, the bands of paterae finely cast in brass and the swags of drops, the shape of which is reminiscent of bellflowers. The shaped canopy at the top with its lambrequin edging recalls some of the crestings noted on rococo mirrors (e.g. p. 421), while the effect of the wrythen cutting on the urn is similar to that of spiral fluting on tripod tables. The chandelier has eight elegantly faceted arms.

A pair of ormolu-mounted Blue John candle vases by Matthew Boulton   Circa 1771

Height 12ins. (30.5cm)

Matthew Boulton, 1728-1802, in partnership with John Fothergill at his workshops at Soho near Birmingham, developed the design and manufacture of ormolu mounts during the 1770s with such accomplishment and commercial skill that he was widely regarded as the leading producer in both England and Europe. In 1772 the Empress Catherine of Russia called his pieces "superior in every respect to the French". He was naturally influenced by French models but, in typical English taste, sought a greater simplicity and elegance than that of typical French work which he himself called *trop chargé*. This, coupled with the superb quality of the chasing and finishing, gave him a reputation which is still just as valid today.

These factors are very apparent in these examples. Boulton was especially keen on the use of Blue John, the fluorspar from Castleton in Derbyshire, each piece of which was carefully chosen for its particularly variegated purple and yellow effect. On to these bodies the mounts were very carefully pinned or screwed, often with twenty or more sections exactly fitted together. The guilloche bands round the stepped bases were stamped out in copper and then, like all the mounts, fire gilded. These, as with lions' heads, laurel swags and other classical motifs, may be compared to other products of the firm. The lids are reversible to become candle sockets when they are inverted.

This form of vase relates to a design in Boulton and Fothergill's Pattern Book I, see Goodison, 1974, fig. 161r. The same vases are illus. as fig. 109 and other similar pieces in adjacent plates. The lids here are very similar to those in figs. 114-5.

A large pair of ormolu-mounted Blue John candle vases by Matthew Boulton　　　Circa 1772

Width of base 3¾ ins. (9.5cm)　Height 12½ ins. (31.8cm)

The finely coloured ovoid bodies of these examples (shown overleaf) are unusually large among Boulton's work. Pattern Book I gives a very close comparison. This has similar scrolled foliage handles, a flared fluted base and even a lid of the same form. Like the previous examples, these lids are reversible as candle holders. The appeal of this combination of ornament and utility was highly thought of by Boulton, as by his French rivals. The detail shows the splendid quality of the chiselling of the sand cast mounts with contrasting matt and burnished areas.

Goodison, 1974, fig. 163, illus. the example in Pattern Book I. It is interesting that in figs. 126-8, Goodison illus. the same lids combined with candle sockets of a different shape. A very similar pair of vases is illus. in Mulliner, fig. 166.

A pair of candle vases by Matthew Boulton described on p. 475.

A pair of ormolu-mounted Blue John and white marble perfume burners   Circa 1774

Height 9ins. (23cm)

Also shown as Colour Plate 45, p. 456. Another favourite form of vase was the perfume burner or cassolette to use its French name, although the purpose of this was much more decorative than functional. Nevertheless, the lids here are attractively pierced and the insides contain gilt copper liners. Of the range of designs that Boulton developed, this proved one of the most popular with its well-balanced proportions and slender loop handles. Sometimes the bodies of the vases were made of white marble like the plinths.

The making of ormolu was only one part of Boulton and Fothergill's business, which extended over a very wide range of metalwork of every description, from steel buckles and buttons in which the firm had its origins, to silver and plate, for which Boulton was instrumental in the establishment of the Birmingham Assay Office. Many of the decorative motifs found on the ormolu work were also found on silverware made at the same period.

Goodison, 1974, fig. 137 shows a silver candlestick made in 1774 which has a concave-sided square base decorated with guilloche and fitting on the flared stem above very similar to these vases. An identical pair of cassolettes appear as fig. 134 and one in fig. 136 dismantled. They relate, apart from the handles, to a design in Pattern Book I (fig. 161f).

A pair of ormolu-mounted white marble candelabra vases by Matthew Boulton   Circa 1775

Height 11½ ins. (29.2cm)

As the 1770s progressed, the use of white marble increased in Boulton's work, perhaps showing a tendency towards greater neo-classical refinement. This model, with detachable twin-scrolled candle arms, shows another variation on the vase theme. The unusual bands of delicate Vitruvian scrollwork and form of the concave-sided bases, as in the previous example decorated with guilloche, are again comparable with pieces of silver. The circular marble bases, bun feet and rings of beading below the drip-pans may be later additions but these do not in the least detract from the overall refinement.

For Boulton the development of ormolu ornaments was a means of making a name for himself in fashionable society. This he achieved both here and abroad, although financially the venture was a disaster because production costs were so high and consequently prices too high for a wide enough market. By the end of the 1770s the demand for the firm's work in this field had practically dried up. It is due to his great commercial skill and perseverance that the legacy of his work is so rich.

The Pattern Books provide a design for these vases including the portrait medallions, see Goodison, 1974, fig. 161i, and with the same handles in fig. 161m; the elegant candle branches are shown in fig. 164d. The pieces themselves are illus. as fig. 146.

BIBLIOGRAPHY
of works referred to in the text

Adam, R. & J., *The Works in Architecture,* 1778, 1786 and 1822 (3 vols.)

Baillie, G.H., *Watchmakers and Clockmakers of the World,* 1951

Brackett, O., *An Encyclopaedia of English Furniture,* 1927

Britten, F.J., *Old Clocks and Watches and Their Makers,* 1911

Cescinsky, H., *English Furniture of the Eighteenth Century,* 1911 (3 vols.)

Cescinsky, H., *The Old World House,* 1924 (2 vols.)

Cescinsky, H., *The Gentle Art of Faking Furniture,* 1931

Cescinsky, H., *English Furniture from Gothic to Sheraton,* 1937

Cescinsky, H., and Webster, M.R., *English Domestic Clocks,* 1914

Chippendale, T., *The Gentleman and Cabinet-Maker's Director,* 1754 (1st) and 1762 (3rd) eds.

Clifford-Smith, H., *Buckingham Palace,* 1931

Coleridge, A., *Chippendale Furniture,* 1968

Edwards, R., *The Dictionary of English Furniture,* 1954 ed. (3 vols.)

Edwards, R., *The Shorter Dictionary of English Furniture,* 1964

Edwards, R., and Jourdain, M., *Georgian Cabinet Makers,* 1955

Fanfare for Europe — The British Art Market, 1973

Fastnedge, R., *Sheraton Furniture,* 1962

Gilbert, C., *Furniture at Temple Newsam House and Lotherton Hall,* 1978 (2 vols.)

Gilbert, C., *The Life and Work of Thomas Chippendale,* 1978 (2 vols.)

Goodison, N., *English Barometers 1680-1860,* 1969

Goodison, N., *Ormolu: The work of Matthew Boulton,* 1974

Hackenbroch, Y., *English Furniture in the Collection of Irwin Untermyer,* 1958

Harris, M., *Old English Furniture,* 1946

Hayward, H., and Kirkham, P., *William and John Linnell,* 1980 (2 vols.)

Heal, Sir Ambrose, *The London Furniture Makers,* 1953

Hepplewhite, G., *The Cabinet Maker and Upholsterer's Guide,* 1788 (1st) and 1794 (3rd) eds.

Hinckley, F.L., *Directory of the Historic Cabinet Woods,* 1960

Hinckley, F.L., *A Directory of Queen Anne, Early Georgian and Chippendale Furniture,* 1971

Hope, T., *Household Furniture and Interior Decoration,* 1807

Ince, W., and Mayhew, J., *The Universal System of Household Furniture,* 1759-62

Jones, W., *The Gentlemens or Builders Companion,* 1739

Jourdain, M., *The Furniture collection of Col. Mark Whitwell,* 1945

Jourdain, M., *Regency Furniture,* 1948

Jourdain, M., and Soane Jenyns, R., *Chinese Export Art,* 1950

Jourdain, M., and Rose, F, *English Furniture: The Georgian Period,* 1953

Macquoid, P., *A History of English Furniture:* Vol. 1, *The Age of Oak,* 1904; Vol. 2, *The Age of Walnut,* 1906; Vol. 3, *The Age of Mahogany,* 1908; Vol. 4, *The Age of Satinwood, 1908*

Mulliner, H.H., *The Decorative Arts in England (1660-1780),* [n.d.]

Musgrave, C., *Adam and Hepplewhite Furniture,* 1966

Redburn, S., *Furniture History, Vol. XIV,* 1978

Robinson, T., *The Longcase Clock,* 1981

Rogers, J.C., *English Furniture,* 1967

Shearer, T., et al., *The Cabinet-Makers' London Book of Prices and Designs of Cabinet Work,* 1788 (1st) and 1793 (2nd) eds.

Sheraton, T., *The Cabinet Maker and Upholsterer's Drawing-Book; The Appendix; The Accompaniment,* 1791-4

Sheraton, T., *The Cabinet Dictionary,* 1803

Sheraton, T., *The General Artist's Encyclopaedia,* 1803-7

Smith, G., *A Collection of Designs for Household Furniture and Interior Decoration,* 1808

Symonds, R.W., *The Present State of Old English Furniture,* 1921

Symonds, R.W., *Old English Walnut and Lacquer Furniture,* 1923

Symonds, R.W., *English Furniture from Charles II to George II,* 1929

Symonds, R.W., *Veneered Walnut Furniture, 1660-1760,* 1946.

Tomlin, M., *Victoria and Albert Museum — Catalogue of Adam Period Furniture,* 1972

Victoria and Albert Museum, *Tables,* 1968

Victoria and Albert Museum, *English Chairs,* 1970

Ward-Jackson, P., *Victoria and Albert Museum — English Furniture Designs of the 18th Century,* 1958

INDEX

Indexer's note: *Where Chippendale, Hepplewhite, etc., is used after an item, the word 'period' is understood. The wood from which a piece is made is indexed if it is other than mahogany under the entry for that piece. Different varieties of woods are only indexed under their own headings where the authors have something particular to say of their qualities. Only names have been indexed from the italicised bibliographic notes in the main text.*

continued

continued

continued

Books from the
Antique Collectors' Club
5 Church Street, Woodbridge, Suffolk, England

Please send for full details of other books published by the Antique Collectors' Club

THE ANTIQUE COLLECTORS' CLUB

The Antique Collectors' Club was formed in 1966 and now has a five figure membership spread throughout the world. It publishes the only independently run monthly antiques magazine *Antique Collecting* which caters for those collectors who are interested in widening their knowledge of antiques, both by greater awareness of quality and by discussion of the factors which influence the price that is likely to be asked. The Antique Collectors' Club pioneered the provision of information on prices for collectors and the magazine still leads in the provision of detailed articles on a variety of subjects.

It was in response to the enormous demand for information on "what to pay" that the price guide series was introduced in 1968 with the first edition of *The Price Guide to Antique Furniture* (completely revised, 1978), a book which broke new ground by illustrating the more common types of antique furniture, the sort that collectors could buy in shops and at auctions rather than the rare museum pieces which had previously been used (and still to a large extent are used) to make up the limited amount of illustrations in books published by commercial publishers. Many other price guides have followed, all copiously illustrated, and greatly appreciated by collectors for the valuable information they contain, quite apart from prices. The Antique Collectors' Club also publishes other books on antiques, including horology and art reference works, and a full book list is available.

Club membership, which is open to all collectors, costs £17.50 per annum. Members receive free of charge *Antique Collecting,* the Club's magazine (published every month except August), which contains well-illustrated articles dealing with the practical aspects of collecting not normally dealt with by magazines. Prices, features of value, investment potential, fakes and forgeries are all given prominence in the magazine.

Among other facilities available to members are private buying and selling facilities, the longest list of "For Sales" of any antiques magazine, an annual ceramics conference and the opportunity to meet other collectors at their local antique collectors' clubs. There are over eighty in Britain and more than a dozen overseas. Members may also buy the Club's publications at special pre-publication prices.

As its motto implies, the Club is an amateur organisation designed to help collectors get the most out of their hobby: it is informal and friendly and gives enormous enjoyment to all concerned.

For Collectors — By Collectors — About Collecting

The Antique Collectors' Club, 5 Church Street, Woodbridge, Suffolk